Kids in Context

Using Family-Based Leisure Education to Enhance Self-Determination in Children with Disabilities

edited by

Charles C. Bullock
University of Nevada, Reno

Danny E. Johnson
University of North Carolina, Wilmington

Mary Agnes Shelton
Family Link in Leisure Education Program

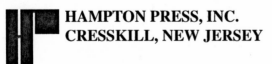
HAMPTON PRESS, INC.
CRESSKILL, NEW JERSEY

Printed in the United States of America

Library of Congress Cataloging-in-Publication-Data

Kids in context : using family-based leisure education to enhance self-determination in
 children with disabilities / edited by Charles C. Bullock, Danny E. Johnson, Mary
 Agnes Shelton
        p. cm. -- (Understanding education and policy)
    ISBN 1-57273-479-5 (cloth) -- ISBN 1-57273-480-9 (pbk.)
    1. Children with disabilities--Recreation--Case studies. 2. Children with
 disabilities--Family relationships--Case studies. I. Bullock, Charles C. II. Johnson,
 Danny E. III. Shelton, Mary Agnes. IV. Series

GV183.6K53 2003
790.1'96--dc21

                                                                    2003044983

Hampton Press, Inc.
23 Broadway
Cresskill, NJ 07626

Contents

Series Preface

Books in this series, Understanding Education and Policy, present and examine various perspectives to better understand the aims, practices, substances, and contexts of schooling, and the meaning of these analyses for educational policy. Our primary intent is to redirect the language used, the voices included, and the range of issues addressed in the current debates concerning schools and policy. In so doing, books in this series explore the varied conceptions and experiences that surface when analysis includes racial, class, gender, ethnicity, sexual orientation, and other salient differences. As a result, books in this series span the social sciences (anthropology, history, philosophy, psychology, sociology, cultural studies, etc.) and research paradigms.

Books in the series will be grounded in the contextualized lives of the major actors in school (students, teachers, administrators, parents, policymakers, etc.) and address major theoretical and methodological issues. The challenge our authors have taken upon themselves is to fully explore life-in-schools, through the multiple lenses of various actors and within the contexts in which these actors and education are situated. The range of empirically sound and theoretically sophisticated works that have been included in this series contribute to a fundamental and necessary rethinking of content, process, and context for school reform. They underscore the reform that all too often disadvantages some for the benefit of others. The challenge we see in these books is that educational policy has a complexity that few are willing to engage. This in turn requires that studies of education and policy have a critical yet constructive stance.

Kids in Context enables the book series to enter three new arenas of research: exceptional children, recreation, and families. It is clear that the wider discourse on educational policy tends to decontextualize the lives of children as is focuses on them as students in schools. In turn, exceptional children are all too often reduced to their learning "disabilities." Children are much more than students and exceptional children are much more than their disabilities. Moreover, as Bullock and his colleagues demonstrate here, it may be that we have focused so much on schooling that researchers are ignoring those aspects of the lives of exceptional children that can significantly enhance the quality of the children's experience. The project on which this book is based, Family Link in Leisure Education, worked with families directly to provide person-centered, contextual learning for leisure education. The cases reveal the power of the families both to help their children and/or to withhold their involvement. They also reveal the kinds of facilitation that families need. This book pushes educational policy to remember its blinders and rethink the conception of education as being bound by the walls of schools and conventional definitions of core curricula. We welcome the consideration this book provides.

Section I

Conceptual Approaches

Chapter 1
A Person-Centered Approach to Family Involvement in Leisure Education

Charles C. Bullock
Danny E. Johnson
Candace Ashton
Michael J. Mahon

A substantial portion of a person's life requires the performance of constructive and personally significant recreation skills. In addition to generally enhancing self-esteem and the quality of a person's life, the ability to occupy one's leisure time in a socially valued and acceptable manner will have a significant impact on where a person is able to live, whether he or she functions successfully in the community, and the quality of relationships they develop.

—Ford et al. (1989, p. 63)

1

A Person-Centered Approach to Family Involvement in Leisure Education

Charles C. Bullock
Danny E. Johnson
Candace Ashton
Michael J. Mahon

The context of a kid's life is her community, her home, her school, her work and her play. Yet, far too often teachers and researchers, even parents, have dealt with these components one at a time. Sometimes, it is just more manageable to deal with only school or only work or any with other single component of a child's life rather than to focus on the totality of the context. In this book, we present in-depth case studies of kids in their context. We have attempted to study kids in the totality of the context. We were particularly concerned about the component of leisure; however, we taught, facilitated, and assisted in that arena only to the extent that it was or became a part of the overall context of that child's life. We learned a lot about leisure and family and community. We learned a lot about professional assumptions as well as cultural and individual realities. We saw the many roles that families play as kids learn, work, play, and grow. In *Kids in Context*, you will read poignant and sometimes comical stories of the lives of kids and their families. You will see what might be considered "success" stories as well as what could be considered "failures." Remember, as you read, that these case studies, rather than being clearly understood "successes" or "failures," are the protracted stories of kids in the context in which they exist.

  Kids in Context grew out of a 5-year research project. In 1993, the Center for Recreation and Disability Studies in the Curriculum in Leisure

Studies and Recreation Administration at the University of North Carolina at Chapel Hill received a 5-year research grant from the U.S. Department of Education's Office of Special Education and Rehabilitation Services to study the effects of an individualized and contextualized leisure education program for school-aged students receiving special education services. Because of this focus given to the students' family in the collaborative process, the project was named Family Link in Leisure Education (FLLE).

The FLLE research project was based on the premise that self-determination and leisure are both important but often neglected skills for children with developmental disabilities. Previous research has shown that both self-determination and recreation skills can be developed through leisure education, but the generalization of these skills is often a barrier to full participation in and enjoyment of leisure experiences (Mahon & Bullock, 1992). Leisure education is being taught in selected schools in a number of states. However, little has been done to ensure that the knowledge and skills learned in leisure education are actually used at home or in the community. In contrast, FLLE sought to develop an experiential leisure education intervention that utilized the participants' natural environments for learning and practice. This is often referred to as contextual learning. The students' classrooms were the entry points into the project, while their schools, homes, and communities were the settings for the interventions.

Leisure education was the intervention which was provided to these special education students. It was provided by Certified Therapeutic Recreation Specialists (CTRSs) and master's level therapeutic recreation students in collaboration with each student's special education teachers, parents and caregivers, and others in their communities. Research participants were students with disabilities in middle schools and high schools in the southeastern United States. The students were referred to the project by their teachers. Over the course of the 5-year project, seven therapeutic recreation TR graduate students and two TRSs/CTRSs provided leisure education interventions to 20 adolescent students with developmental disabilities. The students ranged in age from 13 to 21 years, and their disabilities included mild to severe mental retardation, autism, and blindness. Families were involved in FLLE to varying degrees, with some families being active participants in their adolescents' leisure experiences and with others merely giving their adolescents permission to participate.

The leisure education services were individualized, based on the student's specific leisure and social needs. These needs were determined though the FLLE Student-Centered Strengths/Needs Assessment. This self-report assessment focused on the student's psychosocial strengths and his or her social and leisure needs. The assessments were completed by the student, the student's teacher(s), and the student's parent(s).

Based on the results of the assessments, each student's leisure education intervention was individualized and focused on self-determination, decision-making, problem-solving, planning, friendship, leisure skills, recreation participation, and/or social skills. Leisure education goals and objectives were developed for each student and were often added to the student's Individualized Education Program (IEP) or Individualized Transition Plan (ITP).

Leisure education was delivered in school, home, and community settings over the course of either one semester (4 months) or that of the entire school year (9 months). Data was collected intensively during that time. In school, the students occasionally participated in group and one-to-one leisure education sessions that were conducted by the FLLE staff during the school day on at least a weekly basis. These sessions focused on decision-making and planning, leisure skill development, and social skills training. During after-school programs which sometimes included extracurricular activities (e.g., clubs, sports, and service learning opportunities), FLLE staff provided instruction in recreation activities, social skills, and friendship development. At home, the students and their families were given instruction by FLLE staff in home-based leisure activities, leisure planning, and resource awareness and utilization. In the community, FLLE staff taught students social interaction skills, recreation skills, and how to access and utilize community recreation activities and programs. Students in the project participated for the first time in such activities as attending a swing dancing club, volunteering at a day care center, taking Tae Kwon Do classes, attending YMCA fitness classes, taking golf lessons, bicycling, attending community center teen dances, scouting, taking after school community recreation and parks department classes and joining sports leagues, attending summer science camp, and serving in Habitat for Humanity. Many of these activities became important to the students in the project because they provided them with opportunities to be a part of a new group, to learn new skills and activities, and to choose things which they came to learn that they enjoyed.

It was important that the FLLE interventions were person-centered, contextual, and responsive to the individual needs of each student and his or her family. Typically, students with disabilities have not been encouraged or supported to engage in self-determination in leisure or in any part of their lives. Goals usually have been defined by others, and decisions have been based on stereotypes, low expectations, and the belief that professionals know what is best for people with disabilities. In FLLE, we worked with students and their families to provide the necessary skills so that they could have satisfying and successful lives which include freely chosen and supported recreation and leisure in the settings of their choice. By providing person centered, contextual learning, we hoped to enhance and expand:

- community membership and acceptance,
- the quality and quantity of social supports,
- leisure interests,
- the ability to use problem-solving skills to handle present and future concerns,
- life satisfaction,

- self-esteem, and
- the ability to follow through on personally chosen and planned leisure experiences.

WHY EDUCATION FOR LEISURE?

A substantial portion of a person's life requires the performance of constructive and personally significant recreation skills. In addition to generally enhancing self-esteem and the quality of a person's life, the ability to occupy one's leisure time in a socially valued and acceptable manner will have a significant impact on where a person is able to live, whether he or she functions successfully in the community, and the quality of relationships one develops. The problem is that individuals with disabilities are not afforded the opportunity or education to develop self-determination nor leisure skills. Leisure education is an appropriate mechanism for facilitating both self-determination skills and leisure skills (Mahon & Bullock, 1992).

Leisure education is the use of comprehensive models focusing on the educational process to enhance a person's leisure skills (Chinn & Joswiak, 1981) and participation in recreation activities. According to Peterson and Gunn (1984), leisure education is used to enhance one's awareness and understanding of leisure (e.g., an awareness of the importance and benefits of leisure, an awareness of self in leisure, and a knowledge of leisure resources) and to develop the skills to participate in leisure activities (e.g., decision-making, social skills, and recreation activity skills). Dattilo and St. Peter (1991) and Dattilo, Kleiber, and Williams (1998) have noted that leisure education programs have been designed to encourage individuals to:

1. raise esteem, increase satisfaction, and promote actualization (Tinsley & Tinsley, 1982);
2. make effective leisure choices (Ross, 1983);
3. develop leisure behaviors, skills, and the realization that behaviors can influence the environment (Peterson & Gunn, 1984);
4. increase leisure understanding, awareness, and control (Bregha, 1985);
5. foster selection of meaningful leisure experience, facilitating positive psychological growth by clarifying attitudes and values related to self and leisure (Munson, Baker, & Lundegren, 1985);
6. decrease feelings of boredom by developing knowledge of leisure attitudes, awareness of the psychological benefits of leisure, enhanced motivation to participate in leisure, and a diverse leisure repertoire (Iso-Ahola & Weissinger, 1987);

7. enhance leisure involvement and knowledge retention (Lanagan & Dattilo, 1989);
8. increase wellness and thus contribute to successful transition from school to adult life (Bedini, Bullock, & Driscoll, 1993); and
9. increase recreation participation, satisfaction, and mastery (Luken, 1993).

Work conducted by Bullock, Morris, Mahon, and Jones (1994), Mahon and Bullock (1992), and Mahon (1994) has begun to address a portion of this problem by introducing a comprehensive leisure education program into classrooms for individuals with disabilities. Complimentary work in school-based leisure education curriculum development has been carried out by Voeltz, Wuerch, and Wilcox (1982), Dattilo and St. Peter (1991), and Bedini, Bullock, and Driscoll (1993).

Absent in this leisure education literature is a description of the roles of parents and families in the facilitation of the leisure attitudes, values, and experiences of their children. As stated in America 2000 (1996), "For schools to succeed, we must look beyond their classrooms to our communities and families" (p. 12). Parent-oriented recreation training materials have been developed by the Center for Recreation and Disability Studies (McCann & Bullock, 1991); however little systematic investigation has been conducted relative to the importance of active family participation in this area.

If students with disabilities are exposed to a leisure education program aimed at facilitating self-determination skills, their parents and families must be actively involved in promoting these same skills in their home and community environments (Moon, 1994; Voeltz, Wuerch, & Wilcox, 1982). Unless parents are supportive of the choices that are made by their children with disabilities, the children will themselves be unable to become more self-determining in their leisure lives

The purpose of this project was to understand and document the extent to which self-determination skills can be facilitated using an individualized leisure education planning process with individuals with mental retardation. The intervention used a collaborative school-, home-, and community-based leisure education program to facilitate self-determination skills in leisure, such as leisure awareness, independent leisure decision-making, independent leisure planning, and independent recreation participation.

THE CONCEPTUAL FRAMEWORK OF THE LEISURE EDUCATION INTERVENTION

The leisure education model used as the intervention for this project was based on the principles of personal strengths, self-determination, home-school collaboration and contextual learning. The following brief paragraphs about each of these principles provide the reader with a snapshot of what is behind the leisure education intervention.

Personal Strengths

First utilized in case management with people with severe mental illness, personal strengths-based principles are founded on the belief that all individuals have multiple strengths which give them the capacity to learn, grow, take action, and control their own lives. From a strengths perspective, the client is viewed as a person with vital information, who has gained knowledge through personal experiences, whose cultural and social norms are embraced and celebrated as an integral part of identity, and who should have the locus of control during the decision-making and problem-solving process. The helper aids the student to focus on strengths, guides him or her through the decision-making process, and helps the student access and take advantage of the community and environmental resources, but the client is the catalyst for change. According to Saleeby (1996).

> The strengths perspective demands a different way of looking at individuals, families, and communities. All must be seen in the light of the capacities, talents, competencies, possibilities, visions, values, and hopes. . . . The strengths approach requires an accounting of what people know and what they can do. It requires composing a roster of resources existing within and around the individual, family, and community. (p. 297)

In the early 1990s, strengths-based approaches were extended to people with developmental disabilities (e.g., Fiene & Taylor, 1991; McCallion & Toseland, 1993; Poertner & Ronnau, 1992).

Self-Determination

A major component of the strengths-based perspective is empowerment or self-determination. According to Curtis (1998), Ward (1996), Wehmeyer (1994), and Wehmeyer and Schwartz (1998), self-determination not only consists of the capacity to choose and to carry out choices, but it is also linked to the individual's ability to self-regulate his or her behavior. Self-regulatory behaviors necessary for self-determination include the ability to:

1. identify and express one's own needs, interests, and abilities;
2. set expectations and goals to meet one's needs, interests, and abilities;
3. make choices and plans to meet one's goals and expectations;

4. take action to complete plans;
5. evaluate results and actions; and
6. adjust plans and actions, if necessary, to meet goals more effectively (adapted from Wehmeyer, Agran, & Hughes, 1998).

The definitions and processes of self-determination place the responsibility for self-determination clearly on the person with a disability, even though the amount of self-determination possible for any person depends not only on factors within a person, but also on opportunities outside a person. There is agreement among individuals with disabilities, professionals, and families that one of the most significant ways to empower individuals with disabilities is by allowing them to make their own decisions.

Home-School Collaboration

Central to this project is home-school collaboration. Public Law 99-457 mandated that parents and families of children with disabilities become actively involved in the individualized education planning process for their children. However, parents whose involvement is limited to the IEP conference may not be active and visible participants throughout and across the school years. Parents must be continuous and longitudinal team members in order to be effective. In this project, it was important that parents and families played an active and supportive link between the leisure education program in the school and the most likely settings for recreation participation—the home and community.

Previous work (Bullock, Morris, Mahon, & Jones, 1994) showed that families who were unaware of their child's leisure education outcomes at school could not support or enhance the children's progress. FLLE sought to involve families in their children's learning in natural settings so that they could support and reinforce their children's interests. Families provided assessment information, support (i.e., motivation), resources (e.g., money and transportation), and ideas for participation. It was up to each family to decide the intensity of their involvement in the project. Almost all of the families who participated in the project reported that they engaged in more leisure activities as a family, made more plans for their recreation, got out of the house more, learned new activities, and became more aware of community resources for recreation.

CONTEXTUAL LEARNING

It is in our communities and among our families that we live, work, and play. These contexts are also places where learning occurs and can be enhanced. Contextual learning occurs when one connects subject matter content with the context of application (Parnell, 1996). Learning that occurs in the context of a person's life is more likely to be integrated into his life, such as when a student learns a skill and also how to apply the skill (Bell, 1995). It is easier to learn skills in the context in which the person lives than to learn them in a classroom and plan for transfer. For many years, special education teachers and researchers have insisted that students with disabilities receive community-based as well as school-based vocational training. To learn a job by doing that job has been shown to be more effective than learning that job in a contrived classroom setting. The same is true in other areas of students' lives, such as leisure. Not only does one learn play, recreation, and social skills best within the context in which they naturally occur, but leisure is also a context that is often overlooked, and even devalued (Johnson, Bullock, & Ashton-Shaeffer, 1997).

Family Link in Leisure Education (FLLE) facilitated contextual learning for school-aged students with disabilities by developing individualized, community-based leisure education programming in concert with their families. FLLE was developed in response to previous research (Bullock, Morris, Mahon, & Jones, 1994) which shows that although students who received leisure education in classrooms achieved cognitive gains, the planned transfer to home and the community did not occur.

THE FLLE PROCESS

A systematic process of referral, assessment, planning, intervention, and evaluation was used in the implementation of this project. An ecological, personal strengths perspective guided each phase of the process. The project was ecological in that it attempted not only to increase the students' self-determination and leisure, but also to facilitate positive interrelationships between the students and their environments (i.e., their peers, teachers, family, and community). This perspective recognizes that students cannot be separated from their environments and that self-determination is necessary for shaping those environments (Cowger, 1994). Students' strengths provide the stimulus and force for that self-determination.

The FLLE process is outlined in detail from initial contact with referral sources through follow-up with family, student, and teacher(s). (See FLLE Intervention Protocol in the appendix.)

Referral

At the beginning of the FLLE project, project staff distributed a flyer explaining that the project focused on assisting students and their families in exploring leisure opportunities, developing leisure skills, making decisions, and taking advantage of the leisure choices they make. The flyer was distributed to schools, parent groups, advocacy groups, and related services professionals. The promotional flyer sought referrals for project participants.

Referrals to FLLE were received from both special education and regular education teachers, staff from the local Arc, respite care providers, and other related service personnel. Teachers and families were provided with examples of potential opportunities for meeting education goals in natural settings that might be facilitated by FLLE. Families and students were then contacted to determine their interest in participation. Since far more referrals were received than we could serve, students were chosen for participation in the project based on the following criteria:.

1. Student lacks involvement and connections in the community.
2. Student has been unsuccessful in becoming involved with peers during free time activities.
3. Student lacks partners for recreation participation at home and in school.
4. Student has significant difficulty forming friendships
5. Student lacks leisure interests at home and at school.
6. Student has difficulty with making choices for leisure at home and at school.
7. Student lacks motivation for independent leisure participation at home and at school.
8. Student's family appears to be struggling with family leisure activities.
9. Student needs assistance with development of such skills as social interaction, decision-making, resource awareness, and so forth.

Prior to the assessment process, informed consent was signed by parents for participation in the research process for themselves and their children. Permission was also obtained to seek emergency medical care if needed, for their children to be transported in the researcher's car if needed, and to take photographs of the children and/or the family (copies of each consent form available by contacting Dr. Charlie Bullock at cbullock@unr.edu).

Assessment

The first step in any purposeful intervention should include a "systematic process of gathering and synthesizing information about the individual and his or her world in order to determine the most effective course of intervention" (Selz & Bullock, 2000, p. 288). Two assessment instruments were developed to gather and synthesize information about the students who participated in this project—The Student-Centered Strengths Assessment and The Student-Centered Needs Assessment.[1]

---

[1]We developed six versions of the Student-Centered Needs Assessment (Parent/Caregiver Checklist for Children, Parent/Caregiver Checklist for Adolescents, Student Checklist for Children, Student Checklist for Adolescents, Teacher Checklist for

As explained previously, the assessment process developed and used in this project was based on personal-strengths and ecological models of assessment. It was important that the recreation therapist focus on the students' strengths because, if the therapist were to focus on deficits during the assessment phase, it is likely that deficits would be the focus during the remaining contacts, and that may lead to "self-fulfilling prophecies" (Cowger, 1992, p. 140). Strengths-based assessments should

1. give preeminence to the client's understanding of the situation,
2. discover what the client wants,
3. identify personal and environmental strengths
4. make assessment of strengths multidimensional
5. discover uniqueness
6. use language the client can understand, and
7. give the client a sense of ownership in the assessment process (Cowger, 1994).

Student-Centered Strengths Assessment.   Cowger (1992) developed a model of assessing client strengths that included a strengths/deficits continuum. The strength end of Cowger's continuum identifies the client's strengths related to cognition (understanding), emotions, motivation, coping skills, and interpersonal relationships. The items on the Student-Centered Strengths Assessment were derived from the strength end of Cowger's continuum, with an added environmental component. Six versions of the Student-Centered Strengths Assessment were developed, one to be used with each of the three groups from which assessment data was collected—the students themselves, their parent(s) or caregiver(s), and their teacher(s); and one that reflected the developmental strengths of children and the other adolescents. Each was written with the specific audience in mind.

Student-Centered Needs Assessment.   The second assessment instrument, the Student-Centered Needs Assessment, incorporated Cowger's (1992) deficit end of the strengths/deficits continuum. The items, however, were based on the Leisure Education Content Model (Peterson & Gunn, 1984). The intent was to assess the student's obstacles or barriers to leisure participation. The Student-Centered Needs Assessment identified the student's needs related

Children, Teacher Checklist for Adolescents) and six versions of the Student-Centered Strengths Assessment (Parent/Caregiver Checklist for Children, Parent/Caregiver Checklist for Adolescents, Student Checklist for Children, Student Checklist for Adolescents, Teacher Checklist for Children, Teacher Checklist for Adolescents). There were also two additional assessment instruments (Parent Interview on Student Interests and Student Interests Assessment). All versions are available by contacting Dr. Charlie Bullock at cbullock@unr.edu.

to involvement and success in activities outside his or her home and at school, interpersonal relationships with family and peers, and abilities at finding and utilizing leisure resources, planning for leisure, and self-awareness.

Based on the results of the assessments, each student's leisure education intervention was individualized and focused on self-determination, decision-making and problem-solving, planning, friendship, leisure skills, recreation participation, and/or social skills. Goals were developed with the family and included specific activities, skills, and programs of interest to the student. Leisure education goals and objectives were developed for each student and were usually added to the student's Individualized Education Program (IEP) or Individualized Transition Plan (ITP).

The Intervention

The FLLE leisure education interventions were person-centered, contextual, and responsive to the individual needs of each student and his or her family. The natural contexts for learning were primarily in the student's home and in the community. Each learning plan was based on the student's interests and his or her desire to explore specific activities and interactions. Students and families were encouraged to avoid limiting themselves to recreation programs or activities typically provided for students with disabilities, such as Special Olympics and special populations recreation programs.

FLLE staff worked with students and their families to provide the necessary skills for satisfying and successful leisure experiences. Activities were freely chosen and supported in their natural settings, and they were orchestrated to enhance the students' educational goals. By facilitating leisure experiences that were contextual and person-centered, the goals of FLLE were to enhance and expand the students' community membership and acceptance, and their ability to follow through on personally chosen and planned leisure experiences.

Data Collection

Although FLLE developed and implemented an individual and contextual leisure education program for students with developmental disabilities, the project itself was a research project to study the effects of an individualized and contextualized leisure education program for school-aged students who receive special education services. We wanted to provide students and their families the necessary skills so they could have satisfying and successful lives which include freely chosen and supported recreation and leisure in the settings of their choice. By providing person-centered, contextual learning, we hoped to enhance and expand community membership and acceptance, quality and quantity of social supports, leisure interests, the ability to use problem-solving skills to handle present and future concerns, improve life satisfaction, increase self-esteem, and the ability to follow through on personally chosen and planned leisure experiences. As such, every contact with the student, the student's parents/caregivers, and the student's teachers were opportunities to collect data. In addition, every contact with the student's friends, neighbors, classmates, and activity cohorts were opportunities to collect data.

To collect and analyze all of this data, two qualitative methods were used. Data collection methods included observations and open-ended interviews. Immediately following each observation (i.e., each contact with the student), the researcher would write extensive, detailed field notes. The researcher would then reread the field notes, making notes in the margin. Marginal notes were used to clarify what had been seen and/or heard, and they served to remind the researcher to watch certain behaviors or interactions or to remind the researcher to ask or probe about things that needed clarification. Each interview was tape-recorded and transcribed directly after the interview. Interview transcripts were also read immediately following transcription. Similarly, marginal notes were made. In this way, data collection and analysis occurred simultaneously. Subsequent data collection was therefore informed by the previous data. In that way, the stories built over time. Themes began to emerge through this constant comparison method. By the end of the intervention, there were hundreds of pages of data that had to be condensed into the case study stories. The ongoing analysis was not done in isolation. Rather, the entire research team met weekly throughout the duration of the FLLE research project to discuss the "findings." Each week, one researcher would present his or her student and solicit insight and understandings from the other members of the research team. Field notes and transcriptions were always available for other members of the research team. This collective analysis helped to redirect data collection as needed, as well as validating "hunches" at other times. This team effort helped us to better understand each of the research subjects. When the story became clear, data collection and analysis stopped, and the data was condensed into a story presented in this book.

The Participants

During the course of this 5-year project, 20 school-aged children and adolescents received individualized leisure education services. Of these students, 10 are described in detail in the following chapters. The participants ranged in age from 13 to 21 years old, and all were identified as receiving special education services. They were all enrolled in the same school district in North Carolina. Male students numbered 11, and female students numbered 9. Twelve students were white, 7 were African American, and 1 was Hispanic. Table 1.1 lists the pseudonyms of the students, their disabilities, and the grade levels of the schools they attended.

TABLE 1.1
Participant Data

Disability	Elementary School	Middle School	High School
Mild Mental Retardation	Luis	Ronnie Keisha Stephan Katherine	James David Chuck
Moderate Mental Retardation	Carol	Sally	Eric Windy Katy
Severe Mental Retardation	Marilyn		Sara
Down Syndrome	Tommy	John	
Autism	Mitch		Greg Barney

Nine students were enrolled in self-contained special education classes. Interestingly, four of those students were classified as having mild mental retardation. Another nine students were in self-contained classes for only part of the day. Four of these attended regular education classes for academic subjects, and five were included in nonacademic regular education classes such as dance, chorus, art, and auto mechanics. Two students were fully included in regular education classes for the entire school day.

The students lived in households headed by and composed of various family members. Two students lived in households headed by either one or both grandparents. One student lived with his maternal grandmother and step-grandfather; another student lived with a large extended family headed by her maternal grandmother. However, the household included her mother, aunts, cousins, a great-uncle, and a great-grandmother. Five students lived with their single mothers, and one lived with his single, adoptive father. Ten students lived in two parent homes, one of whom lived with his mother and step-father. Two students lived in group homes. Of the 11 families in this project, 5 received state and/or federal assistance.

This first chapter should provide the reader with an introduction to the FLLE project, as well as a conceptual understanding of the FLLE process. The remainder of the book is that which is really important—the stories of 10 students and how they expanded their leisure skills and knowledge as ways to enhance academic, social, and life skills, as well as to experience success, self-esteem, new friendships, and enjoyment.

WHAT'S TO COME

The remainder of the book contains nine qualitative case studies of family interventions and a summary chapter of our conclusions based on our data. The case
studies have been organized thematically based upon how the families seemed
to view their roles in this process of change.

Section II is entitled, "Tell Us What We Are Going to Do Together,"
and it describes families who sought partners in improving the quality of life of
their child. They invited us into their homes and lives, generously sharing their
family histories. They expressed high interest in the program and exhibited
motivation to succeed. The reader should be cautioned to avoid assuming that,
because a family seemed to categorize us, at least initially, as partners, all interventions ended up with equal zeal from the parents. In fact, it may have been
that motivated families were given much larger roles in this process than they
could handle. Several stories hearken the disadvantages of creating complicated,
involved plans. Chapter 2 tells the story of how Sally increased self-determination. The result of the family's involvement was that Sally learned how to use
public transportation. For her, this was a giant step that enlarged her world. The
story of Luis in Chapter 3 emphasizes the multicultural influences affecting
school services today, Despite a single father's extraordinary involvement,
social inclusion was problematic. Barney's story in Chapter 4 stresses the
importance of expectations from school systems, and it sheds light on increased
"behavior" problems in special education. Barney, like many students involved
in this project, showed us the power of higher expectations and an invitation to
self-determination.

Section III is entitled "Tell Us What You Are Going to Do" to emphasize the role given to FLLE personnel by some families. Families in this category wanted services for their children, but they were not interested in being
deeply involved in the process. They wanted anything that might help their children and any activity that we did with the children. Yet, what they did not seem
to want was any changes that might affect them. This section describes three
families whose lack of efforts ultimately affected the student negatively. Eric's
story in Chapter 5 reveals the difficulty of parents who are not ready to face the
changing needs of an active adolescent who desires acceptance. Their ambivalence overshadows the gains of an energetic teenager from whom little is
expected. Similarly, the parents of James and David stymied their children's
progress by their lack of support, as discussed in Chapter 6. Sara's lengthy story
in Chapter 7 describes her group home and school, which have become her
"family." It dramatically shows that when little is expected from a student with
a disability, little is gained. All three chapters describe barriers from parents and
school systems that failed to support and encourage them. The title of the section, "Tell Us What You Are Going to Do" exemplified their meager efforts.

Section IV, "Tell Us How We Can Do It," typifies families who were actively involved in their children's lives and who needed facilitation from an outside source to succeed. Families in this category were seeking information about which directions to take with their children. Some needed resource information; others needed ideas; others needed "permission" to see that their child's recreation was important. They were ready to go, if only someone could come in and get them going. Marilyn's story in Chapter 8 confirms the difficulty that parents often have when they are the sole caretakers and support for their children. Keisha and her mother needed direction and structure to succeed, as discussed in Chapter 9. Stephan's mother needed a new approach to dealing with him that would be positively reinforcing. Their story, as told in Chapter 10, demonstrates the importance of positive recreation for a youth-at-risk.

The final section, Section V, offers conclusions and recommendations based on our experience with FLLE. The chapter is divided into what we learned about:

1. families of children with disabilities,
2. the provision of family/home leisure education,
3. schools and special education personnel, and
4. students with disabilities.

Recommendations focus upon the importance of self-determination, person-centered planning, strength-based approaches, and the importance of high expectations for student performance.

We hope you enjoy the stories of these kids in the context in which they live and grow. You will probably see bits and pieces of students, parents, caregivers, and teachers you "know." We also hope that these in-depth stories will help you to become better parents, teachers, and/or professionals, as we all strive to provide person-centered, contextual, and responsive services that meet the individual needs of each student and his or her family.

APPENDIX

Researcher: _____   Student: _____

Family Link in Leisure Education
Intervention Protocol
Initial Contact with Teacher—Date
1. Explain project
2. Leave referral criteria list
Classroom Observations
Dates _____
Receive Referral—Date

Teacher Contacts Family by Phone—Date

FLLE Telephone Contact with Family—Date
    1. Confirm interest
    2. Schedule first meeting

First Meeting with Student and Family—Date
    1. Explanation of project
    2. Informed consent form
    3. Consent to transport

       Assessments with Family
       1.   Parent/caregiver demographics   Date _____
       2.   Strengths assessment   Date _____
       3.   Needs assessment   Date _____

       Student Assessments at School
       1.   Strengths assessment   Date _____
       2.   Needs assessment   Date _____
       3.   Interests interview   Date _____

       Assessments with Teacher at School
       1.   Student strengths assessment   Date _____
       2.   Student needs assessment   Date _____

Planning Meeting with Family—Date
    1. Presentation of Six Needs
    2. Presentation of Individualized Leisure Education Plan
    3. Review ILEP with family and student
    4. Confirm family's agreement with ILEP

Planning Meeting with Teacher—Date
    1. Review ILEP
    2. Present possible IEP leisure goals

Continued Family Interventions
    1. On-going review and/or revision of ILEP
    Dates

Continued Contacts with Teacher and Classroom
    Dates _____
    _____

       Discharge Process
    1. Measures   Date _____
    2. Interview with student   Date _____
    3. Interview with parents   Date _____
    4. Recommendations   Date _____
    6. Interview with teacher   Date _____
    7. Summary of intervention
       a. to family   Date _____
       b. to teacher   Date _____

Follow-up with Family and Student

Dates   _____

             _____

             _____

Follow-up with Teacher

Dates   _____

             _____

             _____

Section II

Tell Us What We Can Do Together

"You did it, girl," she said, hugging Sally warmly. MJ told me that the only reason she had let Sally try all this on her own was because of our careful preparation. . . . We were a proud and happy group that day.

—Field notes, chapter 2

2

Watching Pictures Come to Life: Moving Toward Independence

Mary Agnes Shelton

Darkness was closing in on a mid-winter's day when I first drove up to Sally's house. The cold rain that had been falling most of the day had finally slacked off, but gray clouds still churned low overhead. Sally's house, located on the edge of a drainage area for the surrounding residential neighborhoods, was set down about five feet lower than the road. The rain had created a shallow pond in the small front yard. Someone who was obviously used to this eventuality, had placed planks from the driveway to the front porch in an effort to help people stay out of the mud and stay dry. As I tottered cautiously along the planks, I observed the house and surroundings.

The small one-story house appeared to be an old farmhouse covered with dark green siding, chipped and cracked in a number of places. The covered concrete porch that stretched all the way across the front of the house was lined with rusted, broken lawn furniture. A semi-circular driveway surrounded the back of the house, which accessed the main road on either side of the house. I counted 12 cars, in various states of disrepair, parked along the drive all the way around the house. Situated among the cars, a small bubble trailer was parked, and a light was on inside.

Standing on the porch in the darkness and damp, I knocked loudly on the screen door. The main door had plywood nailed where the window had once been, so I heard—rather than saw—someone come to the door. Sally opened the door and greeted me with a big warm smile. "Momma, she's here, she's here," she called into the dark room behind her.

I had first met Sally the week before in her middle school special education class for students with mild mental retardation or learning disabilities. She was a small person; at 16, she was barely 5 feet tall and weighed around 85 pounds. She had dark brown skin and very black, curly, almost shoulder-length hair. Her eyes were large and brown, but she kept them lowered most of the time with her eyelids about half-closed. Sally spoke softly, looking down—people had to frequently ask her to speak up so she could be heard.

The referral from Mr. Wilson, Sally's teacher, was rather unusual, since he described Sally as friendly, wanting to please, very cooperative, a genuinely nice person. Most referrals highlighted all the *problems* that a student manifested or experienced. This one was a recital of her attributes. During the referral interview, Mr. Wilson went on to say that his fears for Sally included her being overlooked and ignored, other people taking advantage of her, and her lack of assertiveness possibly leading to abusive situations.

Mr. Wilson knew of a couple of episodes when Sally had been teased into performing for other students only to be laughed at and scorned. Once, he had heard loud laughter from the girls' bathroom near the cafeteria and had poked his head in to see what was going on. He saw a couple of girls goading Sally into dancing in front of a crowd of other students, with everyone laughing, clapping hands, and telling Sally to "go faster, girl, faster." When Mr. Wilson broke up the scene, the two perpetrators laughed and said, "She's so stupid."

Another time, some students had told Mr. Wilson about a rough, young guy getting off the bus with Sally and following her into her house, having bragged that he was going to "get some" from her. Fortunately, Sally's adult sister was home to head off a possibly dangerous situation. Mr. Wilson was understandably concerned about Sally being able to hold her own against boys trying to "hit" on her for sexual favors. He was hopeful that some one-on-one intervention with a trained recreation therapist might assist Sally in building self-confidence and personal assertiveness, and he felt sure that her family would want to cooperate.

Sally opened the door for me as her mother, MJ, appeared behind her. I could immediately see where Sally got her small stature, as MJ was also a very small person. She was an older version of Sally, but with lighter skin and short, graying hair twisted into a small knot at the back of her head. MJ greeted me with a warm smile. When we had spoken about the Family Link in Leisure Education (FLLE) program on the phone a few days earlier, she had said she would be delighted to become involved.

FLLE was a therapeutic recreation leisure education program that received referrals through the schools, but which sought to increase self-determination and recreation/leisure choices through intensive home- and community-based interventions. Through an assessment process, the goals and desires of the student in regard to leisure choices and pursuits were ascertained and were then developed into a plan of action. Input from the student, the family, and the teacher helped to focus and fine-tune the plan. One-on-one interventions with a recreation therapist to achieve the goals and objectives of the plan then proceeded for as long as it took to accomplish them.

During our phone conversation, MJ had expressed some of the same concerns about Sally that Mr. Wilson had stated, such as the possibility of her being ignored or exploited in social situations, and even her being abused due to her lack of personal assertiveness. She also hoped Sally could work on independence issues, such as transportation and a more diverse use of her free time. MJ agreed to be present at weekly meetings at her home, to provide support and finances for possible outings, and to remain involved in helping pursue whatever goals we developed together. MJ had said she felt very good about getting some help for Sally—this was the first time any special assistance had ever been offered to help her and her family.

At MJ's invitation, I stepped into the living room, and I was directed to sit on one of the two couches. The floor was slanted decidedly toward the left corner of the room, opposite the door, and was covered with a piece of worn, green carpet. The walls and window frames were also slanted in the same direction, indicating a profound shift in the foundation of the house—not surprising, considering the swampy conditions just outside. In a few places, the sheet rock had crumbled behind the wallpaper so that only the wallpaper itself formed the wall.

In addition to the two couches, a couple of overstuffed chairs, two end tables with lamps (no shades), a huge TV covered with dust, and a vase with dusty plastic flowers completed the furnishings. Pictures of Martin Luther King, Jr. on black velvet, John F. Kennedy, and Jesus hung on the walls. A dim fixture in the middle of the ceiling lighted the room. MJ told me she had been born in this house 53 years earlier and she had never lived anywhere else. When she was a child, the house was on the edge of town, with fields stretching off into the country. Now, low-income housing projects, other run-down houses, and miles of city surrounded the small house and lot.

On this first visit with MJ and Sally at their home, we completed the parental portion of the assessment. During the demographics section, I learned that the inhabitants of the small, tilted house included: MJ and Sally; MJ's 23year-old, single-parent daughter, Debra, and her five children; MJ's 24-year-old, unemployed, stock-car-racing son, Jim; and MJ's frail 78-year-old mother who never left the house. Altogether, 10 people lived in their small house. From the outside, there appeared to be only two other rooms besides the kitchen and bathroom. In all the months I worked with Sally, I never did figure out how they all fit in there, not to mention where they slept.

In addition to all of the people who actually lived in MJ's house, I learned about a number of other relatives who were often present. Two doors down the street, MJ's sister, Maude, had a house where she assisted her brother, who had one leg missing, and MJ's 22-year-old daughter with her 7-month-old baby. Traffic between the two houses appeared to be quite constant, with a deep footpath worn from one door to the next. It was quite an extended family.

At Sally's house, MJ was the only one employed, working two after-noons per week as a helper for a nurse's aide. The rest of the family income came from welfare. Although the living conditions appeared to be minimal, all members of the family were typically well-dressed and clean. Despite the many partial cars that surrounded the house, the family had no running car and relied on relatives or friends for essential transportation, such as grocery shopping. The city bus stopped right in front of sister Maude's house and thus provided transportation for MJ to go to work.

During the parental assessment interview, MJ and I initially sat at opposite ends of the couch, with Sally sitting on the couch across the room. By the end of our interview, MJ was sitting next to me with our legs touching and her arm across the back of the couch around my shoulder. MJ had revealed a great deal of her family's personal history to me, displaying a trust and open-ness that was quite moving for me. During our first hour together, MJ and I had developed a warm friendliness that provided a comfortable, solid foundation for our work over the next several months.

GOALS

After completing the assessments with Sally, MJ, and Mr. Wilson, I compared and contrasted them, and I developed a set of possible goals, which combined the opinions, and ideas of all three people. I presented the combined goals to MJ and Sally, and they both approved of them. Then I showed the plan of action to Mr. Wilson, who also approved. We all agreed on the following goals as Sally's plan of action:

1. To increase variety and participation in leisure activities at home,
2. To expand social contacts through school or community activities while practicing planning skills, and
3. To increase transportation resources and skills.

As we began working on the goals, using step-by-step objectives devel-oped from them, MJ became a willing and enthusiastic helper and coach for Sally. She said she had felt for a long time that Sally wasn't getting the attention and assistance she needed, but MJ hadn't known what to do to ameliorate the situa-tion. With suggestions and guidance, she was ready to do all she could. However, MJ faced some inevitable limitations in her ability to spend time with Sally.

MJ's day began at 5:30 a.m. when she got up to get Sally ready for school. She fixed breakfast for Sally and all the other children (ages 2 months to 7 years), who usually got up very early, too. MJ then helped her mother get out of bed and eat breakfast. She also helped feed and clean all of the children—Debra's five and typically a few more that were being baby-sat. She worked two afternoons with an hour ride on the city bus each way, prepared meals for the rest of the family, and took care of shopping and laundry. Her day ended at 11:30 p.m. when she assisted her mother to the bathroom for the last time and put her to bed. MJ was frequently tired and harried, finding little time for relaxation and play. There always seemed to be so much to do—she knew that Sally was neglected in the midst of it all.

Therefore, as MJ helped formulate the goals for us to work on with Sally, she stressed independence skills as an important part of our strategy. Her hope was to help Sally develop enough self-determination and self-confidence that she could proceed to learn and grow by herself, needing less attention and supervision from MJ. Since Sally was already 16 years old, we all agreed that it was appropriate for her to learn to get out on her own as much as possible. Sally was the strongest proponent of all for more independence—she thought it sounded grand!

We began addressing all the goals simultaneously, working at home on the first goal—increasing leisure activities at home, and getting out in the community to address the second and third goals—expanding social contacts and increasing transportation resources. Prior to the FLLE interventions, Sally's main leisure activity at home was listening and dancing to music on tapes and the radio. She rarely watched television and had no hobbies. MJ said Sally spent most evenings in the tilted living room by herself, dancing and humming to music on the radio, while the rest of the family watched TV or hung out in the kitchen. During the assessment, Sally said she would like to make things with her hands and try some art projects.

INCREASING LEISURE ACTIVITIES AT HOME

In order for Sally to experience several different "things to make," I presented her with some options. I brought a paint-by-number project, bead-making supplies, a stencil set, and paint-with-water books. Sally tried them all, using the supplies with MJ and with me. The paint-by-number project was fairly complicated and intricate. Sally enjoyed painting with MJ, but thought it was too hard to try by herself. MJ thought that Sally painted out of the lines so flagrantly that the picture didn't look like what it was supposed to be. When I saw the look of disapproval on MJ's face, I began a discussion about creativity being acceptable however it turned out, and that we weren't looking for any particular result. As we talked it over, I saw MJ's face relax, and I felt her become more approving of Sally's attempts with the paintbrush.

Making necklaces and bracelets with large plastic beads and yarn was fun for Sally; she especially liked giving away the things she created. She made gifts for all of her little nieces and nephews. The two older ones, Jamie and

Lucy, were particularly pleased with their gifts, and I could see the love and admiration they had for their young aunt as they thanked her. However, to do the beading, Sally continually needed help getting the yarn through the holes in the beads, which meant she had to have someone with her to do it. Beading continued to be an activity for Sally that she could do with assistance, but we still wanted to find a project that she could initiate and complete all by herself.

I watched Sally as she worked with the projects. She tended to be very hesitant and looked to MJ or me to see whether she was doing it right. If she didn't receive our constant encouragement, she stopped the task and waited until we were paying attention and approving again. Both MJ and I hoped to see Sally gain the personal confidence and belief in her ability that she needed to continue projects and plans on her own.

Again, stencils were interesting for Sally to do with MJ or me, but she never asked to do them by her own choice. Sally's favorite activity, and the only medium she eventually continued to initiate and use by herself without encouragement, was paint-with-water. Paint-with-water consisted of inexpensive coloring books purchased from the drug store which had pre-applied color on the pictures. By adding water to the picture with a paintbrush, the colors became brilliant and could be spread around on the figures on the page. Sally said she "really liked watching the pictures come to life."

I think one of the reasons Sally enjoyed paint-with-water the most was because she could get all the supplies together herself and paint whenever she wanted. I noticed that if Sally didn't need help getting set up, she was much more likely to participate in the activity. During the intervention, I provided a supply of paint-with-water books, including some with flowers and wildlife from an art supply store which were a bit more age-appropriate than the usual cartoon or Barbie doll books. I told MJ where she could buy them, and she said that she would continue to purchase the paint-with-water books for Sally.

LEISURE ACTION PLANNING

Because we were focusing on independence skills, MJ and I agreed to help Sally learn to make plans concerning how she would use her leisure time, rather than just to try to think of something to do in the moment. Hopefully, planning would also help her expand the variety of activities in which she engaged at home. I provided Leisure Action Planning (LAP) cards and pictures that had been developed in a former project called School-Community Leisure Link, and I showed Sally and MJ how to use them.

The LAP materials included a card with six plastic, see-through pockets on it, which were labeled *What, Who With, Where, When, Things I Need*, and *Name/Date*. (A detailed explanation of the LAP cards can be found in the appendix.) A packet of 20 or more pictures was provided in a labeled envelope for each pocket. There were also several blank "pictures" so Sally could create her own pictures if she couldn't find the appropriate ones for her choices. MJ was quite pleased with the LAP materials and started doing them with Sally right away. Sally caught on to the technique easily, and she and MJ began using the LAP cards together to make plans for things to do at home and for family outings. After a few weeks, MJ told me that making plans with the LAP cards was motivating the whole family to do more together, and they were occasionally getting out of the house together for fun events. One time, MJ and Sally made plans with the LAP cards to take Debra and her five children to the park a few blocks from the house for a picnic lunch. They proudly showed me the LAP card they had put together, with Sally having drawn the *Who With* picture herself—two large stick figures, a medium one, and five little ones.

The event was scheduled to occur on Saturday, so the following week, I asked how things went. Sally looked down, hanging her head and looking sad. MJ said that they hadn't been able to go because one of the kids hadn't been feeling well, and Debra thought it would be too much trouble to get them all ready and down to the park. Sally looked very disappointed. MJ and I spent the next few minutes talking about how plans often change and how that's okay. Then we just make new plans. Life is always changing, so we just learn to go with the flow. Sally looked up at us and smiled.

Although Sally did some paint-with-water activities on her own, her main leisure activity at home remained listening to music on the radio and dancing. However, during the intervention time, she became considerably more creative with this endeavor. Once, while we were on a community outing, Sally came up with the idea all by herself to buy blank tapes, record her favorite tunes from the radio, and choose the tapes for dancing. This way, she could control the music, focus only on her favorites, and omit commercials. Sally developed quite a project for herself with recording, labeling (with help from MJ), classifying, and sorting her tapes. During the 3 months that I watched her develop this project, Sally collected almost a whole shoebox full of tapes. She was very proud of her accomplishment, and so were MJ and I. We felt that Sally's initiative with her tape project was a significant indication of her growing self-determination, motivation, and confidence.

EXPANDING SOCIAL CONTACTS

Sally's second goal involved expanding social contacts through school or community activities while using planning skills. Sally agreed that one place to check for increasing social contacts was through extracurricular activities at school, so we checked into the possibilities there. We learned that the middle school was sponsoring an after-school program in cooperation with area businesses to provide any students who wished to attend with opportunities to be tutored, to visit various job sites, to take special classes, and to socialize. The program ran 5 days per week for 2 hours after school. Transportation to the home was provided.

MJ and Sally had heard of the after-school program, but they didn't know how to gain access to it and they hadn't been aware of the free transportation home. Within a few days, Sally was signed up and attending the program. She was very pleased with this addition to her life, since she was spending more time with people her own age, and she felt included with typical students, as well as special education students, in the various program activities.

The activity that Sally enjoyed the most in the after-school program was taking trips to various businesses in the community to investigate job opportunities. There were three other students with disabilities in the program, and Sally teamed up with the other girl from her class to make the trips. Sally told me that she felt comfortable and close to her friend when they went out into the community together.

MJ appreciated the after-school program because it provided the opportunity for Sally to spend more time with her peers and less time at home on her own. MJ was quite pleased that Sally had made friends with the girl from her class through the after-school program. The friendship hadn't developed during the regular classroom situation. Sally called her new companion her "girlfriend." They talked on the phone often and occasionally went places together, accompanied by someone from one of their families. Sally was proud to have her own friend.

INCREASING SOCIAL CONTACTS AND TRANSPORTATION SKILLS IN THE COMMUNITY

In order to address increased social contacts in the community as well as at school, Sally decided to explore volunteer opportunities available through a youth volunteer agency. We could also bring in our transportation goal at this point, because Sally needed to learn to ride the city bus in order to participate in the volunteer opportunity. During an interview with the director of the area youth volunteers, Mr. T., Sally decided she would like to volunteer with a day care program because she enjoyed children and was used to taking care of them at home. Mr. T. found a position as a helper with infants at a church day care located on the bus route. Sally and I practiced riding the bus to the day care and back home several times to familiarize Sally with the route. No transfer of buses was involved, but we did have to cross a wide, heavily trafficked main street to get from the bus stop to the church.

After school was out for the summer, Sally and I rode the bus to her volunteer job together. I waited in the lobby, working on projects I had brought from my office, while Sally worked. After two sessions, Sally made plans with the day care staff to work for two hours, two afternoons per week. She told me that she enjoyed the job, and the staff at the day care reported that Sally was very good with the babies. Sally decided she was ready to go to her job by herself.

The day after Sally's proposed solo adventure, I called to see how it went. MJ said Sally had been afraid to ride the bus and cross the busy downtown street by herself. MJ also admitted that she had been afraid to let Sally try. Apparently, the idea of Sally getting around independently in the city was easier to accept than the actual event. It seemed that we had been moving too far too fast, and we needed to slow down and back up a bit.

When I saw Sally at our next weekly appointment, we agreed to continue working on independent transportation skills and to let the day care job go for now. We called Mr. T and the day care staff to let them know that Sally wouldn't be able to help during the summer after all. Sally and I focused our attention on bus riding and moving around safely in the city.

LEARNING TO RIDE THE CITY BUS

The focus of our third goal, increasing transportation resources and skills became learning to ride the city bus. Since the bus stopped two doors down and came every 30 minutes, we agreed that it would be a good idea for Sally to attempt to learn to ride it confidently by herself. MJ was hopeful, but hesitant, at the thought of Sally riding the bus alone. She felt there were a number of obstacles to overcome before Sally would be safe. She admitted that she wasn't sure whether Sally would ever be able to ride the bus alone.

During the initial assessment interview with Sally's teacher, Mr. Wilson commented that he thought Sally's mother was overprotective and didn't allow Sally to be as independent as she was capable of being. MJ herself also commented several times that she thought she was overprotective, but she just wanted Sally to be safe. Although I certainly understood her sense of apprehension about Sally's safety, I thought that MJ was over doing it a bit with her reluctance about the bus. During the 5 months that I had worked with Sally during the school year, I had seen her confidence grow, and I knew that we were accessing potential in Sally that had not been tested so far. No one knew how far she could go, including Sally herself. However, we would have to go slowly enough to accommodate MJ's anxiety, so that she could feel confident about her daughter's safety, thereby encouraging rather than discouraging Sally's independence.

Sally had several major obstacles to overcome in order to learn to ride the bus by herself. She couldn't read the names of the bus line destinations on the front of the buses; she couldn't tell time on a clock so she would know the times to catch buses; she couldn't count the correct change for her fare; she was too shy to ask strangers or bus drivers for help; and she lacked the self-confidence to step out and take the lead. MJ was aware of all these obstacles—thus her nervousness about Sally going out by herself.

During the summer months, Sally and I planned and carried out one community outing each week. We used a LAP card to make our plans, with Sally choosing where we would go, how and when we'd get there, and what we would need to take. Sally planned trips to the mall, movies, and to go out to eat. We used public transportation for all of our outings, addressing each of Sally's obstacles and practicing how to overcome them.

First, Sally and I collected bus schedules for all the bus lines in the city. I attempted to teach Sally how to read them, but all the numbers and columns were just too confusing for her. After a few times of Sally trying to read the schedules and feeling disappointed that it was so hard, we decided that I would initially read the schedules and figure out our route while she watched.

Although Sally couldn't read the names of the bus line destinations on the front of the buses, she could read the route numbers that were displayed on every side of each bus. So, we devised a plan for me to use bus numbers, times, and arrows to outline each bus trip that we took, including transfers, on a piece of paper. Sally could follow the diagram and refer to it during the trip. If she needed assistance, she could show her paper to the bus driver or another passenger to get help. MJ watched us create and use this process, and she agreed that she would continue to diagram bus trips for Sally when my intervention time with them ended. After we had developed this technique, I could feel that all three of us had become more confident that Sally would actually be able to pull this off.

Another barrier to independent bus riding for Sally concerned her inability to tell time on a clock. She was able to read digital time, though, and compare it to the times I had written on the paper. After making a few phone calls to some community organizations, I was directed to a local charitable agency to inquire about helping Sally to buy a digital watch. The lady at the agency said they would be glad to do that—they were always looking for local ways to be helpful and make a difference for people in the community.

After receiving money from the charitable agency, I bought the watch and took it to Sally for a surprise. Sally and MJ were very pleased. Sally squealed and jumped up and down when she realized that the watch was for her. MJ said it was the nicest gift Sally had ever received, and she helped Sally write a "thank you" letter to the agency. A few weeks later, MJ told me that Sally only took her watch off to take a bath and would then put it right back on. She even slept with it on. On all of our subsequent trips, Sally watched the time and reported when it was time for us to get to the bus stop to catch our bus. Being able to handle the time was a strong confidence builder for Sally, and it improved her self-esteem. She always looked up proudly and smiled when she announced the time.

To overcome Sally's barrier about counting money for her bus fare, we practiced having Sally pick out the coins by sight that she would need to ride the bus. She picked that up right away, easily learning to recognize a quarter and a nickel or three dimes. Though Sally had worked with money and coins frequently at school, she had never been able to remember the values of various coins for very long. The ease with which she learned the coins for riding the bus appeared to be related to the fact that she was actually going to use what she learned for a real task in the real world. Abstract concepts for use "someday" just didn't seem to stick with Sally, but useful information in the present moment, repeated only a few times, became a part of her permanent knowledge base. However, just in case, we also practiced a back-up plan of having Sally hold out her change to let the bus driver select the coins she needed.

We dealt with Sally's shyness when she was out in the community by having her ask for transfers and directions from bus drivers, order food items when we ate out, and ask for directions from people on the street. In order to accomplish this, Sally had to raise her head, look at the people directly, and speak up more than she was used to doing. Talking to the bus drivers was fairly easy for Sally, but ordering food at restaurants proved to be a challenge.

Through Sally's choice, we often ate at fast food places that were busy and noisy. The staff people were in a hurry and sometimes became annoyed when Sally spoke too softly. At first, I frequently had to restrain myself from attempting to ease the situation by telling the staff person what Sally wanted. Instead, I encouraged Sally to raise her head and speak louder. The more she practiced, the better she accomplished the task of ordering food and the more comfortable she felt. By the end of the intervention, Sally could speak up easily without any coaching. The last few times we went out to eat, Sally did all the ordering while I sat at the table. We were both proud.

We also practiced having Sally ask for directions from strangers on the street and at bus stops. I wanted her to be able to ask for help if she needed it when she was out by herself. Sally typically seemed to select women to ask for assistance—she said she felt more comfortable with them. All of the people she encountered when I was with her were quite helpful and kind. After only a few successful approaches to strangers. Sally became much more at ease with speaking up and interacting. MJ mentioned to me how much more outgoing and talkative Sally was becoming when they went places together. MJ was both pleased and proud of her daughter.

While working on Sally's independence skills, the most difficult task for her to accomplish concerned the ability to take the lead when we went places. Sally and I talked over how we could help her learn to take the lead, and we decided on a plan. When we were walking together, I began hanging back and walking a couple of paces behind Sally. I wanted her to set the pace and make the decisions about how to get where we planned to go. We started this process in the mall where Sally felt comfortable.

On our first attempt at Sally taking the lead, it was very difficult for her. She felt hesitant walking out in front of me, and she kept slowing down. I stayed two paces back. Soon, we virtually came to a stop. I walked beside her again, and then slowly fell back while encouraging her to keep up her pace.

We soon learned that it was much easier for Sally to take the lead when she had a clear idea of where she was going. We read the map in the mall, talked over how to get where we wanted to go, and allowed Sally to proceed at her own pace. It still required four or five practice trips with Sally in the lead before she felt at ease. Since Sally had always been accompanied and led when she went anywhere, this was a big change for her.

After Sally could take the lead and move easily around the mall, we took our endeavor out into the streets. Since the traffic and people moved so fast and seemed so intimidating to Sally, we had to start all over, slowly letting Sally take the lead. Practicing was the key, and I learned to allow progress at Sally's pace. The last big hurdle was for Sally to take the lead when crossing streets. Since she really couldn't judge the movements of traffic very well, we decided to only cross at traffic lights that said "walk," even if we had to go a couple of blocks out of our way to find one. With practice, Sally was able to move around town in the lead, but she remained a bit nervous about crossing streets during heavy traffic times, even with the lights.

As we practiced Sally's new skills, we always reported back to MJ, who said she could feel the confidence growing in Sally. Still, when we were ready for Sally to take her first ride alone on the bus, MJ was apprehensive. I told her that I would follow the bus in my car and meet Sally at the downtown terminal as soon as she got off. MJ reluctantly agreed that it should be okay. Sally felt thoroughly ready and thought it would be "no problem."

Since Sally and I had been catching the bus in front of sister Maude's house for several months, the bus driver noticed when Sally got on the bus alone and I waved from the door. Sally gave him a confident smile, and he winked at me before he closed the door. Sally sat at the back of the bus so she could look out and see me following in my car. She smiled and waved. I hadn't realized how fast buses move around the city, and I was hard-pressed to keep up. I had to park and race to the downtown terminal in order to be there when Sally got off. I arrived just in time to see a beaming Sally disembark from her first solo ride. Sally said she had felt quite comfortable on the bus alone. I drove her home to MJ, who was relieved that everything had gone smoothly.

Sally and I proceeded to plan trips where Sally would increasingly undertake more and more independence. We planned several solo rides for Sally to the downtown terminal where I met her. We walked around town a bit, had lunch, and then Sally rode home alone on the bus. The next step was for Sally to ride to the terminal and transfer alone.

On the day of Sally's first solo transfer, I drove to the terminal ahead of Sally's bus, watched from the sidelines while she transferred, and then met her at our destination, the movies. Sally said she had known just what to do the whole time and hadn't felt nervous or had to ask for help. Sally's self-confidence and my confidence in her abilities soared. After repeating that scenario on several different occasions, Sally's confidence grew strong and firm.

Our final independence task was for Sally to catch the bus from home, ride to the terminal, transfer, meet me at the mall for lunch, and then reverse the process to get back home. Sally felt quite confident about the trip, but MJ and I were a bit nervous. Sally seemed so small and the world so large, but we knew we would have to just trust and go for it at some point—and this seemed to be it. I took off for the mall, and Sally confidently got on the bus.

About 20 minutes later, I stood at the bus stop at the mall waiting for Sally's bus. This was the first time that I hadn't been at the terminal to be sure she made the transfer safely. One bus went by—no Sally. It was probably the wrong one. Another bus went by—no Sally. I was pretty sure that it was the one she should have been on. I nervously began planning how I would track down what had happened to her—call the police, call the main bus depot to trace her . . . what? Suddenly, there was a smiling Sally right in front of me. She had been walking behind the big guy who got off before her, and I hadn't been able to see her. What a relief! "No problem," Sally said, smiling confidently and looking me in the eyes.

After lunch, Sally rode home, transferring alone again. I drove on to her house to meet her when she got off the bus. Sister Maude was on the porch when I arrived. She congratulated me for helping Sally to get out on her own. She had always known that Sally could be more independent, but she never would have believed that MJ would let Sally out of the house by herself, much less let her ride the bus alone. Maude laughed and clapped me on the back. "Good job," she said. "Good job."

MJ was delighted when a beaming Sally got off the bus in front of the house. "You did it, girl," she said, hugging Sally warmly. MJ told me that the only reason she had let Sally try all this on her *own* was because of our careful preparation—we had *shown* her that Sally could do it. We were a proud and happy group that day. As it turned out, when Sally started high school the next year, she had to walk almost a mile through a dangerous neighborhood to catch the school bus, while the city bus that stopped near her house also stopped in front of her school. Sally began riding the city bus to and from school every day. MJ said she never could have done it without the independence training we had done the previous year.

Although MJ was perhaps initially overprotective, we were able to build up her confidence in Sally's abilities by taking slow, steady steps and letting her see that Sally could be successful. As we planned and took our trips, I also saw Sally's self-determination and confidence grow and blossom. During our final interview, MJ said:

> The program has changed how we do everything in the family. Sally never used to ask to do anything or go anywhere. I guess she just didn't know to ask. Now she wants to go all the time, so we are all getting out and doing things. Sally has gained a lot of self-confidence from the program. She speaks up a lot more for herself now. She used to hardly say anything—she talks a lot more now. . . . This program has really changed Sally's life.

SUMMARY

With the support and encouragement of Sally's mother and other relatives, we were able to bring about changes in Sally's self-confidence and self-determination that had important and lasting effects in her life. When I envision Sally as I saw her when we first met and I compare that shy, withdrawn little girl with the blossoming young woman that Sally is today, my heart is truly warmed. I would not contend that all of Sally's progress could be attributed to the FLLE program, since she was at a crucial maturing age all on her own. However, I do believe that we were able to come into Sally's life at just the right time for her to accomplish amazing, satisfying successes that should serve her well, now and in her future.

APPENDIX: LEISURE ACTION PLANNING

Once students had made a decision regarding what they would like to do for leisure, they were then taught to make a Leisure Action Plan (LAP). The student was given a LAP card on which they were taught to create their plan (see FIG. A.1). The card was a 5- by 8-inch piece of paper of card stock. Five 2- by 2inch boxes were arranged on the card, each with one of five words representing the components of the plan: *What, With Whom, Where, Stuff, When.* The students were instructed by the TRS to create their plan by selecting something for each of the five categories. An example of a planning process follows:

1. *What?* I am going to play cards. (Facilitated by the decision-making process).
2. *Who With?* I am going to play with my two classmates, Jim and Peter.
3. *Where?* At the large table in the classroom.
4. *Stuff?* We will need a deck of cards.
5. *When?* During sixth period leisure time.

The reading and writing skills of the students sometimes precluded them from writing key words in the boxes to represent each component of the plan. In those cases, students were taught to select pictures to represent each component. Each time the student engaged in planning, the TRS provided them with a large binder filled with stickers of pictures representing an array of activities (*What*), locations (*Who With*), and materials for participation (*Stuff*). The binder also contained stickers with pictures of one person, two people, three people, and a group of people. These stickers were used for the "who with" box. Finally, stickers with clocks were also included in the binder. Students were taught to draw the time during which they would participate in leisure on the clock. Students learned to first identify an answer for a given category, and only then did they search through the binder to find pictures to represent their selections. This process was emphasized to ensure that the students created their action plans without being cued by the pictures. If the students identified an activity that did not have a corresponding picture within the binder, the TRS would draw a figure to represent the activity, materials, and so forth.

Students were encouraged to independently engage in the planning process. Each time the student made a decision about their leisure activity, the TRS would say "OK. Now, make a plan for your leisure." She would first wait for the student to initiate the planning by asking for a card and the binder. If, however, the student did not initiate, the TRS would bring out these materials. During the planning process, the TRS would first allow the student time to initiate an idea for each of the five components. Only after the TRS had waited for 5 to 10 seconds did she prod the students by saying, for example: "Who are you going to play Uno with?" Students were also encouraged to independently select their stickers, and they were only assisted when they appeared unsure of what picture to select.

Once the student had created a leisure action plan, the TRS would end the session by saying, "Now you have a plan for today's leisure time. Make sure you do your activity this afternoon." Each student was given a 6- by 9-inch portfolio in which to keep their plan, with a brightly colored marker attached to the folder. During this baseline period, the students were not told to do anything with the plan. Students were verbally lashed if they carried out their leisure action plan, and also if they self-monitored using the card.

Leisure Action Planning and Self-Monitoring

Once students exhibited stable baseline behavior related to self-monitoring and participation, the self-monitoring intervention was introduced by the TRS. This training involved the TRS explaining to the students how they could use their cards to remind them what they had planned to do for sixth-period leisure. In order to assist the students in understanding the self-monitoring process, during the first intervention session, the TRS made her own leisure action plan: to draw a picture by herself. Following this, the TRS carried out the plan in front of the students, and checked off each of the pictures on the plan when appropriate. The TRS then had the students make their own plans. She then encouraged them to carry out the plans, and monitor themselves by checking off the pictures of the plan.

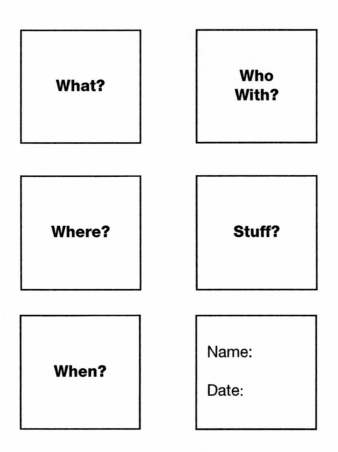

FIG. A.1. Leisure Action Plan.

3

When a Rescue Is Not Enough: A Clash of Three Cultures

Mary Agnes Shelton

Though I didn't know quite what was happening, the fellow escorting me did, and we had to make a break for it. The fellow led me and my new child out the back way and into a taxi. We headed straight for the airport, leaving all of my traveling gear at the hotel. Somehow, the adoption fellow got Luis and I on the next plane out of the country, and we took off with only the clothes I had been wearing. The whole thing was like some spy movie or something, but a lot scarier.

—Dennis (interview)

Dennis was the most rare kind of parent, a single father. I received a referral for Luis, Dennis' son, from the elementary school psychologist, Ms. Godwin. Ms. Godwin had mentioned Luis right away when I asked her about possible suitable students for our Family Link in Leisure Education (FLLE) program. Luis was a bright child, but he had numerous learning difficulties which had caused him to be classified as LD in the public school system. According to Ms. Godwin, Luis had been adopted by Dennis from a Brazilian orphanage several years earlier.

Luis was dark-skinned with black hair, whereas Dennis was quite fair—they were obviously not blood related. So, for father and son, they made quite an unusual pair. Ms. Godwin said, "Luis' dad can use all the help he can get. He's a conscientious, dedicated father, but Luis gives him a run for his money, that's for sure."

The family dynamics of a single-father parent situation seemed interesting to explore because it was so unusual, so I called Dennis to see if he would be interested in participating in FLLE. Dennis' response was overwhelming—he was absolutely jubilant! He kept repeating over and over how glad he was that I had asked him. I agreed to meet with Dennis during lunch at his workplace to fill him in on the FLLE program and what we could offer.

I met with Dennis at South Side Hospital where he works in pharmacology. We talked on the phone first, and we described ourselves to each other so that we could find each other in the lobby. Dennis described himself as almost bald with brown hair, wearing a lab coat and khaki slacks. I told him I would be wearing a maroon woven shawl with black fringe. We walked right to each other. (Dennis really only has a receding hairline.)

Dennis showed me to a corner of the lobby where we sat in comfortable chairs and began our interview. I went over some of the possibilities for Luis through Family Link, and I explained what we might work on. Dennis said he was particularly interested in working on social skills with Luis. I asked Dennis how he came to adopt Luis, and he told me this story:

> Six years ago, while I was working for an organization that helped find homes for orphaned children on a global scale, I heard about a 3-year-old orphan in a Brazilian orphanage who was not doing well. Without improved medical treatment, the child was in danger of losing his hearing and sight, and possibly even dying. The adoption agency was desperately trying to find a home for the child, but without much success. I made the radical decision to adopt the child myself, even though I felt entirely inadequate as a parent. Friends and co-workers agreed to be supportive and helpful, and they rallied around me to help me proceed with the adoption. I flew to Brazil to pick up the child myself.
>
> The orphanage contained 8,000 residents, with one adult caretaker for about every 50 kids. Children were strapped into cribs, hosed down in large rooms for baths, and fed minimal foodstuffs in giant warehouse rooms full of picnic tables. Children never received personal attention at all. The conditions were unbelievable. My heart was broken by what I saw there. Many of the children were sick, malnourished, and dying. The staff was overwhelmed to the point of exhaustion.
>
> When I met Luisersone (which I shortened to Luis), Luis had never spoken a word, even at 3. Luis had skinny little arms and legs and a swollen belly from malnutrition. When I was ready to take Luis away, the staff person said that they would have to leave the clothes that Luis was wearing because the orphanage couldn't afford to let any clothes leave with the kids.

I had to wrap Luis in my own undershirt, so I wouldn't be carrying a naked child down the street.

When I and the fellow from the South American branch of the adoption agency who was helping me returned to the hotel carrying Luis, we saw a uniformed immigration agent in the lobby. Though I didn't know quite what was happening, the fellow escorting me did, and we had to make a break for it. The fellow led me and my new child out the back way and into a taxi. We headed straight for the airport, leaving all of my traveling gear at the hotel. Somehow, the adoption fellow got Luis and I on the next plane out of the country, and we took off with only the clothes I had been wearing. The whole thing was like some spy movie or something, but a lot scarier. Apparently, the Brazilian government would often hold kids hostage who were up for adoption to Americans to try to get more money before letting them go.

Upon returning to the States, I learned that Luis had been sexually and physically abused and that his vision and hearing damage was due to repeated blows to the head. At first, doctors thought perhaps Luis vision and hearing would continue to deteriorate and that he would be deaf and blind by the time he was ten. Fortunately, the degeneration has leveled off and stabilized. Luis wears thick glasses and a hearing aid, but he gets along okay in school despite his handicaps.

I don't know anything about Luis parents except that his mother was *indigenos* and his father was African-American. I don't know the circumstances of Luis ending up in the orphanage. I'm glad I don't know because when Luis asks about it, there is nothing to tell—no secrets to hide.

Dennis was a single father. He had no support from his natural family, but he had an excellent network of friends in Iowa where he first took Luis. At first, Luis medical and behavioral problems were overwhelming, and Dennis was really frightened about the situation that he had created for himself. His network of friends had been essential for him to make it with Luis at all. When Luis finally began to talk and respond to loving attention, many people rejoiced along with the new father.

Three years ago, Dennis and Luis moved to this area so that Dennis could work at South Side. The first year was hard because they didn't know anyone well, but they have now built a new network of friends that feels like a family for them. Dennis also said, "We have been really lucky with teachers for Luis at Brentwood. He has had excellent teachers every year."

Dennis said he would very much like to work with FLLE and he signed the forms for informed consent and transportation. We made arrangements to meet the following week at Dennis and Luis home.

What a story! I teared up as Dennis was telling it. I felt really good for Luis that Dennis was able to rescue him. Dennis appears to be sort of an odd fellow. He has a very serious expression and speaks precisely and a little more slowly than is usual. However, when he smiles, it is a bright experience, as his whole face lights up and his eyes dance. But then the smile disappears immediately. His smile is like a flash of light. Sometimes, he almost smiles, so that his eyes sort of crinkle up but his mouth stays serious. He seems really reserved at first, but has a lot to say and goes into great detail about his topics. I enjoyed our time together and am looking forward to getting to know him and Luis. (Field notes)

I was very impressed with Dennis and the life he had undertaken by adopting Luis. He had created a nontraditional family for himself with possible social ostracism as a built-in component, especially here in the South. I thought that Dennis was a likable fellow and would be a very interesting person with whom to work. I was soon to find out that there was an even more interesting and unusual history involved with this small, atypical family

ASSESSMENTS

The next visit with Dennis was designated for completing the needs, strengths, and activity assessments concerning Luis. It was also the first time I met Luis in person.

I arrived at Dennis and Luis house at 8 p.m. on a cold night. The house is located on a circle drive about five blocks from Luis school, Brentwood. Many of the houses nearby had Christmas lights up, since Christmas is in 3 weeks, but not Dennis'. The neighborhood felt safe and comfortable—well-established with lots of trees and not much traffic. Dennis' house is red brick with white trim and looks neat and tidy. There were no lights on that I could see from the outside, and I thought perhaps they had forgotten I was coming. But when I walked up the driveway, I could see lights in the depths of the house. Dennis answered the door when I rang the bell.

Dennis was wearing a white sweatshirt and blue jeans. He is a slender, small-boned man, probably in his mid-30s. He has a fair complexion that looks as if he might have had freckles as a youth. Dennis greeted me with a warm smile and led me through the apparently rarely used, dark living room into the kitchen. Luis was sitting at the kitchen counter finishing his dinner.

Luis is a little on the small side for 9 years old. He has a round face, golden brown skin, black curly hair cut short, and a very wide grin. He was wearing thick glasses that made his eyes look even bigger than they already are. I noticed he was wearing a hearing aid in each ear. An outstanding feature of Luis face were his lips, which are perfectly formed with a very distinct outline. He is really a very attractive child and will probably be quite handsome as a man.

Luis said "Hi" to me as soon as I entered the room. Dennis introduced us. Luis wanted to show me some Christmas presents that he had already received from friends who celebrate early. He bounced exuberantly next to Dennis, seeking permission, until a nod from Dennis gave the okay. Luis disappeared into his room and returned in seconds with a basket full of gifts. He pulled me to the dining room table, pointed out the chair I was to sit in, and chattered excitedly as he displayed each gift. I was charmed by Luis immediate acceptance of me as a new friend and his ready sharing of his delight. Dennis smiled and shook his head at my exuberant welcome by his son. (Field notes)

During my conversation with Luis, I described the FLLE program to him and told him some of the things we might work on together. Luis seemed particularly interested in the part about making and keeping friends. He said he would like to have lots of friends. I asked him if he wanted to participate in our program, and he said, "Yes, definitely."

Dennis sent Luis off to bed then, reminding him to brush his teeth. Luis reappeared twice for more scraps of conversation, until Dennis said that if he showed up again, he'd be in trouble. The last time out, Dennis and I both received hugs. Dennis served a pot of tea, and I handed him the assessment sheets. (Field notes)

As Dennis filled out the strengths assessment, he commented on a number of the questions:

Luis has a great deal of hope—he is very positive about life. Sometimes, Luis lies. Luis is very outgoing. He responds particularly well to adults, not so well with peers. Luis would like to have relationships with peers, but that he really doesn't know how to relate. (Interview)

As we continued, Dennis began reporting details about Luis and himself. For the first 3 years, it was very hard with Luis. He was violent, acting out all the time, and people were afraid of him. At one point, Dennis said:

I checked into annulling the adoption because I didn't think I could make it. But the past 3 years have been getting steadily better. We have done a lot of family therapy, and Luis is growing up. I attend parenting workshops three or four times per year. I really try to be a good parent—some of the kids' parents I see don't seem to be trying very hard. (Interview)

We discussed TV, and parents letting the TV raise their kids. Dennis and Luis don't watch TV except for occasional programs on PBS. Dennis considers commercial TV to be a complete waste of time. Luis watches it sometimes at the after-school babysitter's, and Dennis wishes there were something he could do about that.

Dennis said that he and Luis had found a nice local church there in the neighborhood. They had tried several churches when they were searching for friends and had felt like outsiders until they went to this church. He said:

> We felt included in the congregation as one of its own. The minister and the people were all supportive and helpful. Luis had a good time in Sunday School, and we liked the church socials and such. We had met some other families that we could be friends with who lived here in the community. (Interview)

One important strength that Dennis described has to do with Luis ability to "read" a crowd. Dennis said,

> Luis can be in a gathering of people and assess who they are and what they want, and use that to his advantage. He can be very charming, getting people to do things he wants. When we get home from an event with adults, I am often amazed at the level of observation and intuition that Luis displays when he talks about the people he met. Luis doesn't have the same skill with children, only adults. (Interview)

Another important strength that Dennis described was that Luis was willing to work really hard at something, like his homework and at school. His retention was short, so he had to keep routines going or he would lose momentum. For example, he had to keep reading over the summer every day or he would lose ground. Dennis helped him with all of this. They would do about 2 hours of studying and homework every night. Just recently, Luis had begun to enjoy reading on his own for its own sake. Dennis felt that this is a big turning point. Dennis clearly wanted Luis to have good reading skills and good math skills. Whatever he would do from then on would be okay with Dennis—to go to college or not. According to Dennis, "Luis has strong self-esteem and is a happy kid."

During the needs assessment, Dennis said that he thought Luis could use help during recess and at lunch at school. He wasn't sure that was going well. Dennis felt that social skills are the big one for Luis. When looking at the use of free time, Dennis said that Luis hardly had any. He rarely got to choose what he wanted to do. Most of his time was filled with necessities and school work. During the parental assessment, Dennis told me about his own background:

> I was raised Amish in South Dakota. My mother was Native American, and my parents were Mennonite. We moved into the Amish community of 800-1,000 people in South Dakota and were always considered outsiders. I felt our family was always discriminated against. I had a very hard childhood, working constantly on the farm. During the summers, I wouldn't see any other people except my own family, two sisters and my parents. I couldn't wait for school to start each year. My family was very somber and serious. I have NO happy memories from childhood.

When I was 18 years old, I left the community and went to the University of South Dakota on scholarship. My parents disowned me. They said if I left the community, they had no son. The years in college were difficult—I didn't know anyone, was deserted by my family, and had no social skills. I loved school though, and loved being around all the people. (Interview)

Although Dennis' parents knew about Luis, "they still aren't warm, but they do acknowledge us [Dennis and Luis] as part of their family."

When we talked about the interests Luis had, Dennis said Luis liked to be outdoors—he "likes to do boy things with sticks." Sometimes, Dennis and Luis would walk to the school playground in the summer, and Luis liked to play there. They both enjoyed active stuff. Since money was tight for Dennis and Luis, they liked to find free things to do, such as going to the art museum, attending free movies at the museum in the summer, watching local neighborhood sports, and visiting friends.

Dennis said he had been very pleased with the neighborhood sports programs for the kids. Luis liked baseball.

He [Luis] tried and liked soccer, but he played too rough. He would hit other kids and get too revved. He wanted to win at all costs. He did better with baseball, not so much physical contact where he might hurt someone. (Interview)

Dennis liked going to the games because he could meet parents there. They had a chance to chat, and he learned about parenting from them.

During the assessment, Dennis told me that Luis had a neighborhood friend who sometimes came over to spend the night.

His name is Joseph, and he is a "slow learner," too. He is a quiet, low-key kind of kid, and he and Luis complement each other. Luis revs Joseph up, and Joseph calms Luis down. Both I and Joseph's parents like the effect they have on each other. (Interview)

I had spent 3 hours with Dennis, so I began to squirm a bit to help him head for a conclusion. I felt that he could have talked for hours. Dennis may have felt a bit isolated from other adults despite his network of friends. Dennis took the hint and wrapped it up. He thanked me and said he had enjoyed the evening. In my field notes, I wrote:

A very interesting guy. Perhaps the Amish bit relates to his apparent seriousness and strictness of routine for Luis. He is certainly an involved parent and is devoting all of his energies to creating what he feels is a good life for Luis. Luis is one lucky kid to have ended up with Dennis. I feel I am really going to enjoy working with this family.

The next assessment to undertake was the one with Luis. I was looking forward to meeting with Luis because he had appeared so energetic and enthusiastic on the night I had first met him. Dennis said we should probably schedule the interview for a Friday night because of Luis rigorous homework schedule, which didn't leave him much extra time on school nights.

I arrived at Dennis and Luis house at 8 p.m. on Friday. When we made the appointment, Dennis had said it would be okay for Luis to stay up until 10 p.m. because it was the weekend. When I rang the bell, Dennis answered the door with Luis right behind him. Luis was jumping around and looking excited that I was there. Dennis showed us to the den where the TV and all their plants were kept. It was a dark room, all done in tones of brown. There wasn't much around to make it attractive or homey. Dennis said he was going to leave us alone—he would be reading in his room.

I asked Luis how it was going at school. He said it was all okay. Luis asked me about my job—just what I did and why. He wanted to know with whom else I worked and what I had done with them. He wanted to know what we would do together, but I told him we didn't know yet, and that's why we were doing the assessment. He appeared to take it all in and be satisfied.

I sat on the couch with Luis right next to me. As we went over the assessment, he leaned over to read what I was reading. Several times he read ahead of me and answered the question before I even got it asked. He appeared to read quickly and accurately. Luis was quite lively and interested in answering the questions. He enjoyed thinking and talking about himself. He answered the questions accurately—the same way I would have answered them for him. He displayed a very positive attitude about himself and his life. He enjoyed most things and felt good about himself. He rated himself quite highly on attitudes about people and having good relationships. The needs that Luis felt were most pressing for him included having people to do things with, spending more time with friends, and controlling anger and disappointment. Luis favorite activities centered around sports, especially baseball and soccer, and doing arts and crafts, particularly drawing, painting, and working with clay.

Luis paid attention and remained focused throughout the entire assessment. When we finished, he hopped up and ran to get his video games to show me. He had gotten a new one for Christmas—something about dragons, so he put that one on. He didn't do very well with it—he kept sinking in the swamp on the second level. Then he put in Mario Brothers, and he cleaned up there. I could tell he'd done that one a lot. It demonstrated how good he could get with practice on something.

We spent about 45 minutes with the video games—with him showing me how he played. I said I really needed to go, and Luis begged me to stay and play some more. I had to virtually pry myself away because he wanted to me stay so badly.

As I was walking to the door, Dennis came out and said "good-night." I told them both I'd be in touch about the leisure plan.

Luis is a great kid. He is intelligent and interested and fun. From what I've heard from people, it seems that he has recently rounded a milestone in his development, and that things are getting better for everyone. Luis is learning to understand that other people have feelings, too and that cooperation is really key in getting along with others. (Field notes)

The last assessment was with Ms. Conrad, Luis teacher. Ms. Conrad was a young, pretty woman who appeared a bit harried and overwhelmed every time I saw her. She was responsible for 28 nine-year-olds with only the help of a part-time teacher's aide. When I took the assessment to her after school, she asked me to leave it for her to fill out and give back to me. I really preferred to do an interview because I received so.much extra information during the conversation, but I acquiesced to her wishes.

Ms. Conrad saw Luis major needs as having more friends, improving his social skills, and gaining better control of his emotions. During observations in the classroom, I saw that Luis hyperactivity and need for recognition combined to make him one of her more difficult students. Luis could be quite a pest to other students when he wanted their attention while they were otherwise engaged. I felt that being in such a large classroom was not in Luis best interest because he just couldn't get the attention he needed. When I mentioned this situation to Dennis later, he said he thought the same thing. He had looked into private schools which had a much better teacher-to-student ratio, but the costs were prohibitive. Dennis said he had decided he would just have to deal with what he could get in the public schools.

GOALS

After comparing, contrasting, and combining the assessments, I presented the following goals and some possible techniques for attaining them to Dennis, Luis, and Ms. Conrad:

1. To improve social skills
   a. weekly social skills training
   b. observation and assistance with personal interactions
2. To increase community involvement
   a. Boy Scouts (mentioned by Luis as a possibility)
   b. karate (mentioned by Ms. Conrad as a way to channel excessive energy)
   c. Brentwood library programs (available in the neighborhood)
   d. Brentwood sports program (Luis was already successful in this program for baseball)

Dennis, Luis, and Ms. Conrad agreed that these looked like the main areas to pursue and that the ideas for accomplishing them were reasonable. In discussions with Dennis and Ms. Conrad, it was decided that Luis really only had time to pursue one of the community activities. When the full range of possible activities was presented to Luis, he chose baseball. Since Dennis enjoyed participating in baseball with Luis, I didn't really need to get involved in that activity. Therefore, my work with Luis became focused on social skills.

SOCIAL SKILLS

I began working on social skills with Luis by consulting with Dennis and Ms. Conrad and observing Luis interacting with his peers at school. During observations, I could see that Luis had some areas to work on in order to get along better with his peers, but I didn't think it was anything very serious. I felt that Dennis was considerably more concerned than he needed to be. I tried to communicate my feelings that Luis would settle down and fit in better as he grew up. I felt that the most important thing Dennis could do for Luis was to be sure that his son knew that Dennis loved him, no matter what. Dennis received all this by saying, "Yes, but he needs to be really good in math and reading and be able to get along with peers, if he's going to succeed in this world." Since I felt that Dennis wasn't able to hear what I was saying, I just tried to model the behavior I thought would be helpful.

Since I could see that Luis might use some help with his social skills, I asked Dennis and Ms. Conrad to help me come up with a list of behaviors to address. Our list included:

1. personal space (standing or sitting the "right" distance from another person for conversation),
2. interrupting (dominating conversations),
3. waiting one's turn, and
4. observing social cues from other people and what they mean.

We felt that these four behaviors were the ones causing the most difficulty for Luis. I developed worksheets for Luis to use to draw his attention to each of the behaviors, and I presented them to him at our weekly sessions. Dennis participated in the sessions with us.

PERSONAL SPACE

The first social behavior that we addressed was about personal space and the distance that people maintain while conversing, or even when being next to each other. Ms. Conrad in particular had stressed that Luis often stood too close and made people feel that he was "up in their face." We thought that it probably had to do with Luis' being hard of hearing, but he would still need to learn to adjust his distance from other people to allow them to feel comfortable.

During one session at his home, while Dennis finished putting the clean dishes away, I discussed "social skills" with Luis and that it means "how people get along with each other in a polite and friendly way." Luis had a good understanding of what I was talking about. I explained the "Close Encounter" worksheet to him—that we were talking about the distance that people place themselves from each other when they interact (see the appendix). Dennis came over and sat down next to Luis. I had Luis move various distances from Dennis' face as he talked to him to see how it felt. Luis got the idea. Luis comfortable distance was considerably closer than is usual.

We went through the exercises on the worksheet with Luis reading them aloud and discussing what it would mean for him to do each one. Two of the six exercises were for homework—things he was supposed to do at school and on which he would report back the following week.

The last exercise was for Luis to draw two people standing too close and then draw two people standing just right. Luis said he was drawing his dad and himself standing just right. Then he was drawing his dad and his dad's girlfriend standing too close because he thought they would like that. Dennis was listening and smiled. Luis said he was drawing her as very beautiful because she was. Dennis agreed that she was beautiful.

APPENDIX: CLOSE ENCOUNTERS WORKSHEET

When we talk to people, or even stand near them, there is a certain distance that is comfortable for most people. How far this is depends on social custom. In our culture, about two feet is a normal distance to be apart to talk or listen to each other. Some people may want a bit more distance. Here are some exercises to see how you handle your "close encounters."

1. When you are talking to your dad, stop at some point and stand very still. With a yardstick, measure how close your faces are to each other. Does this distance feel comfortable to you? Ask your dad if it is comfortable for him.
    Answers:

2. At school, watch three different students and see how far they are from people they are talking to. Is it the same for all of them? Which one are you the most comfortable talking to?
    Answers:

3. Do you sometimes need to stand closer to someone so you can hear him or her better? What would you say if you needed someone to speak up?
   Answers:

4. How would you know if someone felt that you were standing too close when you were talking to him? What would you do?
   Answers:

5. For next time, watch kids and teachers at school to see if you see anyone standing or leaning too close to someone else. How did you know they were too close? See if you notice yourself being too close to someone else. How did you know? What did you do?
   Answers:

6. Draw two people standing too close together when they are talking. Then draw two people standing together having a conversation and being just the right distance apart.

The following week, Luis said he had enjoyed the worksheet. We talked about his observations and what he felt he was learning from the experience. Luis said he had observed kids standing too close several times and that it made people back away from them. He said he thought he would be able to tell when he was standing too close because people would draw back from him.

Interrupting and Waiting Your Turn

Since it appeared that Luis had the gist of the personal space lesson, we went on to the next one, "Talkus Interruptus." Dennis, Ms. Conrad, and I had all observed that this was a problem for Luis. The following is the worksheet I created for Luis on interrupting.

Talkus Interruptus

There is an old social dinosaur that we all wish would become extinct. He is called the "talkus interruptus." He rears his ugly head when someone begins speaking while another person is already talking. Do you know this dinosaur? Have you ever seen someone turn into him right in the middle of a conversation? Have you ever turned into him? Here are some exercises to help you recognize and defeat (at least for yourself) the terrible "talkus interruptus."

1. Pick one evening this next week for you and your dad to pay attention to see if you interrupt each other. Decide which night it will be

in advance. Then for two hours, including dinner, both of you listen to see if you can catch each other or yourself interrupting. If you do, raise your hand and say, "Excuse me, you were interrupting," or "Excuse me, I was interrupting." Make an "X" by your name if you interrupted. See who gets the most "X"s.

Luis:

Dennis:

2. Pick a day at school to watch for "talkus interruptus." Choose one of your friends to listen to during one lesson, and see if he interrupts during that time. Write down his name and make an "X" for every interruption. During another lesson, listen for how many times a student interrupts Ms. Conrad. Make an "X" for every interruption. Also, make an "X" for every time Ms. Conrad interrupts a student.

Friend:

Students interrupt Ms. C.:

Ms. C. interrupts students:

3. Here is a harder one. On a different day, pay attention to yourself during a whole morning in class. Keep track of how many times someone interrupts you when you are talking AND keep track of how many times you interrupt someone else when he or she is talking.

Someone interrupts you:

You interrupt someone:

4. If you are talking and someone else starts talking before you are finished, what could you say? If someone else is talking and you start talking by mistake, what could you say?

Answers:

5. Draw a picture here of "talkus interruptus."

At the next session, Luis reported back on his observations of interrupting behavior. Then, we moved on to waiting one's turn and sharing. Here is the story from my field notes:

Luis said he had listened to hear people interrupting or being interrupted at school during the week. He said (and had marked on his paper) that the kids interrupted Ms. Conrad 9 times when he was listening for it. He also showed that Ms. Conrad had interrupted kids 7 times. He had marked about kids interrupting him and his doing it to them. The question about him and Dennis interrupting each other wasn't marked yet, so Luis did it right then. He marked that he interrupted Dennis 5 times, and Dennis interrupted him 10 times. We talked about interruption a bit, and I felt that Luis had gotten the point. I told Luis that tonight's session was going to be on sharing and taking turns. We would work on that by playing the games I had brought. Luis thought that was a great plan.

Luis wanted to try out one of the games right away, so we did. The game was Ker-Plunk. We both had a good time, stressing the taking turns part of playing. Luis was a little disappointed when he lost, but he was a good sport about it.

Then Dennis joined us, and we all played the games. We played Ker-Plunk, Ants in the Pants, and Jenga several times. We stressed taking turns and sharing as we played. Sometimes Luis' enthusiasm would lead him to jump ahead of his turn, but he was easily redirected. Luis really liked it when Dennis messed up or made an error. Finally, Luis began to get fidgety, so we wrapped it up. Dennis and I congratulated Luis on a good job of taking turns and sharing.

The next plan is to work on sharing and taking turns, along with noticing social cues with a friend of Luis, probably Joseph. (Field notes)

Observing Social Cues From Other People

Luis and I began exploring social cues by talking about what that means and how one recognizes how another person is feeling in ways besides words. Luis seemed to have a good understanding of the concept, but he tended to run right over other people anyway. Luis and I decided to work on the idea of social cues with a real live participant, Luis friend Joseph.

Joseph was spending a few days with Dennis and Luis during Spring Break, so I went to Dennis and Luis' house while he was there.

I met Joseph, who shook my hand, as soon as I went in. He seemed to be a nice kid, mild-mannered and wearing glasses. Luis was playing Mario Brothers when I walked into the den. He didn't appear to be sharing with Joseph but was hogging it all himself. Joseph was letting that pass—it appeared that he really didn't care. When Luis got stuck, Joseph said he could get him past the barrier. After several attempts, Luis let Joseph take him past. Then, Luis took the stick back and kept playing himself. I said that I didn't think that seemed very fair, and we were here together to work on sharing and noticing social cues. The three of us talked about that, and Luis agreed that he should remember to take turns.

> I brought several games to play, and we got them out. Luis was sort of all
> over the place wanting to start right in without telling Joseph how to play. I
> made him wait and slow down, pointing out how he could tell that he was
> going too fast for Joseph. Joseph was polite and reticent. I urged Joseph to
> speak up for his turn and not let Luis run all over him. (Field notes)

Luis really wanted to win at all the games. He felt shamed when he
made a mistake, as if it were something personal. When he did win, he gloated
and bragged. Joseph and I both talked about how we would rather just have fun
and that winning wasn't very important. Luis heard us, but he really didn't buy
it. I pointed out how it might not be fun for someone else to play with him if he
bragged so much about winning. Luis said he thought that was true, but he didn't
back off much.

Luis is a difficult kid to play with, more so for a peer than an adult. He is
so revved and enthusiastic that he tends to just run over the other person. It seemed
to me that it would take a kid as laid back as Joseph to even put up with him.

Follow-Up

During the final interviews with Luis, Dennis, and Ms. Conrad, they all agreed
that they thought the social skills lessons had been helpful. Luis said that he
hadn't really thought about trying to see how other people felt before and that
he would try to do that now. Dennis said he loved the extra help and having
another adult work with Luis at home besides himself. Ms. Conrad said she was
hopeful that Luis would continue to develop his social skills and learn to get
along better with his classmates as he grew older.

A year later, I did a follow-up interview with Dennis and Luis. Dennis
said that things were going quite well. Luis had another very good teacher and
was making good academic progress. He also had two friends, and one was a
girlfriend. Dennis felt that Luis was learning how to get along with peers better
as he got older. Luis agreed that his life was going quite well. He said he had a
very good time at school, but he wished he didn't have so much homework.
Dennis and Luis both said that the most important aspect of the FLLE program
had been that it had been in the home and had been directed toward Luis' real
needs. They had really liked it that I came to their house and interacted with
them in their everyday surroundings. They both felt that directing Luis' attention to his social behavior in a very personal way had helped him see how he
could change to get along better with his friends.

Summary

I really enjoyed working with this unusual family. Dennis was ready to participate fully, as long as he had guidance on what to do. Dennis was more con-

cerned with Luis academic status than I thought was necessary. I suspected that Luis was a bit developmentally delayed and that he would make entirely adequate progress in his own time. I tried to model a more relaxed, easy-going style of parenting for Dennis while I was working with them. I thought that perhaps some of Luis' hard-hitting drive to win and aggressive interactions were related to the pressure he felt from Dennis.

I attempted to relate some of the thoughts about being relaxed to Dennis in my discharge summary. I reminded him to try to allow himself to discover Luis' talents and interests as they evolved naturally, rather than superimposing his own ideas and desires over Luis innate abilities. I wasn't sure how much Dennis took in my advice, but he assured me that he had been quite grateful for our time together.

I felt that my experiences with Dennis and Luis corroborated two major insights that we had discovered in FLLE about working with students. The first insight involved the importance of knowing a student's family history and situation in order to work with him or her effectively. I felt that it made a vast difference in working with Luis to know his history and his father's history—where they had come from and what they had been through. If I had just met Luis in school and had tried to help him design a leisure and recreation program without knowing what he had to deal with in his life, I feel sure that our entire exchange would not have been nearly as meaningful for either of us.

The second insight centered around the fact that, as recreation therapists, we are not psychologists or family counselors. I felt that Dennis was unnecessarily strict and rigorous in discipline with Luis, probably due to his programming as a child in the Amish community where he grew up. I thought that Dennis could have achieved even better results with Luis by demonstrating his love and caring and using lots of praise rather than maintaining such high expectations for his son. I tried to share my feelings several times, but Dennis really wasn't hearing me. I decided that modeling the behavior that I thought would be positive was the best way to go. People will make the choices they need to in their lives, and I can offer the best of what I have—and that's it.

4

When Boredom
Is Not Chosen

Jacqueline Cavadi

*We need relationships which open us to ourselves, relationships which help
us to be more than what we are. And above all, we need more than one.
[Relationships] are like windows through which you see out in the world
and then back into yourself.*

—Shain (1978, p. 24)

This is a story about Barney, a young man with autism, and the people in his
life; it is about their expectations and the choices they made—to open the door
to his world or to keep his talents locked inside him. For this young man with
autism, the choice belonged to others—to invite him into social interplay or to
force him into a self-focused, isolated existence. This is a story about how others in Barney's life defined who he was through the interactions of their relationship with him. It is about how others chose what reflection Barney would
see, and how he mirrored that reflection.

MEETING BARNEY . . .

At 19 years of age, Barney was no longer an adolescent, but a young man. By late afternoon, bearded stubble shadowed his large, square face, physically marking his adulthood. Standing 5'6" tall, Barney had inherited the not-so-tall stature of both his parents. His ash blond hair was worn military style. The sides and back were short and fuzzy, like a crew cut, while straight bangs, often pushed to the side, framed his forehead. Clear, crystal blue eyes could capture one's gaze and stare with such intensity that it seemed as if he were looking into and beyond the depth of one's eyes.

His brown leather belt or red suspenders served not only for fashion, but also for the true purpose of securing his blue jeans. His rotund belly frequently peeked out from an untucked shirt. As if imitating an image of Santa Claus, Barney often leaned back, patted his belly, and finished with a few circular strokes. Photographs, along with teacher and parent comments, revealed that Barney's heftiness had only been a recent development. Limited exercise, coupled with his fondness for foods, especially bread and fast-food hamburgers, had played a major role in his expansion. The extra pounds seemed to pull his body forward into a perpetual state of unbalance. With his head and torso slightly bent as if to propel himself forward, Barney moved with a quick but awkward momentum. His feet shuffled along the ground, never raised more than an inch, while his eyes cautiously surveyed the ground just a few steps ahead. In movement, he presented an image of an old man on a mission to quickly reach his destination.

As Barney's autism emerged soon after his second birthday, he rapidly began to lose his verbal language skills. When he was younger, his parents' hope that he would regain his speech led to intensive speech therapy, but to no avail. Once able to imitate his favorite cartoon character, Donald Duck, Barney now expressed himself through his own mosaic of communication. This mosaic included expressive body language, sign language symbols, facial expressions, and verbal noises that inevitably required others to rely upon and expand their skills of interpretation.

Barney knew several American Sign Language (ASL) symbols, but he used them less frequently than in the past because he had not been made to consistently use them by others. The signs he chose to use were ones that expressed his immediate desires, such as bread, hamburger, crackers, work, finish, and bathroom. Although he did not use words, Barney played with his voice in a variety of sounds and pitches. His vocal expressions were mostly "inner noises," requiring him to inhale rather than to exhale. His facial expressions ranged from serious intent to humorous contortions. He seemed to enjoy experimenting with his ability to contort his face. His mother commented, "Barney loves to look in the mirror . . . to make funny faces," such as puckering his lips like a blowfish and wiggling them up and down.

Throughout life, people shape and model themselves in response to the messages they receive from others. As we develop and grow, we become more cognizant of the expectations which drive our behaviors and interactions. We receive these expectation cues from our relationships with people, the environment, and the situation. As we mature as individuals, we develop our own self-expectations and learn to choose where we want to be—and with whom we want to be—in order to express ourselves.

> There are friends who feed the spirit, and those that feed the senses, and some whom the attachment is emotional and warm. And you can be different with each of them, so it makes sense to choose one's friends for the different sides of yourself that you want to express. It is in the choice of friends that we decide what we shall feed and what we are willing to let starve. (Shain, 1978, p. 83)

What happens, then, to a young man with autism, who does not have the opportunity to choose where he wants to be and with whom he wants to be? The power to feed, as well as the power to starve, his self-expression belong not to Barney but to the people in his life—family, teachers, professionals. It is others' expectations and attention that dominate his choices, his interactions, and his behaviors, and thus either feed or starve his connection to the social world.

When people reflected low expectations for his potential, Barney responded to these confines by seeking stimulation within his own world. He chose self-stimulatory, repetitive activities for long periods of time: bouncing a ball, spinning objects, sifting objects through his hands, winding and rewinding cassettes. When attention-seeking behavioral expressions were ignored or received negative responses, Barney turned to his mode of repetitious, self-stimulation, unchallenged and unmotivated. With low expectations and minimal positive attention, Barney was like a record, caught in a rut, spinning monotonously while the same cadence played over and over, never changing, never moving forward. Barney was waiting for someone to notice that he was on hold, stuck in the groove—his potential existed, but it remained stifled and untapped.

When others reflected high expectations for his potential and gave him positive attention, Barney ventured beyond his ritualistic activities to express a higher level of talent and capabilities. He made a wider range of choices in activities. He initiated and participated in more activities while behaving in socially appropriate ways. He displayed curiosity and playfulness. Like the spinning record, after one gentle push of the needle, Barney rose to the occasion and released a beautiful expression. The belief that possibilities existed beyond the tiresome groove, combined with personal attention, created a supportive environment for Barney to experience a higher level of talent and skill.

> Friends are people who help you to be more yourself, more the person you are intended to be, and it possible that without them we don't recognize

ourselves, or grow to be what it is in us to be. Our lives are in fact many lives, and we can all be much more than what we are, so there cannot be any doubt that the secret of who we become is whom we meet along the way. (Shain, 1978, pp. 83–84)

Barney's talents lay dormant, waiting for an external influence to stir them awake. The people whom he had met along the way were the external influences—the ones that controlled his connection and relationship to the outside world. This is a story about choice—to stir Barney to recognize himself and grow to be what was in him to be or to sit by complacently and let Barney slip into solitary activity.

HOME SWEET HOME

Barney lived with his father and mother, Mitch and Betty. Barney, his parents, and his only sibling, an older sister named Lynda, moved from their home in the northeastern United States to this state six years earlier. This relocation physically separated them from their extended families. A few years ago, Lynda moved away to the southeast, and since then, has married and moved to Europe. Barney's parents planned to have him live with them indefinitely.

A year and a half earlier, they had sold their ranch-style brick home in a suburban development. While deciding whether to buy or build a new home, they resided in a rented, small, two-bedroom house. A thin line of tall bushes afforded little protection and privacy from the happenings of a convenience store and the stop and go traffic of a major intersection.

Although the ensemble of the rooms was quite inviting and comfortable, the furniture, large in relation to the size of the rooms, gave the house the appearance of having been shrunken. This small house did not provide Barney with the same opportunities of the houses of his youth. Within this house, Barney moved from his bedroom to the kitchen and to the family room; yet, he was never more than 30 feet from his parents. In his early years, Barney had shared a two-story home with his family. The backyard had held a large pool where, at age 3, Barney had first learned to swim and jump off the diving board. A photograph of Barney at age 11 showed him poised in mid-air, high above his trampoline in a large, grassy backyard. Another photograph portrayed a young Barney on a bicycle along the sidewalk on a tree-lined suburban street. Within his last house, a large basement with "perfect-for-balls" linoleum had been his favorite domain, along with a rear patio, both of which he had used independently. In contrast, the logistics of his present home dictated that the doors were latched for safety. Barney could lounge on the front porch on the wooden Adirondack chairs, but never without a parent nearby.

Barney's favorite refuge was in his mauve leather recliner in his dark, paneled bedroom. A bookcase beside him held several framed photographs depicting his father in the service, his sister, a favorite cousin, and a family wedding. Loose photographs of Barney beside a race car, in a race car, and in a school bus rested on a shelf. The indentations and smudges from Barney's fingers had worn the photographs. Sitting cross-legged in his chair, Barney listened to ABBA, his favorite musical group, on his Fisher Price cassette player. His parents were concerned about the age appropriateness of this cassette player, but they had had difficulty finding another one that was both durable and easy to operate. They had conceded the age-appropriate look of toys to ensure Barney's enjoyment.

During an initial meeting with Betty and Mitch, they offered what they called "the history of Barney." They described Barney

> ". . . as a normal baby until he was 2 years old." Mitch said "his gross-motor skills, his speech, everything was normal." Betty said that Barney knew lots of words and that his speech was developing fine. Barney could imitate Donald Duck. Their "first indication that something was wrong was on Barney's second birthday. Barney was sitting in his high chair. Then his head fell forward and hit the high chair and we knew something was wrong." (Field notes)

Doctors placed Barney on several medications to control his seizures. Although the medication helped stop the seizures, they also "made him a vegetable." Betty and Mitch reflected that "they were young and thought doctors were gods," but that they eventually got to a point where they felt that they needed to do something other than keeping him medicated. Another children's doctor agreed to find a way to have Barney remain on a lower level of seizure-controlling medication. Betty and Mitch decided that they "would rather risk a breakthrough of a seizure to have him be able to function." The doctor was able to get the seizures under control and wean Barney off all the medications except for Tegratol, which is "the only drug he was put on and he's been on it ever since."

Betty and Mitch believed that Barney's seizures, and his development of autism, resulted from his DTP immunizations. They felt that the government did not disclose all of the risk factors associated with the immunization. Betty and Mitch had an opportunity to participate in a class action suit filed against the government, but they "decided that it wasn't worth the time they would have to sacrifice, and it wasn't going to change Barney."

Barney had been involved in special education services since he was a small child. When he was younger, Betty and Mitch hoped he would regain his lost speech skills, and thus Barney received intensive speech therapy, but to no avail. Before moving to their present location, Barney was in special education classes with children with varying levels of disabilities. According to his mother, when he was younger, he was in a class "where they wanted him to be able to write his name, whereas all I wanted was for him to be able to pull up his pants." Because of his autism, they had to change their perception of what they wanted for him and what was most important, such as being able to dress himself rather than being able to write his name. They had to adjust to making decisions in regards to what would help Barney, and what would not, such as a lengthy involvement in the class action suit; Mitch and Betty were like other parents— parents with and without children with disabilities. Barney's mother stated:

> We have certain expectations and things [we] want for [our] children. We have to live with Barney and make adjustments, but Barney also needs to learn to conform. Barney needs to learn that there are appropriate behaviors and inappropriate behaviors. We have to meet in the middle on some things. (Field notes)

Barney was an integral part of their family and their social life. As Betty and Mitch pursued meaningful experiences in their lives, they sought for Barney to also experience the same experiences. They did not want him to be merely a content observer of life, but an active participant, and thus, they included him in their community activities. With his participation, Betty and Mitch had high expectations for Barney to have happiness, acceptance, and good social behaviors, and to have choices. His parents' high expectations and their efforts to involve him provided a positive influence for Barney; and thus, he was able to successfully and appropriately participate, have acceptance, and have enjoyment.

For the family, participation in stock car racing was a large part of their leisure life. They had found a community which provided enjoyment, excitement, friendship, and acceptance for themselves and for Barney. On weekends, Barney attended races with his parents. He knew when it was race day, wearing his team jacket to the events. Mitch had commented that Barney got excited, jumped up and down, and clapped his hands when the cars came around the track. Barney had many photographs of himself with the race car. Most were worn and crinkled from his carrying and touching them.

Barney was considered a part of the racing team, and thus he was expected to participate in team activities both on and off of the racetrack. On weekends, he spent time in the car shop with Mitch and the team members. He was not there just to observe, but also to work, and as he completed assigned responsibilities, such as sweeping and helping with the tool cart. On race days, Barney continued to contribute to the team. Barney had been given the tasks of helping with the tool cart and setting up the team chairs because, "you can tell Barney where something goes and he'll remember . . . so, then you just have to tell him, and he knows just where to put it," Barney's father shared.

Equally important to the family were the social acceptance and interaction which Barney received through his participation with the race car team. The family who owned the race car had become good friends with them. According to Betty, they had "always . . . been accepting of Barney" and "always talk[ed] to him and include[d] him." Barney recently attended one of their daughter's weddings with Betty and Mitch. During the reception, the family's foster son, the father reported, "sat with Barney and talked with him. Barney really liked him and kept smiling and smiling. They would have been disappointed if [Barney] didn't come to the wedding."

The Staten's commitment to Barney's inclusion in this family recreation was evidenced by their financial investment in a race car trailer that included a cabin area with a sleeping bunk. Additionally, Betty and Mitch had to invest in a new truck that could pull the trailer. One of the most important factors influencing their decision to purchase the trailer was Barney's enjoyment and comfort. Race days are often long, stretching from early morning to late evening. Tiring easily, Barney's only option was to stretch out and try to sleep on the bleachers amidst the noise of the car races in progress. The new trailer provided Barney with an appropriate and comfortable place in which to rest during these long days, thus enabling him to enjoy the entire experience.

Since he was 3 years old, Barney had loved swimming. He swam weekly with his public school class, but because he enjoyed it so much, his parents enrolled him in the local parks and recreation special populations swimming program for a few years. Members from a local high school's female swim team helped train participants. Two high school students were then in their second year of swimming with Barney. Throughout the session I observed, Barney smiled and giggled as he interacted with his two coaches. Playing a game of pool tag, Barney swam away from the girls, but he looked back to make sure they were chasing him. With their encouragement, he climbed out the pool and he jumped back into the water. During his time in the pool, Barney was completely engaged in the swimming and the interaction with the high school girls. His parents had observed that the importance of the swimming experience was that "Barney was having fun once a week swimming with friends." Their observation was not limited to the benefits for Barney, but they felt "it was [also] good for the girls to be with people like Barney" because it increased their awareness and acceptance of others.

According to Betty and Mitch, one of Barney's favorite activities was to eat out. Betty and Mitch included Barney in all their community outings, especially dining out. About once a month, the family dined out at a private dining club. According to Mitch, when they would tell Barney they were going out and "give him a jacket and tie to put on, Barney gets very excited because he knows [they] are going to the club." The staff at the club knew and welcomed Barney. One staff member always cut Barney's bread into small slices for him before bringing it to the table. During this dining out experience, Barney did quite well with his manners. Mitch pointed out that he did better with his manners in more formal settings than informal ones, which is typical of most people.

During my final week of working with Barney, I was invited by Betty and Mitch to the club for dinner. Barney was dressed in a shirt and tie, a blue blazer, and khaki pants. During our car ride, Betty, Mitch, and I talked, while Barney spent his time looking out the window. Periodically, Barney turned and grinned at me. Once in the club, Barney sat and participated in our conversations by listening and smiling. As his mother had often pointed out, "Barney loves to sit among company." The only assistance he required was in cutting his food and occasionally being reminded by his parents to drink his ice tea more slowly. Every so often, Barney's teasing, humorous side surfaced as he leaned toward his dad, smiled, and "stole" one of Mitch's utensils. Then he would sit back and laugh. I was struck by the fact that had any other diners glanced towards our table, they would have been unaware that Barney had any disability.

The expectation for Barney's happiness was also a guiding force in how Betty and Mitch viewed his future as an adult. Because they "are only in their forties and healthy," they planned for Barney to live with them "until [they] are too old to take care of him." However, it was his happiness that was the main concern in regards to residential considerations. As Barney moved into adulthood, they thought that they might explore residential options "if a group home could give Barney more of what he needs and he would be happy there." In considering residential options, they wished "that group homes allowed a person to come stay for a few hours or a night" to see how they liked it and how they adjusted to it. Barney had only stayed away from his parent's home when he had been with grandparents. Betty and Mitch were concerned about his being comfortable, safe, and happy in another living environment.

At the time, Betty and Mitch were aware that as a young adult, time away from them might have been good for Barney and for them. The consideration was more than just basic respite from each other; instead, the important factor again was Barney's happiness. "Our mothers [could] take him for a week every once in a while, but I don't think hanging around your grandmother's house would be very much fun for Barney." Betty and Mitch believed that "it would be better for Barney to be in a program where they had activities, than to be with just one person." Without a planned program, what "happens all too often" is that people failed to engage him in interactions or activities if he seemed occupied and was not causing any problems.

Additionally, Betty and Mitch considered Barney's future in employment. With his teacher, they had discussed work experience through the schools at the local sheltered workshop. While Betty and Mitch thought this "structured and high level of supervision program" would best meet Barney's needs, they remained concerned about how he might do. Mitch talked about some of his concerns:

> Seeing him at the ARC dance, where he really did not interact with anyone except to shake hands, made Betty think more about how he will do at the sheltered workshop. "It makes me nervous, because Barney would not know if someone were being mean or hurtful to him." Betty worried that he wouldn't be able to distinguish between what was appropriate or inappropriate for someone to do and that she "worried about him being taken advantage of." (Field notes)

Betty and Mitch had other concerns for Barney beyond the long-range future of living and working environments. They had concerns about his present life and enjoyment within their own home. Within his home, Barney had a restricted range of activities in which he participated and enjoyed. On any given afternoon, Barney could be found involved in watching an ABBA video, listening to tapes on his Fisher Price tape recorder, or bouncing on the bed. On occasion, Betty and Mitch could involve Barney in other play activities, but they were "not sure if it is because he really wants to." Their goals were seeing him independently choose and initiate activities and "knowing that he wants to do them and it's not just us giving him something to do." Thus, my goal for working with Barney within his home and classroom was to introduce him to new games that he might independently pursue during his free time. As Betty and Mitch had identified as their priority, "it was really finding him things to do that he wants to do at home."

SCHOOL DAYS

Although there is a high school within a few miles of his home, Barney rode the bus across the county to attend another high school. When the bus arrived in the morning, Barney eagerly hastened out the door to his bus, a short, squat version of the longer, typical school buses. This bus only transported a small number of passengers, all of whom had disabilities. Each morning, the bus rolled into the school parking lot and veered off from the other buses, delivering its charges to the farthest entrance on the right side of school.

To most of the students who attended the high school, their experience occurred across various environs: within different classrooms, the hallways, the cafeteria, the library, the gymnasium, the auditorium, the stairwells, and even the restrooms. For Barney, his school experiences were confined to limited environs: one classroom, the "special" school bus, and structured community excursions with his special education classmates.

At 19, Barney was the youngest of four students who shared this classroom. Barney had attended school in the classroom for 3 years. Only two of the students, Felix and Thomas, spent their day with Barney and the teachers. The oldest, Robert, spent only a brief time with the class, once in the morning and once in the afternoon. The remainder of the day, Robert worked at the local sheltered workshop.

Barney's classroom had no formal walls or partitions, yet imposed boundaries were evident from strategically placed furniture. Two large rectangular tables were pushed together to form a larger multipurpose table for eating, playing with toys, and assembling pizza boxes for a local pizza parlor. Close by, a large, gray metal cabinet stored various games and toys. A side door connected to a classroom for students with severe and profound disabilities, which shared its kitchen and bathroom facilities with Barney's class.

In the far right corner of the room, a gray carpet, two small couches, and few chairs established the limits of the "relaxation" area. Along one wall, the television was always turned on to talk shows, game shows, or soap operas. When Robert returned from the workshop, he announced his entrance by requesting his favorite soap opera characters, "Erica Kane, Max Holden." He was never disappointed. On the wall behind the television, a poster board framed photographs of Barney and his classmates from the previous year's activities, such as Special Olympics and swimming. On any given afternoon, Barney could be found sitting in a chair in the corner, bouncing his favorite blue ball against the wall and/or floor. On some afternoons, Barney would curl up on the couch and sleep.

In the front, right corner of the room, four adjacent desks resembled study carrels from a library, serving as a work station for a student to perform a task—typically sorting objects by type, size, or color. When I first met Barney, he was sifting colored, plastic beads—green and purple—into containers. He scooped an entire handful of mixed colors into his fist. Then, as if performing a magic trick for his audience, he held his fist high above the target container and precisely sifted out only the green beads, while still grasping the purple ones within his fist.

Barney's educational agenda included 2 more years of school. Those 2 years were to be spent within this same self-contained special education class-room. The only anticipated change would be the introduction of new classmates as Robert, Thomas, and Felix would move on. During my visits to his class-room over a 6-month period, teacher comments and classroom observations reflected an atmosphere of low expectations for Barney's potential and capabili-ties. Remarkably, these expectations never wavered, despite the fact that Barney often demonstrated skills and abilities which negated the teachers' perceptions of him. The atmosphere seemed to express that the teachers decided that this was the end of the line as far as Barney's development was conceived.

During an initial interview, his teacher, Barbara, described Barney's ability to understand verbal language as being "like a dog" because "he responds more to the tone of your voice than to the words." This description was incomprehensible to me in light of the fact that Barney consistently responded to verbal directions from many adults, including Barbara, his assis-tant teacher, his parents, and me. And yet, his teacher failed to integrate these invalidations of her perception into her overall view of Barney.

The pervasive message that prevailed within Barney's classroom was that Barney had already reached his maximum potential for learning and devel-oping. When specifically asked what the school's expectations for Barney were for the next 2 years, Barbara responded, "At this point, Barney can't . . . ." She stopped herself in mid sentence and looked up at me. "At this point in the game, we are going to monitor his behavior." The next 2 years of school would consist of a possible 360 days of instructional time and opportunities, and the overall expectation for Barney would be restricted to behavior management.

As indicated by the intent for 2 years of behavior management, Barney's behavior was the primary concern for his Barbara and Grady, the assistant teacher. Repeatedly, they commented how his behavior had changed from the previous year. Barney now seemed more anxious and was demonstrating more negative and inappropriate behaviors, such as masturbating, head banging, putting his feet on the table, and pulling other people's hair. On several occasions, Barbara, his special education teacher remarked, "He has been acting strange"; "I wish he were the way he used to be"; "Grady and I used to say we'd take a lot more kids if they were all as good as Barney." Barbara perceived that the meaning of these behaviors were Barney's effort to gain attention.

> He does this to seek negative attention because he knows he is going to get a reaction. It's like he thinks, "hmmm, they don't like it when I put my hands in my pants, so that's what I'll do to get their attention." (Field notes)

In the past, all Barbara "had to do was to scold him, and he would look up sort of surprised or upset and stop, but now he just looks at you, laughs, and continues."

Barbara clearly and accurately recognized that Barney demonstrated inappropriate behaviors in an effort to seek attention. She felt these behaviors would dissipate if his antianxiety medication levels were adjusted. The ultimate motivation seemed to be to have Barney content and compliant not for his sake or happiness, but for Barbara and Grady's sake. It seemed more important to control his behavior, rather than to address what his actions may have been expressing. For example, one day Barney ran into the bathroom of the adjacent classroom, and

> Suddenly, Barney ran out without his shirt on and holding it in his hands. He was laughing and ran past where Barbara was sitting. He stopped right in front of me. I teased him about not wanting to see his body and told him, "Let's put your shirt back on." I held it for him and he ducked his head and arms into it. Barbara commented, "I told you he has been acting weird lately." She asked me, "Don't you want to stay for the rest of the day?" [I felt as though she wanted me there so she could relax.] (Field notes)

On many occasions that I visited Barney's classroom, I was consistently struck by the fact that *not once* were the teachers actively engaged with Barney in an activity or in social interaction. No one was ever with him. No one was ever talking to him. The communication the teachers had with Barney was primarily restricted to verbal directions and reprimands. I observed one positive engagement between Barbara and Barney, which occurred at my initiation. With my encouragement, Barbara sang "Itsy Bitsy Spider" to Barney. Barney smiled, laughed, and did the hand motions. When the song was over, Barney immediately requested the song again by doing the hand motions. In spite of Barney's overwhelming positive response to this interaction, I never again witnessed any similar interplay between Barbara and Barney.

Each time I entered Barney's classroom, I found him self-absorbed in one of three activities: repetitively bouncing the ball, repetitively spinning an object, or sleeping. In a classroom, among other people, Barney was very much alone. Barbara was reading a newspaper, working on the computer, or talking with another teacher. Grady, the teacher's assistant, was reading a tabloid, watching television, or doing both simultaneously. A typical field note of a classroom visit was:

> Barney was sitting in a chair in the far right corner of the classroom. He was bouncing the ball against the wall. Thomas was lying on the couch; Felix was sitting on the other couch; and Grady was watching some talk show about women who think they are too beautiful. (Field notes)

This was typical for my observations in this classroom and I was often struck by the thought that it was quite possible that Barney might sit alone, bouncing the ball for 2 hours until the school day ended. As long as Barney was not displaying any bothersome behaviors, then he was assumed to be content. Once I posed the question to Barbara regarding indications of whether or not Barney was bored. She responded, "I think sometimes we interpret that he is bored because he is doing repetitive actions, but he is probably content." This perceived contentment appeared to be the accepted goal for Barney within the school environment.

This indifference toward Barney, as well as toward other students, proved to extend beyond the immediate classroom. On an early spring day, I arrived at Barney's classroom to find out that he was outside by the running track with other students. My field note that day read,

> As I approached the track, I could see a group of students and two women sitting on the bench. The bench was situated just inside the asphalt track on the field. Two students were sitting in wheelchairs; three were sitting on the benches. Felix was squatting on the ground just in front of the bench and was using his finger to draw in the dirt. Barney was sitting in his cross-legged fashion on the ground about 10 feet in front of the bench. He was reaching down and grabbing handfuls of dirt and sifting them through his hands. As I got close to him, I realized that his hands were filthy with dirt from sifting it. He had dirt on his jeans, his sweatshirt, and his tennis shoes. Apparently, he had not been discriminating as to where he was allowing the dirt to fall as he sifted. He also had dirt on his face, along with dried ketchup or tomato sauce. (Field notes)

The same complacent attitude prevailed; as long as the students appeared content because they were not demonstrating annoying, attention-seeking behaviors, then any interaction by the teacher was not deemed necessary. That day on the track, Barney and I played; for 20 minutes, Barney laughed, giggled, and teased with me. We played a game of "tickle and chase"; we kicked the ball and ran after it; we played an arm pull version of tug-of-war. As we returned to the two teachers,

One of the teachers said in a concerned tone, "Was Barney running away from you?" I perceived this to be a question of whether or not he was giving me trouble. I laughed and told her, "Oh, no, we were just playing and teasing. I was pretending to chase after him. You know, getting him going, walking, running, and having a good time." (Field notes)

WORKING WITH BARNEY AT SCHOOL

When I was first getting to know Barney, I tried to engage in the repetitive activities he was already doing, such as spinning objects and bouncing a ball. One day while he was spinning a small top, I asked Barney if I could have a turn, and the following occurred:

After it stopped spinning, he picked it up and gave it to me. It was very small; and at first, I had difficulty getting it to spin. Once it stopped spinning, I returned the top to Barney. I asked him again if I could have a turn, and he gave it to me a second time. However, this time he placed the top in front of me and then demonstrated with his fingers in the air how to spin it. (Field notes)

Interestingly, while I observed him, Barney also observed me, and offered me guidance in my spinning technique. This experience laid the foundation for my expectations that Barney had many hidden capabilities that somehow just needed to be tapped. I believed that there was a lot going on inside Barney's head, and that he was thinking and evaluating the present situation all the time. My belief and curiosity prompted me to comment to his teacher that "I would give $100 for just 10 seconds of Barney's thoughts." Barbara responded, "Wouldn't it be funny if he were thinking, 'bounce, bounce, bounce?'" The division in our perceptions of Barney was confirmed.

Arriving at Barney's classroom, I always greeted Barney verbally and with a handshake. After greeting one another, I asked, "Barney, do you want to play?" while also using the ASL symbol for play. The symbol involves placing the hands in a fist, extending the thumbs and pinkie fingers, while rocking the fists back and forth. Over a few months, Barney progressed from responding with a partial imitation using one hand to eventually using both hands held in fists in a close approximation of the sign. This progression of skill development reinforced my perception of Barney's ability and his potential to connect words with symbols to communicate.

Throughout the course of working with Barney, Barbara, his teacher, repeatedly told others and me that "Barney does not attend to pictures" and that "he is object-oriented." However, because of the advantage of spending time with Barney at home, I was exposed to Barney responding to photographs of himself and family members. This exposure led to the idea that Barney could use photographs to respond to and make activity choices. I incorporated photographs of Barney engaged in various activities (i.e. playing Perfection, playing Connect Four, listening to tapes) onto a communication device. With this device, pressing the photograph makes a selection of an activity, and a verbally recorded message is activated. My field note describes how it went on the first day of using the device:

> I had gotten Dan to record the responses so that Barney would hear a male's voice saying, for example, "I would like to play with the ball." I placed the device in front of Barney and before I could even prompt him, he looked at the board, reached out and pressed the picture of himself playing with the ball. The machine, of course, responded with "I would like to play with the ball." Barney looked at me and signed his version of the play symbol—two fists rocking back and forth. I immediately gave him the ball, and he began bouncing it off the table, keeping it to a very low dribble. When he paused with the ball, I asked him, "Barney show me how you say play." Barney immediately signed his play symbol. (Field notes)

Until that moment, Barney had never done the play symbol without my having done it first. I was disappointed that his teachers were not present to witness this event. Over time, Barney had moved from partially imitating a symbol to understanding the conceptual connection of the sign to the word "play," as well as to the action of playing.

Barney and I usually sat by ourselves at the large, rectangular table in his classroom. During the first month, I brought a variety of games and toys with me. As I plopped down the bag onto the table, Barney was curious about what I had brought with me. He scooted to the edge of his seat, strained his body and neck forward, and eyed what was in the bag. Many times, he reached in and pulled the games out onto the table. This view of Barney's curiosity presented a marked contrast to the view of him just moments earlier when I first arrived, when he was sitting alone, completely involved in spinning a play dough lid or bouncing a blue ball. His curiosity and initiation toward the games implied his awareness of the intent of my presence, to play games with him. However, it also indicated his level of interest and desire to participate in activity and interaction beyond his ritualistic, repetitive patterns.

During the early weeks of my intervention, I presented Barney with choices by placing two or three activities on the table and asking him with which one he would like to play. Without physical prompts or cues, Barney always made an independent choice, either by pointing to the game, tapping on it, or just going ahead and taking the pieces out. Barney always self-determined when he was finished by signing "finished," by pushing the game away, or by putting the pieces away. I described our interaction in a field note:

> I took out three toys: Perfection, the sorting game, and the colored peg manipulative toy. At this point, Barney has demonstrated an interest in

Perfection and the sorting game as he has chosen them and played with them for several sessions. I asked Barney, "Which one do you want to play with now?" Barney looked at the three activities and reached for the sorting game. He independently opened the box and took the game out. I spread the pieces out and Barney began picking them up, one by one, and placing them on the peg according to color. When Barney was done, he pushed the game away from him. I asked him, "Barney, are you finished with this game?" He signed "finished" and began putting the game back in the box. (Field notes)

Throughout the 30- to 60-minute sessions, Barney consistently made choices and participated in games. Sometimes, he completed an entire game or puzzle; other times, he signed finished and/or pushed the game away after only partially completing the game. Usually, he then chose another activity from among the other games; however, on a few occasions he chose to find and play with his blue ball.

During one of my last sessions at his school, I entered to find Barney in typical fashion, sitting in a chair in the far, right corner, bouncing a ball against the wall. He came over and we began to play:

Barney took out the shape sorter from the cabinet. I also took out the Perfection game, and returned the ball to the shelf. We sat down at the table, catty-corner to one another. I offered Barney the two games. He took the shape sorter, opened the lid, and dumped all the pieces on the table. On his own, he began putting all the pieces through the geometric slots. Barney was able to fit many of the shapes in the correct place. Frequently, he turned the sorter around to find the correct place. When he was finished, he signed finished, and then got up from the table and returned the shape sorter to the cabinet. I thought Barney might take the ball out, but he did not. He just put the shape sorter back, closed the cabinet, and returned to the table. I thanked him for putting the game away. Barney initiated taking the Perfection game and tried to open the compartment to get the pieces. I asked him if I could help, and he handed the game to me. Once the pieces were on the table, Barney grabbed them and sifted them a few times. As he was playing the game, I took some photographs of him. When I called his name and told him to look up and smile, Barney raised his head and grinned . . . (Field notes)

Similarly, on another day near the conclusion of our months together, the following occurred:

I approached Barney, said hello, and asked him if he wanted to play. He shook his head in a sort of "no" side to side way, but at the same time, he did the play symbol. I asked him again, and he got up and ran away from me. However, Barney ran over to the cabinet, opened it, and took out the game Perfection. Barney and I sat at the table with the game. He dumped all the pieces out onto the table and had to pick up several pieces off the floor. His style of play was fairly typical for this activity: periodic sifting, looking and putting some pieces in correctly, forcing other pieces anywhere. When he was done, Barney signed finished. I asked him to put the game away. We went to the cabinet together, and I asked him to pick something else to play. I was curious as to what he would pick. His cassette player was on the middle shelf, right up front. Instead, Barney pulled out a wooden puzzle. I verbally reinforced him by saying "Good choice. You must really like that puzzle." He dumped all the pieces on the table and proceeded to try to place them into the specific slots. Each time he sifted the piece and let it bounce off the table. Sometimes he redirected himself after anywhere from 10 seconds to a minute. Two or three times I verbally redirected him by asking him where the piece goes or to show me where it fits. He completed the entire puzzle. I asked him if he were finished or did he want to do it again. Barney dumped all the pieces on the table and redid the puzzle. We walked over to the cabinet and I asked him to find something else he wanted to play. He reached in and took out the shape sorter. I chatted to him about how it was like the one he had at home, and how his mom thinks it his favorite activity. He played the game as he usually does: dumping out pieces, sometimes sifting, getting pieces to fit, forcing other pieces. (Field notes)

In the early weeks of my intervention with Barney, he made choices and participated in games based upon having the specific games physically presented to him. As our time together drew to an end, Barney was selecting and initiating playing games on his own. The only outside influence he needed was to have my positive attention and verbal guidance to choose a game. Barney's higher level of choice making and activity initiation grew out of my consistency of personal attention, expectations for him to be involved, and the development of a positive relationship over time.

BARNEY AT HOME

Arriving at their house once a week in the late afternoon, I would find Barney engaged in one of several self-involved activities: sitting in his recliner listening to cassette tapes, watching an ABBA video, or bouncing on his bed. In contrast to his engagement in solitary activities within his classroom, at home he smiled, laughed, and bounced frequently while engaged in his activities. The difference in his affect led me to wonder if his solitary activities at school were used to fill his time, whereas the solitary activities at home were used for enjoyment.

Consistent with my interactions with Barney in his classroom, I always verbally greeted him as well as shook his hand. I then asked him if he wanted to play, as I also signed the ASL "play" symbol:

Barney made his hands into fists and rocked them back and forth similar to the play symbol. I held out my hand, and Barney took it and stood up. We went into the kitchen and sat down at the table. (Field notes)

Just as during our sessions at school, Barney chose the games with which he wanted to play and also self-determined when he was finished with each game:

I offered Barney a choice between Perfection and Connect Four by presenting the games to him. He reached over and took the Perfection game . . . Barney placed several pieces in the board, although a few pieces he was able to fit into different spaces than the ones for which they were intended. . . . There were two pieces for which Barney could not find the proper place. With each piece he made several attempts at trying to finding its slot, but then handed the pieces to me. . . . As Barney was putting the pieces in, Betty and I both offered verbal prompts, such as, "Look at the piece, Barney" and "Look at the board." Barney pushed the game away and signed "finished," although there were still pieces left to fit in the board. He leaned over and tried to peer in the bag of toys which was sitting beside me. Barney reached for the Magna Doodle. (Field notes)

On several occasions, Barney chose a game, played with it, put it away, and then chose another game to play. After a period of 15 to 20 minutes, Barney chose to be finished with all the games, as well as with me. He usually indicated he was finished with me by simply leaving the room. For example, on one such occasion, he selected and played with a puzzle, Perfection, the sorting game, and was next involved with Connect Four when

he accidentally dropped a piece under the table. When he leaned down to pick it up, he also found a Perfection piece. Barney took the Perfection box to put the piece away. Barney returned to the Connect Four game and continued to spin and place the pieces in the game. When he was done, he signed "finished," and then got up and went into his room. I followed him into his room, where he sat down in the recliner with his cassette player. Betty came in and told Barney to show me how he rides the exercise bike which is in his room. With Betty's encouragement, Barney got on the bike and peddled and did the arm poles for about 20 seconds. . . . After that, he got off and brushed by me, took his cassette player off the chair and went into the living room. (Field notes)

Throughout my time with Barney, he developed specific preferences for the games I introduced to him. I left the games at his house for him to use during the week. When I gave them to him,

he added the games to two other toys that were already on the chest and then pushed them so that they were neat. I also handed him the Magna

Doodle and the colored peg manipulative board. Interestingly, he handed the pegboard back to me. (Field notes)

Despite his awareness of what games he liked, he primarily only engaged in the activities if either his parents or I invited him to choose one to play, although, on a few occasions he sought out some on his own. Barney's parents spoke of his involvements:

> I told Betty I wanted to get her feeling for how these activities were working. She said, "He'll do things when we give them to him and get him to sit down. But then he'll do them for a few minutes and sign 'finish' and go back to what he wants to do. It's like 'okay, I did what you wanted me to do, now I am going to do what I want to do.'" She said he still goes for the ball, the tape player, and the video most often. She said that of the games, "Connect Four and the sorting game are his favorites." She said of the manipulative peg game, "he only touches that to move it out of his way." She said that once in awhile after they have played a few games, he'll sign "finish" and stack up all the games. (Field notes)
>
> Mitch said that "The biggest thing has been his initiating choices and things he wants to do. Did Betty tell you that two or three times this weekend he brought the shape sorter out on his own? He also brought the Connect Four out once or twice." He continued saying something like, "It is great to see him doing things and knowing that he wants to do them and it's not just me giving him something to do." (Field notes)

As I worked with Barney both at home and in school, I began to notice that his behaviors and interactions with me were different between the two settings. Within his classroom, Barney seemed more subdued and more focused on the objective of the activity, while at home, Barney seemed less focused on the game and more focused on seeking my reaction. Some of his behaviors involved putting objects in his mouth while laughing, banging his head, and/or touching himself inappropriately. If I paid attention to him and ignored the inappropriate behavior, Barney usually redirected himself. A typical example follows:

> I offered him Connect Four and the sorting game, from which he chose Connect Four by taking the game and opening it up. He periodically stopped and either sifted, spun, or put the pieces in his mouth. When he put the pieces in his mouth, he looked at me and laughed. With prompts to go "faster and faster" or "Barney it's your turn," Barney focused and put several pieces in a row in the board. (Field notes)

Within his home, but not at school, Barney requested other playful interactions, such as singing songs. For Barney, that meant that he did the motions while the other person sang the words. Within these singing interactions with others, Barney expressed such enjoyment and pleasure that did not seem to exist in any other activity in which I have observed him.

I asked Barney if he wanted to play, and I did the ASL "play" symbol. He continued to bounce and laugh. He looked up at me, and then he made his motion for the "Wheels on the Bus" song—he sticks his right arm out with his hand in a fist and his thumb pointing down and then he moves his arm in a circular motion. In response to his initiation, I sang two stanzas for him about the wheels going round and the people going up and down. Barney kept looking right at my face and smiling at me. Barney reached out and took my hand. I thought he might be shaking it "good bye," so I asked him if he wanted me to leave. Barney shook his head in a combination "yes" nod, "no" shake. Barney was holding my left hand with his right hand. He reached over and took Betty's right hand with his left hand and continued to smile. After about 5 seconds, he let go of Betty's hand and took hold of both of my hands and started rocking his upper body forward and backward. I took this to mean sing "Row Row Row Your Boat." While I was signing, Barney continued to push and pull and smile and laugh. He kept laughing and whipping his head down toward his chest. Betty also sang to. . . "Wheels on the Bus." Barney did the motions to the song, smiled and laughed, and bounced up and down several times. (Field notes)

CONCLUSION

The relationships in your life are very important to you—they are a big part of who you are. We truly do very little alone in life. Many people have played a part in helping you arrive where you are now, for better or for worse. People have the capacity to touch your life, teach you, and help you grow. (Negley, 1997, p. 1)

In working with and observing Barney, the questions I kept asking myself were: "In what capacity do the people he has met, and is presently meeting, along the way effect his life, his choices, his self-expression? What part do the people in his life play regarding where has arrived and where he is going?" For Barney, living his life with autism had put him in a position in which he had little choice about with whom and where he spent his time, and therefore, the influence of others played a primary and powerful role in directing his actions. His teachers, his parents, and I all had different beliefs and expectations, different experiences, and different relationships with him. And, thus, logically, Barney had different expectations, different experiences, and different relationships with each of us. And, the ultimate outcome, was that Barney expressed himself in relation to the varying relationships.

His teachers apparently did not believe in Barney's potential to grow further as an individual. Their relationship with him was almost empty, a one-way directional relationship that focused on little more than custodial care. The teacher's low expectations for him to have meaningful relationships were evident in how they responded when Barney reached out in the only ways he knew how. Instead of recognizing his social desires, his teachers viewed any behavior as one to be terminated rather than to be explored. They were not windows for him to reflect himself and his potential. The teachers reflected to Barney that his attempts at interacting were not worthy of a reciprocal, meaningful relationship. Instead, they personally responded to close him off from social interaction. They ultimately forced him into self-reliance to stimulate himself within an environment that offered minimal human or activity enjoyment. As his attempts at socialization were shunned, Barney retreated into a solitary existence of repetitive motions, bouncing balls, spinning tops, and sifting beads. Within this relationship-starved environment, maybe his reliance on these repetitive activities reflected more than his autism; maybe his actions reflected loneliness.

As his parents, Mitch and Betty have experienced and loved Barney for 19 years. They have been with him and have supported him through his loss of skills and his onset of autism and his years of special education; but, most importantly, they have loved him for being their son and part of their family. Not only do they believe Barney can experience meaningful relationships and activities, they expected it and actively pursued it for him. They were no different from other parents whose primary goal for their child is to be happy in life. Their beliefs, their expectations, and their love showed in their relationship with Barney. Their relationship was truly a window, reflecting to Barney who he was, showing him the outer world of possibilities. When he experienced those possibilities in supportive environments, such as at the car races and the club, Barney rose to the occasion to enjoy meaningful interactions and relationships.

Barney's parents, like other parents, also have had to divide their attention among many things, jobs, home, chores, friends, recreation, and family. Although Mitch and Betty wanted Barney to be happy, to make choices on things he enjoys, their time and energy were limited. And thus, at times Barney must fall back on himself—listening to his tape, watching his ABBA video. Within this loving and relationship-enriched environment, maybe his reliance on these repetitive activities reflected more than his autism, may be what his actions reflected was a need for alone time, just as I might escape my daily activities to read a book.

My relationship with Barney was different from the ones he had with his parents and teachers. Unlike his family, I did not have a lifetime of experiences and love with Barney. Unlike his teachers, I did not spend 6 hours a day with him. Even though my relationship with Barney was limited by time (a few hours per week for a few months), it was enriched by my belief that Barney's capabilities would rise to the surface through the provision of activities and personal attention, and they did. By offering him choices, giving him my personal attention, respecting his choices, and accepting his communicating behaviors, my relationship with Barney was another window in his life. That window reflected acceptance, but it also gave him a glimpse of possibilities beyond solitary, repetitive tasks. And again, in experiencing the possibilities in a supportive environment, Barney consistently rose to the occasion and consistently made independent choices, actively engaged in games, and enjoyed reciprocal involvements. At those moments, he was not locked into his own world, but reached out to connect to the larger world, And then he was the window— reflecting back what he saw and understood in me, while providing a view into present and potential being.

.

Section III

Tell Us What You Are Going to Do

Chapter 5
"Mad, Angry, and Ill—What That Mean?": A Struggle to be Accepted
Jennifer Laughrun

Chapter 6
Lots of Talk, But No Action: The Quiet Saboteurs
Mary Agnes Shelton

Chapter 7
Can't Anyone See?: When Caretakers Are Also Blind
Kathy Fletcher

. . . Although they condoned my work with Eric, they did not have any free time that they were willing to give the project and to Eric. In retrospect, I realize that taking on Eric as a client without his family's commitment to the project went against the very mission of the project—to work together supportively with students and their families. However, at the time, I thought I could sway the family to work with us eventually. I had a hard lesson yet to learn.

—Field notes, chapter 5

5

"Mad Angry, and Ill— What That Mean": A Struggle to Be Accepted

Jennifer Laughrun

Children of Special Education are children of Small Expectations, not great ones. Little is expected and little is demanded. Gradually, these children— no matter their IQ level—learn to be cozy in the category of being "special." They learn to be less than they are.
—Granger and Granger (1986, p. 26)

INTRODUCTION: ACCEPTANCE

How do we learn to be accepted? How do children, teenagers, or adults learn to embrace friendships—learn to become an active, accepted, and an integrated piece of a community? Is acceptance learned, given, taken, innate, selective? Does acceptance differ for people with disabilities?

Beginning with Public Law 94-142, passed in 1975, and through the Individuals with Disabilities Education Act (PL 101-476), passed in 1990, children in Special Education have been routinely guaranteed a free and public education in the "least restrictive environment," an environment as "normative" as possible. They are also were assured of receiving recreational therapy as a related service, if needed, to enhance the education that they receive. Providing inclusive classrooms and mainstreaming has quickly become a way of fulfilling the requirements of these laws. However, these laws state nothing about acceptance—acceptance from classmates, from parents, from teachers, and from the community for these children labeled as "Special." How does one mandate acceptance? Belief in one's abilities, approval of one as an integral part of a group, acknowledgment of the importance of one's presence and the positive effect that one's behavior, attitude, and spirit have on an environment: these are things that we all seek from childhood to adulthood.

ERIC

This is the story of Eric and his struggle with acceptance. Eric was an energetic 17-year-old male, diagnosed as moderately mentally handicapped, with an IQ of 50. He had sandy brown hair and deep teakwood eyes, and he was handsome in a "puppy dog" sort of way. He dreamed of one day driving a low-rider truck, with his girlfriend tucked neatly in the crook of his arm. He loved football and carpentry and girls. Eric was full of hopes and dreams of things that he wanted to do and see—fantasies of the reality that many 17- and 18-year-old males live. What Eric wanted was to be accepted—to have his self-concept acknowledged by those around him, to be viewed by others as a person capable of obtaining and maintaining typical relationships and vocational opportunities, and engaging in "teenage behavior" (i.e., driving a car, having a girlfriend, going out on Friday nights). Eric wanted to be accepted not only in his trainable mentally handicapped (TMH) classroom, but also by his triad of support. This triad consisted of his other high school peers, his parents, and the community at large.

I worked with Eric for 8 months. When Eric and I worked together, he would often goof off, unrelentingly ask to write Shirley, his girlfriend, a letter (a task that became the reward at the end of a good lesson), or become distracted by those students around him. More than grasping the concept of how to make a decision, Eric was enthused by my attention and that which he received from his peers when he was with me. For example, he would often brag to the other kids about "working with me"; he would take whatever we had done that day back to show to the class or he would tell other peers that I was his "friend." Eric received status and acceptance through our interactions, and thus the themes of Eric's life and our intervention began to emerge.

The glimpse I got into the life of Eric was priceless to me. By observing Eric's interactions with others as we walked down the hall to go to the cafeteria to "work" (learn a new skill), or by watching how he related to the students as they paraded through the cafeteria during class changes, I was given insight into who Eric was. His need and desire to be accepted by his peers and his unsuccessful way of achieving this could not be denied. It was through my observations that I began to notice how important being a teenager was to Eric. I noticed him wearing Stetson cologne, I noticed him hold up his fingers in the peace symbol while making a barking noise at the guys who walked down the hall, and I saw the toughness he exuded by jumping up and touching a door frame or hitting a wall when a girl walked by. I was reminded consistently throughout the intervention of Eric's inability, or rather lack of skills, to be accepted by others. I realized how little was demanded and expected from Eric by those around him.

THE INTERVENTION

I worked with Eric for 8 months as a part of the Family Link in Leisure Education (FLLE) project, carried out at the Center for Recreation and Disability Studies at the University of North Carolina at Chapel Hill. The grant's purpose was to document the impact of an individualized comprehensive leisure education program as an educational enhancement in the lives of students with disabilities and their parents. Students with disabilities who also lack leisure and recreation opportunities, social skills, and/or decision-making choices were referred via special education teachers for participation. Students were taught the life skills and self-determination techniques that are natural components to the acquisition of satisfying leisure and recreation. Family participation and awareness were key elements. The qualitative methods used for collecting data included observation, transcribed open-ended interviews, and extensive, detailed field notes of all the sessions. The protocol of the intervention as established by this project was: referral, assessment, planning of goals and objectives/interventions, implementation, and evaluation. The sequence of the intervention established within FLLE, which I used for Eric, is shown in Fig. 5.1.

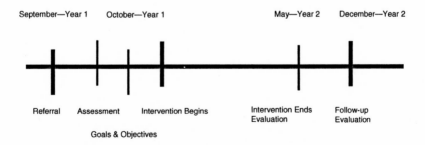

FIG. 5.1. Intervention Sequence.

ASSESSMENT

Using a Strengths and Needs Assessment designed especially for the intervention, Eric, his parents, and his teacher were interviewed separately in regard to Eric's strengths and needs (both psychosocial and environmental) and his interests. The results of the assessments were then compared and goals were developed based on the highest ranking strengths, needs, and interests.

Goals and Objectives

Three goals were set for Eric:

- Goal 1: To learn and utilize a process to decide how to use his free time.
- Goal 2: To expand leisure interests and meet new people by increasing participation in school activities.
- Goal 3: To learn and to display independently appropriate social interactions in the community.

Fortunately, these three goals flowed smoothly together by sequentially building upon one another. These goals are discussed and exemplified as the themes that emerged are discussed. The climax of our efforts was getting Eric involved in Habitat for Humanity, a national volunteer program that builds houses for low-income families.

ACCEPTANCE: THE OVERRIDING THEME

Acceptance emerged from the data as the main theme. Eric desired to be accepted by others. In all of the realms in which Eric interacted, he continuously strove to participate, to fit in, and to become an integrated member of that "world." This theme can be best understood by breaking it down into two subthemes: goofiness and being 18 years old.

Goofiness

Eric tended to use humor and random, wild behavior to get attention from the people he was around. Showing off, running, yelling, making exaggerated movements, mimicking, and falling down were all tools that Eric used (he thought) to get the positive interaction and acceptance he desired. Eric's mother told me that he had behaved this way for the majority of his life—primarily in public and social situations. On the other side of goofiness was the way that Eric's triad of support—home, school, and community—neglected to accept Eric on his terms. People reacted to Eric's goofiness in one of three ways: (a) they ignored or avoided him, (b) they made fun of or looked strangely at Eric, or (c) they denied that Eric could be anything more than "Special."

Being 18

Eric also had a clear definition of what his age meant. Although he was immature and childlike at times, he knew that other "normal" guys his age were driving cars, carrying backpacks, dating girls, and holding down jobs. Eric strongly expressed the desire to have some of these responsibilities, too. Once again, Eric's strong need to physically and emotionally engage in the normal rituals and behaviors of teenagers his age were not acknowledged by Eric's support system. He was considered to be less than he was.

The theme and subthemes will be best illustrated by exploring and discussing them separately in each of the settings in which I observed Eric: home, school, community—his potential "triad of support."

HOME: "LOOK MOM, NO HANDS!"

Eric's family was a quiet, reserved, working-class family. They lived in a three-bedroom, ranch-style house, spending their weekends at home, watching television and doing yard work. They participated in few activities except for going to church and attending the baseball games of their 16-year-old son, Bobby. Jan, Eric's mom, was a petite woman of about 4'11" and 100 pounds. She had wispy blonde hair, sprayed into place, and a Southern "country" accent. Her expressive teakwood eyes and round cheeks were reflected in Eric. She was a secretary at a law firm, and she worked from 9 to 5, five days a week.

Doug, Eric's stepdad, was a 5'6", muscular man with brown hair, cropped on top, a mustache, and closed-off brown eyes. I noticed immediately that he rarely made eye contact and was usually quiet when I was around. He seemed to be the controller of the family, silencing Jan with a look, or directing Eric with a stern voice.

Eric's brother, Bobby seemed to want nothing to do with Eric. For example, one morning on the way to school, he dropped Eric off on the side of the road about 2 miles from school because he was too embarrassed to be seen with him. Eric ended up walking to school. Bobby avoided Eric in the hall and only acknowledged him with a mock punch in the air near Eric's head. In contrast, Jan maintained that Bobby would "stand up for Eric when he gets teased at school." Eric seemed to respect his brother, talking about him lovingly and with admiration—"Bobby is my best friend." He saw Bobby's aloofness towards him as part of his "coolness."

When I first approached Eric's parents about the FLLE program, they seemed somewhat reluctant about the idea. However, they agreed to allow Eric to participate in the project and they willingly went through the assessment process with me. They seemed somewhat distant, and they made it clear that, although they condoned my work with Eric, they did not have any free time that they were willing to give to the project and to Eric. In retrospect, I realize that taking on Eric as a client without his family's commitment to the project went against the very mission of the project—to work together supportively with students and their families. However, at the time, I thought I could sway the family to work with us eventually. I had a hard lesson yet to learn.

When I interviewed the family, they talked a lot about surface issues, alternating between sugar-coating and debasing their interactions with Eric, and they offered only what I initially asked of them. Eric's father and brother distanced themselves from the intervention and me. Whenever I visited their home or called, I was directed to go through Jan, with Doug often hovering in the background. As a result, most of my discussion involving the family will center on my conversations with Jan.

Goofiness

When I asked Eric's parents about his behavior—his "goofiness"—they did not appear to know about that which I was referring to. Jan said, "Sure Eric gets out of control sometimes . . . he will talk to anyone in the grocery store. But we just reprimand him." Eric's parents controlled his actions in the home and when they were out in the community with a stern voice and threats. Eric was never held responsible for controlling his own behavior. So, when his parents were not around, Eric would easily get out of control—falling down, yelling, and so forth.

When Eric and I began building at Habitat for Humanity, my interactions with the family became more frequent, but they were not necessarily more involved. They usually consisted of greeting me when I picked Eric up and dropped him off, and sometimes they did not even do that.

The lack of interest and involvement from Eric's parents, a key resource to any child's growth, was frustrating and heart-breaking for me. Eric and I could only do so much without reinforcement, support, and consistency from the home. The intervention, and the ultimate goal of acceptance, would be limited, if Eric's parents refused to be actively involved and enthusiastic. To them, Eric was accepted as Eric, nothing more and nothing less. He was an ageless human with special needs and limited potentials that were worth everything, except their time.

Being 18

Eric's mother spoke of Eric fondly, talking in a quiet, empathic tone with a loving smile on her face. She seemed to see Eric in two different lights, and she was struggling to converge the two. On the one hand, Eric was the child who needed a night light. This was the Eric who still believed in the Easter Bunny, who needed help shaving and tying his shoes, and the one who played best with the 4-year-old next door. Eric was the child who "when he was 4 years old, got a knife and opened up the Lite-brite, and took the light bulb out and stuck the knife in." He was the child who she perpetually worried about getting hurt ever since she heard the words, "Look, Mom, no hands!" and glanced up to find Eric rushing head first off of his bike into a parked truck. The boy seemed to have no cognitive understanding of death. When asked what Eric's diagnosis was, she hesitated for a long time before finally saying that Eric had "special needs," but "can do anything . . . except color in the lines." This was the light that blinded her from seeing Eric's potential and that kept him in his "special" labeled box.

Then, there was the 18-year-old Eric: the young adult fond of cars, the child Jan was struggling to set free. The Eric who took care of her when she was feeling ill, the teenager who she hoped would one day hold a job, the child about whom she got teary-eyed when I proposed taking him to his first dance. She says of this Eric, "Well, I think he is a pretty happy kid. It breaks my heart that he will never be able to do things like drive a car. We try to be really honest with him about things like that."

However, when it came to issues of sex, a topic that Eric was actively involved in learning about, honesty became silence. Eric's capacity to grow and be responsible was lost in Jan's lack of motivation and insight into the capabilities and opportunities available to Eric. Similar to the reaction of a deer in car headlights, Jan was paralyzed when it came to actively helping Eric to reach his potential, to become the teenager he wanted to be, to accept Eric as he was.

Perhaps this is why the responses that I received from Jan were so hot and cold." Jan was always cordial when I called to update her on Eric's progress, give her a piece of insight, or ask to visit Eric. However, she and Doug were apprehensive about getting involved themselves. When I told her about Habitat for Humanity (a community activity in which Eric and I eventually got involved), she said:

> Eric already has his wardrobe picked out for it. He told me yesterday that you two are going to lunch. I think it is a great idea. I am very pleased. You could not have picked a better activity to do with him . . . but I sure don't want to do it. (Field notes)

Jan often seemed tired and exasperated over the phone, as if she would rather not be bothered. For example, when I called to tell her about going to Habitat for the second time, initially she acted as if she did not know what I was talking about, kept the conversation short, and hesitantly gave me permission to take him. Another time, she had trouble containing her excitement over Eric "working." Her mood seemed to dictate her response to the intervention and her acceptance or expectations of Eric's abilities.

CLASSROOM: "COME ON DOWN"

Shawn, a 20-year-old black male, was printing out a note on the 1980's Macintosh computer. Shawn, who was diagnosed with moderate mental retardation, used a wheelchair as a result of an adverse drug reaction when he was a toddler. His large, egg-shaped head, adorned with glasses and a sparkling smile, rocked back and forth with the motion of his body as he sang an Elvis tune, *Love Me Tender*. Shawn was perceptive about the emotional and social issues he dealt with as a result of his disability; he had a great sense of humor, and he was full of hope for his future.

Shawn was quite verbal compared to his classmates, and although he often persevered on thoughts or ideas, he was a very insightful and compassionate person. On this day, Shawn wheeled over to Eric with panache and proudly handed Eric a letter. Eric took the letter from Shawn and stumbled over the words. He read slowly, pronouncing some words with a thick stutter, as if he were trying to get peanut butter off the roof of his mouth with his tongue:

> Dear Eric,
> You are a really good friend and I am glad that I have you.
> You make me laugh.
> > Sincerely,
> > Shawn

Eric's face turned bright red as he blushed. He yelled loud enough to get attention from the rest of his classmates, "Oh gosh, how sweet!" Eric then got up and intentionally fell against the wall, trying to handle the embarrassment caused by the acceptance from another peer.

Eric had attended school at Foster's High School for the preceding 2 years. The school was a large cement-block building that had approximately 2,000 students in attendance. Eric was in a classroom of 15 students who were labeled TMH—a high number of students, it seemed to me, for the one teacher and two assistants. The teacher was Carla Brady, a laid-back Caucasian woman in her late 30s. Carla had an expressionless face and small, brown eyes masked by round, brown glasses. Her thinning chestnut hair, delicate gestures, and quiet manner made her seem almost fragile. She talked in a soft, nasal Southern drawl, and she quietly maneuvered her way from student to student, trying to take care of everyone's physical, emotional, and educational needs.

The classroom was rectangular, with bright lights, white walls, and few adornments. There was one poster of the Flintstones movie characters. The brown desks were arranged in a "U" formation. A refrigerator stood against one wall, next to a big gray metal cabinet. which was filled with a hodgepodge of manipulatives (clothes pins, pencils, Legos, beads), worksheets, and toys. The air was usually heavy with the heat and with the smell of rubber and vinyl wheelchairs, pizza, and cleaning fluid.

Eric was one of the highest functioning students (both socially and cognitively) in the classroom. Whereas other students worked more on physical gross and fine motor skills throughout the day, Eric was busy working on academics at the level of a second or third grader. He was not hard to notice, calling attention to himself quickly as he cracked jokes or raced around the room without intention. The first time I walked in the classroom, Eric immediately saw me and yelled— disrupting the group lesson in which he had been participating— "Come on down!" I felt immediately drawn to work with this exuberant student.

As I began my observations, I noticed that there were unique forms of interaction and acceptance within the classroom. The students all participated in activities alone. Each student had his or her own assignment and conducted that assignment within his or her own world. Carl was clipping a clothes pin onto the rim of a cardboard box; Helen was doing simple addition flash cards; Maria was matching words to pictures on the computer; Eric was listening to music. Each activity was individualized, with little interaction among the students. However, there were also activities, such as making pizza boxes, that allowed the students to joke, laugh, argue, and develop friendships. These secure and isolated friendships seemed to separate the students more deeply in their TMH classroom, making it harder to generalize interpersonal skills beyond the classroom walls. They were "cozy in the category of being special." When I asked Carla Brady and Sam (an assistant) about the classroom, they concurred with my observations:

> "This whole class is made up of loners really—they don't really interact as friends," said Carla. Sam replied, "Yeah, you are right . . . they are all loners. Even though they don't interact, they always have a very close unit. A real sense of family—brother/sister. It's like, 'we see each other everyday, there is no need for small talk.' I know how you are, and you know how I am." Carla, nodding her head slowly and apathetically replies, "Yeah, there is a real sense of support and security. Everybody stands up for each other. . . . The kids in this classroom are secure with each other and themselves within this classroom. We are segregated from the rest of the school. This makes it hard for the students to leave the school—the transition." (Field notes)

There appeared to be a pattern of how Eric coped and interacted within the classroom—how he acquired the attention and acceptance that he desired. In a typical classroom, they call kids like Eric the "class clowns." Eric, an extreme version of a class clown, was at one time labeled with attention deficit disorder and put on the drug Ritalin. His parents became upset with the "zombie effect" that the drug had and took him off it within a year. Unlike the class clowns in "normal" classes, Eric had never learned to self-monitor his behavior—to differentiate between funny and goofy. He often yelled, fell on the floor or against the wall, or asked questions repeatedly to get acknowledged. The following excerpt from the field notes provides an example:

> It is a cold day, and the students in Carla's class were inside a large gym playing a loose game of basketball. A cacophony of squeaking wheelchairs, slapping rubber soles against the tile floor, and incoherent cheers to make a basket filled the gym. Eric, stimulated by all of the excitement, is similar to a puppy that is overly aroused. He is running circles around the other kids, knocking other students down, yelling loudly, and demanding everyone's attention when he is at the basket. (Field notes)

I soon learned that moments like this were not uncommon for Eric. He seemed to be in desperate need of recognition and attention—validation that he is a positively functioning teenager who could play ball with the best of them.

Being 18 and Goofiness

Although Eric was at the cognitive level of about a 9-year-old, he was acutely aware that socially he was 17 going on 18. He often talked about his girlfriend, Shirley, driving a car, having a job and wearing a backpack—all status symbols to Eric of what "being 18" meant. Ironically, because of Eric's disability and the lack of opportunities available for persons like Eric, a girlfriend was the only one of these status symbols that Eric could attain. With the exception of Shirley, Eric lied about the other "status symbols." For example, one day Eric told me, "I have a purple low-rider truck," moving his hand up and down and making a buzzing noise to signify the sound of a truck moving up and down. Eric did not even have a driver's license.

Shirley was a 21-year-old female with an outgoing personality and a crooked-toothed smile to match. She had cerebral palsy, and she alternated her time between using a wheelchair and walking with the aid of a walker or a friend (usually Eric). Shirley's social and cognitive levels were lower than Eric's, but she made up for that with her dynamic character and token sayings. The first time I met Shirley, she quickly pulled me aside for a personal conference, telling me, "You are gorgeous. You are pretty; you are 101 Dalmatian cute, Jennifer."

Eric was Shirley's biggest advocate—a telling sign of his compassionate and caring soul. He was constantly aware of their "relationship," looking for presents for her in magazines, gift stores, and at home. He desperately wanted to have a normal relationship with Shirley—to take her on a date to a football game, out to dinner, and even to marry her.

Eric wanted their relationship to be accepted by others. He lied about the extent of their relationship to his teacher, his parents, his brother, and his peers: "Jennifer, Shirley and I went to a football game on Friday night. . . . I spent the night at Shirley's house" or "Shirley gave me this ring for my birthday." He appeared to know and want the same dynamics of a relationship that his peers had. He even talked about kissing Shirley or having sex with her, a topic that was quickly dismissed and avoided by his teacher and his parents.

The issue of a girlfriend is a perfect example of how Eric wanted to be accepted as a teenager and how that was denied or ignored by those around him. One day, near the end of my intervention, I was talking with Carla, Sam, and Debbie (the other teacher's assistant) about Eric's future. Debbie said, "Someone needs to talk to Eric about sex education. He has been doing things in class and I think he is scared to ask his parents about stuff like that." Apparently, Carla, as well as Eric's parents, had a hard time accepting Eric's typical sexual urges as "normal," but they rather viewed them as something to be repressed. Carla looked at me that day inquisitively, as if to ask me if I would talk to Eric's parents.

SCHOOL: "LOOK AT ME"

From the classroom, I branched out to see how the other typical peers accepted Eric in his school. Eric was already attending a "regular" physical education (PE) class as part of his Individualized Education Plan (IEP). Eric was physically fit—a trim, muscular, and coordinated teenager. Based on this strength, his teacher had requested that Eric be integrated into a PE class. Integrated, not necessarily accepted. When Eric first started to go to his "inclusive" PE class, he was gung-ho. However, once I had begun working with him, Carla became concerned that Eric did not want to go to PE. She said, "Coach Jones didn't want Eric to come to class for a few days last week because he is being observed teaching . . . and maybe Eric is getting picked on by the kids." Eric's need to be accepted as 18 and his "goofy" means of trying to achieve that can best be illustrated by describing a day in his inclusive PE class.

Being 18

I decided to observe Eric in his PE class so as to try to get an idea of what was going on. The Coach was a tall, heavy set man in his 30's with dark hair and a bulldog-looking face (but not so fearsome). He was wearing a tee shirt and those polyester shorts that all coaches seem to wear. His eyes were averted when he talked to me, and he appeared a little uneasy. During the interview, he told me that he thought that Eric was doing pretty well, saying, "The class is starting a new unit in volleyball on Wednesday, and I don't know if Eric can handle that . . . [he seems to have a hard time grasping rules] and sometimes he just takes off running up and down the court. I got some kids that adjust and include real well; now, I got some others that don't." He also told me that sometimes would Eric hit the other kids in the arm or the back, "just trying to be one of the guys."

I walked up the stairs to the gym. There were four basketball goals lining each long wall, with a goal also at each end. The coach's class utilized the ones on each of the side walls and one on the end wall. I sat to the side in a chair and observed:

> Eric was on a basketball team with two other males. They were playing against a team of two guys. One of them was the cherubic kid with the long hair that I had seen Eric interact with before. Eric clapped whenever a goal was made. He was guarding the kid with the long hair and blocked his shots 50% of the time. His teammates cheered him on to "Shoot, Eric, make a goal." They smiled at him, and everybody occasionally punched everyone else in the arm. Eric seemed to be having fun and was tolerated by the other people. They seemed to like him. However, he was on the outskirts of the game. (Field notes)

The frank, insightful words of a small, 14-year-old girl enlightened me as to the dynamics of Eric's inclusion into the classroom. Her name was Tammy. She was about 4'9" and weighed about 80 pounds. She had her sandy brown hair pulled back into a ponytail. She was wearing gray stretch pants and a pink windbreaker. She looked very innocent, but I soon found out that she was tough. I told her that I was working with Eric, and I had come to watch him today in his PE class. Tammy told me that Eric was "loud" and didn't understand the rules of games. Tammy told me, "One time in football, it is cold outside, and we finally got the ball. Eric took off running up and down the field, and we lost the ball. It took us about 10 minutes to get it back." Tammy also told me that the girls stayed away from Eric:

> One time we were playing football—it is cold again—and Smyrna, that girl over there, is wearing shorts. Eric walked over to her and said, "Are you cold?" When Smyrna said, "yes," Eric said, "I'll warm you up." After that, we all stay away from him. But not me, I'll beat him up if he tries to touch me. (Field notes)

I assured Tammy that I did not think that Eric would touch her. The guys, according to Tammy, put up with Eric, saying, "Some of them get along well with him." The students seemed to like Eric as a person, but they could not tolerate his inability to understand the rules of a game. Tammy went on to ask me, "Is his mama like him?" I said, "His mom is just like us." Tammy replied, while smiling at Eric, "Eric is like us, just different. He's wild."

The beauty of this interaction stemmed from the frank impression I got from one of his peers. Eric's behavior was recognized as inappropriate and interpreted by this peer as annoying. Eric appeared to act "goofy" in his PE class—trying to get my attention, hitting other guys, falling, saying age-appropriate "pick-up lines" to the girls, and adhering to the silly orders of his peers, all in order to be "cool," to be accepted. However, this acceptance seemed to be returned only half-heartedly. Eric was a nice guy, so he was accepted somewhat, but he appeared to be the brunt of others' jokes and leering looks. He was accepted as "that goofy kid from the TMH classroom," not as "Eric, a funny kid in my PE class."

Goofiness

Eric appeared to be a very impulsive and easily influenced teenager—acquiescing to the wants and desires of others. For example, on the day I observed Eric in his inclusive PE class, a large kid came up and told Eric to "get" another guy. Eric hit the student but he ignored Eric. The large kid put his arm around Eric's neck and said, "You a good guy. Do this: AAAAAAWWWWWW," waving his arms in the air and screaming. Eric did it. A girl behind me shook her head and said, "Eric's a trip."

"A trip," "wild," "goofy," "TMH"—all labels to describe Eric's behavior, but none to describe Eric the person. Eric seemed to not have the tools or techniques to control himself, to be "cool." Together, we worked very hard on this, and eventually, Eric gained control over himself and began to act like a "teenager." Eventually, he was accepted in one community setting as a person, not as a label. This event is described in the next section.

COMMUNITY: "BUILDING THE FRAMEWORK"

Throughout the intervention, Eric and I worked first on developing a decision-making process for him, and second on turning his "goofy" behaviors into "cool" ones. The decision-making process was based on the Decision Making in Leisure model (see Mahon & Bullock, 1992). The "cool" lessons involved Eric in a dual process of first identifying desirable "cool" behaviors, and then replacing those "goofy" behaviors with the new "cool" behaviors through role-playing and modeling. Once Eric had the processes down, he and I surveyed the school club registrar for a club with which Eric would like to get involved. After interviewing several different club sponsors and attending several different club meetings, Eric chose to join Habitat for Humanity. We worked at Habitat for Humanity for 4 months. His interactions, acceptance, and relationships there cannot be generalized to the population as a whole or to Eric's involvement in other community arenas. It was a slice of life, one specific and special example of how Eric, when given the tools, chance, and encouragement from others, could gain the acceptance that he so desired. His success had as much to do with the patience, guidance, and advocacy of the people we worked with, as it did with Eric's enthusiasm, perseverance, and need to be accepted.

Being 18 and Goofiness

A baseline idea of where we started behaviorally can be provided by a description of the first time Eric and I went out into the community. It was December 8, and Eric had chosen to go help decorate a Christmas tree at the National Armory. Carla, his teacher, had told Eric and I that several students from a neighboring high school would be joining several of the students in his Special Education class to decorate a tree to be auctioned at the symphony. The following scene is described in my field notes from that outing:

> It is around 4:00 p.m., and Eric is ready to get going—"Come on, Jen, we are going to be late." Carla leaned over and whispered to me, "Eric is really excited to go to this today."
>
> Eric and I got in the car. He insisted on carrying my backpack—another "status symbol" of being 18. His main concern was whether or not I had a tape deck. He brought a tape of rap music along with him. He insisted that we pump up the bass, turn up the tunes, and roll down the windows—"We'll look cool." This turned into a ritual every time we got in the car. The car ride is obviously exciting for Eric. He kept asking me if we were going to ride on the "big highway."
>
> We walked into the Civic Center, and there were around 10 bare, fake Christmas trees. The room is a big, barren room with a stage at one end and a balcony at the other. The room is lit by natural light and by the luminous glow of Christmas lights that adorn the balcony and some of the Christmas trees.
>
> Eric and I walked over to the far right-hand corner. About 10 females and one male—high school age—were decorating the tree. Eric walked up and said, "Hello, girls," with his arms flung wide open. No one said a thing. For the duration of the decorating, the other kids pushed Eric to the side. Once in a while, he would try to talk to a girl, but he would touch her hair or back, and she would shriek away. I pulled Eric over and told him that it is not okay to touch someone that you do not know. Eric said, "But she is pretty," fully believing that anything pretty is worthy of touching.
>
> Once the tree decorating was complete, Eric decided that they needed to view the tree from afar. So, Eric and two girls moved over to the far right wall to admire the tree. It is quite comical. The three of them standing there

with their arms crossed shaking their heads and saying, "What a great tree." For some reason it reminded me of the Grand Canyon scene in *National Lampoon's Vacation* where Chevy Chase and his son stop to admire the Grand Canyon, shake their heads once, and exclaim, "Okay, let's go."

Eric took off suddenly. He ran toward the tree and fell right beside it. He almost knocked the tree down and knocked his forehead on the floor pretty hard. He then got up and ran to me. He was laughing loudly. I tried to stop him from running into me by putting my hand out. He dodged me. He picked up a spare Christmas tree part and started to twirl it around in the air. It was a pretty big piece of tree—it could have been dangerous. Eric wasn't dangerously out of control, but he was definitely not in control. He also did not follow my directions to stop. The girls decided that it was time for them to leave and said, "Good-bye, thanks for letting us help." Their eyes were opened wide, and they looked a little shocked by Eric's behavior. (Field notes)

This was an eye-opening experience for me. I realized how "normal" and accepted Eric seemed within the confines of his classroom or home. I now understood why his teacher or his parents had not called Eric "goofy." Within Eric's protective world—his home and classroom—Eric did not seem so goofy. His antics were accepted because "Eric was Eric," and his dysfunctional behaviors didn't really stand out when one saw him everyday. I found that even I had gotten used to him. However, once I saw him out in a different environment with far different norms, Eric's behavior shocked me. He seemed much more out of control, much more isolated, and much more developmentally disabled. I was shown that, although Eric was a sweet, lovable, and funny child, he needed to work on his social and self-control skills to be able to function in society outside of his "world." Eric's goals to be included, self-determining, and self-controlling seemed all the more important and relevant for him to gain acceptance as an 18-year-old.

Following the Christmas tree decorating experience, Eric and I began to work on following rules, self-monitoring, and "being cool." All of these were practiced within the environment of Habitat for Humanity, an activity Eric had chosen to become involved in. Habitat for Humanity proved to be an ideal place for Eric to work on his self-control skills and interactions with others.

In February, the building began. Typically, I would pick Eric up at noon, we would go eat lunch, and then we would drive to the Habitat for Humanity site on Main Street. Main Street was a bumpy paved road, lined with old, beautiful homes whose heydays were long past. Children played out in the front yards, vying for attention from the adults out in the yards with them. The Habitat site was at the very end of the road. The site consisted of two houses on the right side of the street. The house at the very end was totally finished on the outside but it was bare on the inside. The house second to the end was the outline of a house that we would fill in together. We would be working on the siding, roof, front porch, and insulation. There were two more sites across the street. A huge blue school bus sat on the front lawn. It was inscribed with "HABITAT FOR HUMANITY" on the side, and it was full of tools, ladders, and water buckets—all neatly labeled and placed—heaven for Eric.

As we got out of the car, Dan, the site supervisor, greeted us. Dan was a thin, 5'8" man in his early 30s. He had a booming, jovial voice, and he embraced both Eric and me with every "Hello." His shoulder-length brown hair was matted to his baseball cap with sweat, and he wore a flannel shirt with his boots. To Eric, Dan was his employer, his mentor, and his supporter. Dan included Eric in all aspects of Habitat for Humanity—from set-up, to work, to break, to clean-up. Eric was treated with the same respect, responsibilities, and humor from Dan as was everyone else. For example, one time he asked Eric to go "onto the Habitat bus and get an orange extension cord," and another time to "go on the roof of the bus and get a ladder." He did not limit his expectations of Eric to Eric's label.

Eric had both good days and bad days. On good days, Eric was attentive, his eyes sparkled, and peels of loud laughter readily sprang from his lips. On bad days, Eric appeared to have a very short attention span, his eyes were glassy, and the invisible strings that usually held his malleable face up in a smiling position, pulled his face way down, almost creating a bulldog look. I began to be able to gauge what Eric and I would be able to do, based on how Eric looked. But how would people with whom Eric came into contact in other places be able to do this? Everyone, of course, has good and bad days. However, the difference with Eric was that he did not verbalize—"I'm having a bad day," and so people who met him once may have attributed his behavior to his label. He was accepted at school and at home on these terms. How could the community be different?

The tasks we were assigned to complete for Habitat, in the 2 hours we were there, usually guided how our day would go. Three out of four times, we were assigned tasks that Eric could fully grasp. However, on the first day we were assigned to help some other builders put on vinyl siding. The task was too intricate for Eric, and he ended up being very obstinate, inattentive, and out of control. He was fairly unsafe, jumping on the ladders and hammering anything and everything. We had to leave early that day and our nerves were worn thin.

It became clear to me that, in order for Eric to be successful at Habitat, he would need some self-monitoring cues, and clear rules to follow. To help Eric control himself, we devised a self-monitoring cue. Eric chose the gesture of holding one's hand like a gun, pointing it at the person out of control (usually Eric, not me), and winking at that person. When I did this, Eric was supposed to recognize it as his sign that he was getting out of control and then verbally say, "I need to get control of myself." If Eric did not calm down after that, we would leave.

We also had a list of rules that Eric and I drafted. Included on the list were, "Do not yell, Do not cuss, Follow directions, Have fun, and Do not touch people." I carried the list of rules everywhere we went. We reviewed the rules before and during building sessions as needed. Eventually, my gesture of reaching into my pocket to pull out the rules when Eric was out of control became a cue for him.

When we first started building with Habitat, not only did I notice Eric's behavior, but I also noticed the behavior of other people toward us. Dan immediately embraced Eric and treated him as "one of the guys." However, other people tended to watch us from a distance with the veiled look of curiosity that we fine tune in adulthood—the same one neighbors use to watch each others' comings and goings through the kitchen window. As Eric became more proficient at cementing and waterproofing walls on his own, the other builders seemed to overcome their own barriers, interacting with Eric on a peer level. I noticed that the other builders began modeling my positive reinforcements with Eric both verbally—"Good job" or "Nice hammering," and maybe "Good listening"—and physically—high fives and pats on the back by everyone. People began to address Eric when they wanted to ask him something or wanted to tell him something—not me, as they first had. He was accepted, reprimanded, supported, and encouraged like everyone else at the site. If Eric was acting inappropriately or off task, people did not hesitate to redirect him and sometimes scold him. Eric's abilities—and not his disabilities—were the focus.

I think Eric felt this. He was able, by the fourth Saturday of building, to recognize when he was being unsafe and alter his behavior. He was self-monitoring, and—after practicing—he was able to do almost any task alone—without the guidance of an adult. However, I was forced to ask myself—"What happens when I am gone? Will this last?"

The following is an excerpt from my field notes for the last time that we worked at Habitat in April:

Eric and I were assigned to waterproof the concrete foundation of the house. After around 30 minutes, Eric put the cement on the wall like I was doing as I guided his hand. About this time, we had to make more cement. Eric got the good idea to go and bring a bag of cement and a cup of water up to us, instead of us toting the wheelbarrow down the slight, bumpy incline to the hose across the street. He came back covered in dry cement (there was a hole in the bag). We laughed, and Eric slammed down the bag. The bag burst open. Eric yelled loudly. I gave Eric the double-gun sign and said, "Now, what did you do just then that is not okay?" Eric said, "Slam down the bag." "And?" I replied. Eric said, "And yelled." I said, "Right. Now what are you supposed to do instead?" Eric thought for a moment and then said, "Put it down gently." I said, "Right. And what happens if you do not control yourself and put things down gently?" Eric said, "We leave." [Eric knew what was needed for acceptance, but he also knew that he often didn't do it. He needed support.] After that, occasionally Eric would slam the shovel down or drop something hard without thinking. Before I could even look at him, he would say, "I'm sorry about that Jen," or "excuse me." Eric was actually monitoring himself without me saying anything. Dan came to help us do the job. He said, "You guys are doing a great job—you are a lot quicker than me." Dan said, "Eric is really great." I said, "Yeah, he is awesome. He loves to build." Dan said, "Well, he has gotten really good being here." That day, one of the other regular workers said, "It is great to have Eric here! It is good to see someone who loves working here so much." Eric was accepted and even embraced as an integral part of the Habitat team. (Field notes)

As we left that day, I remember feeling both elated and frustrated. I was elated that Eric's potential was accepted both by Eric and by others who had worked side-by-side with him. I was elated that Eric actually self-monitored and worked at Habitat semi-independently. And I was elated that, when I asked Eric how working made him feel, he said that he felt, "Proud!" We finally had built a foundation upon which Eric's expectations and the expectations of others for him were congruous.

However, I also was frustrated. I was frustrated that there was a good chance that Eric's parents would not continue what we had started. I was frustrated that Carla Brady still believed that Eric needed to be on Ritalin in all environments in order to control himself. I was frustrated that Eric succeeded in being "cool," in "being 18," and in being accepted, but that these would not last unless he was supported. And, I was frustrated that only one of Eric's triads of support could learn how to accept a teenager's expectations and realize his potential. I knew in my heart that the successes Eric and I had shared would end up as short-lived memories. Although I tried to set up supports for Eric that would guarantee his continued participation in Habitat for Humanity, I failed.

I asked Eric on the last day that I worked with him how he would feel when he woke up on a Saturday and realized that he would not be going to Habitat. Eric replied with unusual clarity, "Mad, angry, and ill . . . what that mean?"

IMPLICATIONS

What does all of this mean to practitioners, to teachers, to parents, and to people with disabilities? There are two main implications that can be gleaned from this case study. First, when given the tools, opportunities, and supervision, it is possible for some adolescents with developmental disabilities to succeed in being accepted as an integral part of a "normal" community. Second, this success will not happen without on-going support from the family, school, and community. In order to get out of the "cozy category of being special," it takes collaborative effort and support from a variety of resources.

It became blatantly apparent throughout the intervention that acceptance is given, as well as earned. Acceptance is not innate. Self-monitoring, taking responsibility for one's actions, and functioning in a community are also skills that were learned. Some people can do this more quickly than others. When the strengths and abilities of a person are focused on, almost anything can be accomplished. Opportunities for community involvement for people with disabilities are limited because of the intense training, time, and continued guidance that is needed for some people with disabilities to develop the necessary social and vocational skills. However, when the involvement is a collaborative effort, the inclusion flows, and the results received by the organization, the family, and the individual are priceless.

Unfortunately, if just one element of the triad of support—home, school, or community—is absent, the effectiveness of the intervention is often lost to a significant degree. It is important for support to come from many different areas, people, and diverse environments. Support systems are not made up of one practitioner, one volunteer, or one graduate student who initially offers services. With Eric, the support was limited from school and home, and thus what Eric and I could accomplish—acceptance—could only really occur in one arena, the community. Once the intervention was over, Eric's outlet to the community ended, too. His teacher and his mother did not have the time, energy, knowledge, or belief in Eric's abilities to make it continue. I also do not think that they understood Eric's yearning to be accepted and the self-esteem he gained from being an included member of Habitat for Humanity. Acceptance, for Eric, meant support from a variety of people. It meant understanding Eric from Eric's perspective. It meant listening and valuing the wants and desires of a person with a disability.

It is also important for the practitioner to listen to what those support groups (family, friends, teachers) are willing to give. I neglected to listen and value the family's orientation to leisure and to Eric. I knew from the beginning that the family did not want to be involved. Yet, I clung to the hope that I could change their minds and their orientation, once they saw what Eric and I could accomplish. Family orientations, no matter how incongruent they are with the practitioner's, need to be acknowledged and seen for their value. It was a hard lesson to learn.

CONCLUSION—ACCEPTANCE

Eric and I each wrote letters to Eric's parents asking them to continue taking him to Habitat for Humanity (see the appendix for a copy of my letter). I set up contact people through Dan at Habitat who were willing to help Eric monitor himself and work cooperatively. However, when I returned to do a follow-up interview in December, my fears had been realized—Eric had not been back to Habitat.

In December, Eric and I sat and talked for an hour about our time together. To my amazement, he remembered precisely how to use the decision-making model, our rules, the self-monitoring cue, how to be "cool," and most importantly, his work at Habitat for Humanity. He reiterated how "warm" and "proud" going to Habitat had made him feel. His teacher exclaimed, "It really is too bad that no one carried that on." It really is too bad that people blame "no one" for a lack of continuity and continuance in an intervention.

As for his "goofiness," Carla, the assistants, and Jan all agreed that Eric had a lot more control over his behavior. Carla stated, "He never falls down anymore, and he monitors himself." Jan stated,

> He really listens now . . . Habitat for Humanity is all he would talk about for awhile. It's too bad we can't take him. . . . But, I see a difference in him this year. He seems a lot more focused and his attention span is longer. He follows directions more and is in more control of himself. . . . I really think that you have made a difference. I am very pleased. (Field notes)

This story is about the struggle of one adolescent, Eric, to be accepted in his world. As I observed Eric in all of his worlds—home, school, community, and self—I realized that Eric's ideas of who he was and where he was going were radically different from those established by his caregivers. It was as if Eric were a kite—a childlike image just waiting for a good wind to help him fly and reach his adult potential. Once, I asked Eric what he thought he would be doing when he was age 21. Eric replied frankly, "Living with Shirley in New York and working as a carpenter." At times, Eric could take off for a few seconds, only to be pulled back down. The limited expectations, roles, and "special" boxes that his primary caregivers tied to his string served to ground Eric:

- "Eric has 'special needs'," but he "can do anything . . . except color in the lines." (mother)
- "Eric is like us, just different. He's wild." (peer)
- "Eric needs to be at a group home where he is independent." (classroom teacher)
- "It's funny [that Eric] doesn't really care if he is a part [of the school], if he is included or not. It is probably just from being in here [the special education classroom] too much, the security." (classroom assistant)

While Eric dreamed of living independently with his wife and working at a job, others saw only an outline of Eric's potential—certain that they would have to be responsible for coloring it in.

There are many Erics out there, struggling to find their niches, their identities, and their acceptance. Is Eric's a story of success? I think anyone as exuberant, determined, and lovable as Eric cannot fail, but he can be failed by a society that leaves him out. And those who pass up the chance to accept and understand such a giving and lovable person, they make me, in the sage words of Eric, "mad, angry, and ill—what that mean?"

APPENDIX

Dear Jan and Doug,

I saw Eric for the last time a couple of months after the end of my intervention with Eric. I just wanted to make you aware of all of the things that Eric and I did together. Included in the packet is a summary of Eric's goals, how he met them and the outcomes, along with recommendations for keeping them going. I also included a letter from Eric, a map to Habitat for Humanity, and a short list of alternative opportunities for Eric this summer.

Eric and I were talking on my last day, and I asked him what he would like to continue to do. Eric strongly felt that he should continue to go to Habitat for Humanity. In fact, when I asked him how he would feel when he woke up on a Saturday and realized that he would not be working at Habitat, Eric said he would feel "mad, angry, and ill." I think that Habitat was an incredible experience for Eric. It strengthened his building skills, listening and self-control skills, and most importantly, boosted his self-esteem. I cannot continue to go with him, but I would be happy to supply you with the supports and connections to help you take Eric to Habitat on Saturdays. The students at school are going to continue to work at the site throughout the summer. It is my belief that with a little supervision, Eric could even be dropped off for an hour or so to work at the site. I have talked with Dan, the construction coordinator and foreman that has worked with Eric and me, and he supports this also. The Center for Recreation and Disability Studies would be more than willing to help monitor Eric, and keep in touch with Dan. If you are interested, call Charlie at the Center—555-0534.

I told Eric that I was going to be writing you a letter. He decided on his own that he wanted to write you a letter, too. The letter included is Eric's note that he dictated to me. The words and phrases are Eric's and were written down exactly as he said them to me. He then copied from my paper what he had dictated.

You have an amazing son. He is vibrant, caring, funny, and full of potential. I attribute a lot of this to the loving environment that he was brought up in. As Eric grows up and realizes that he in fact is 18, I think that it would be a tragedy if he were not involved in the community, not included in the things he so desperately wants to be a part of. Sharing himself with others and having others share with him. Unfortunately, the "system" does not make this inclusion an automatic task. The expectations of people with disabilities are lowered, and along with this, the programs and options open to them are lessened. I hope that what he has accomplished through this opportunity to work with me will allow the doors to be opened and the steps to be taken to keep him involved. You've seen him shine after a day of building, going to a dance, or winning a medal at the Special Olympics. I have felt the strong love that you feel for Eric. My ending hope is that that love continues to be shown in a way that is constructive and productive for Eric. Aim high, I know you know as much as I do that Eric is awesome.

Sincerely,

Jennifer Laughrun

6

Lots of Talk, But No Action: The Quiet Saboteurs

Mary Agnes Shelton

INTRODUCTION

"Are you sure these guys are brothers? They have the same parents?" I asked incredulously. Jessica, the special education teacher for students with mild mental retardation in a large high school, and I were standing in the glassed-in office in a corner of her classroom. The blinds were down over the windows, but they were opened so we could see the students although they weren't paying much attention to us. Jessica had just pointed out the two African-American brothers whom she had referred to our Family Link in Leisure Education (FLLE) program. Their names were David and James—David was 17, and James was 15.

David was a tall, slender young man with dark brown skin, close-cropped hair, long arms and legs, and a rather small head set on a long neck. He walked with a shuffling-type gait, head hanging forward and eyes down. At first he appeared to be rather sullen and withdrawn, but then he suddenly smiled. David had a truly remarkable smile. It was broad and warm and sweet, lighting up his whole face. Something almost tangible seemed to flow through that smile which made me feel all warm and fuzzy inside as I watched him through the office window.

"Did you see that?" Jessica gushed in her charming Southern-belle accent. "That boy has the sweetest smile you ever did see. Why, when he smiles like that at me, I would just give him anything. He's my favorite, you know. I don't tell the kids that, but they all know."

We then turned our attention to James, the younger brother. James was short and stocky, with a much lighter complexion and a more muscular build. His head was large and set close to his shoulders. James had a mischievous look in his eye and a rather belligerent expression on his face.

"James is just a whole other story," Jessica said, shaking her head. "He is only after what he can get for himself, and he gives poor David such a hard time. These two should give you plenty to work with. I'm sure their parents will want to participate in your program—they're very involved with the boys."

MEETING THE PARENTS

With the two brothers appearing to be so different, I was quite interested to meet with their parents. Here's how my field notes tell that story:

> It was a lovely fall morning at 11 a.m., as I turned onto Bolton, the street where David and James lived. It was a quiet, lightly traveled, old neighborhood street with small, well-kept lower income houses. From the few people I could see here and there, it appeared to be a racially mixed neighborhood, though predominantly black. David and James' house was at the end of the "no outlet" street.
>
> The house was small and square, covered with forest green siding. It had a block concrete porch with five steps—no overhead covering. There was very little landscaping—a couple of scraggly bushes, no trees. Two old cars sat in the driveway looking unused. I rang the bell.
>
> A small, round, beaming woman answered the door. She was a glowing brown color, with round cheeks and sparkly eyes. I immediately recognized her as looking just like James, though her expression was happier than James' usually was. Her hair was slightly straightened and cut short. She wore a muted red dress and house slippers. I asked if Margaret was home, and she said "Yes," as she opened the door for me to come in.
>
> I assumed that the young-looking, rather shy woman was an older sister of the boys, so I waited for her to go get Margaret. When she just stood there, I asked for Margaret again. She said, "I'm Margaret," and giggled. I said, "Oh, you don't look old enough to have two teenage boys!" She giggled again and waved me toward a seat on the couch. The rather elaborate stereo/radio set was playing loudly—the blues.
>
> The living room was sparsely furnished with two over-stuffed chairs and a couch to match, a low table, and the large stereo equipment. No carpeting, a small throw rug near the front door, no wall decoration. I could see into a kitchen at the back of the house, and also down a hall, probably toward bedrooms.

A man, looking more than twice the age of Margaret, was sweeping the hall. When he looked up at me briefly, I saw that he looked just like David, only much older—the same gangly build and sloping shoulders, but minus the engaging smile. I assumed he was Jackson, the boys' father, though I wasn't introduced. He acknowledged me with his eyes when I first came in, but he never paid any attention to me again. (Field notes)

ASSESSMENTS

As I completed assessments with each of the boys separately and with Margaret and Jackson, I saw many more genetically passed attributes besides just physical appearance. David looked unmistakably like a younger version of his father, but he also displayed the laid-back, easy-going, indifferent attitude that I came to know in Jackson. On the other hand, James presented the spitting image of Margaret in his appearance, as well as in his feisty, energetic, mischievous personality.

During the initial interviews, Margaret did virtually all of the talking and she was lively and upbeat. Jackson sat quietly, showing little expression and appearing to go along with whatever seemed to be happening. While Jackson appeared to have no opinion, Margaret rated both boys very high on all their *strengths*, even creating a new category above the highest one to accommodate how completely excellent she found the boys to be on some items. In the *needs* section, Margaret wanted the boys to focus on independence skills and community involvement—Jackson said nothing. From Margaret I learned that Jackson had been injured in a construction accident years ago and received a disability pension, so now he functioned as the "house husband." Margaret worked as a nurse's assistant at the regional hospital on the 3 to 11 p.m. shift.

During the assessment interviews with the boys, I discovered specific characteristics and individual interests that would become the focus of their Individualized Leisure Education Plans. David had just received his driver's license. Though he said his father wasn't letting him drive much yet, he was really looking forward to the freedom and independence that driving on his own promised. During the assessment, David rated himself very highly on all the *strength* items, especially in the area of independence and family support. *Needs* with which he wanted help focused around community involvement and peer interactions. David said that what he really wanted to do was "go clubbing," meaning "hitting the night spots where music was played." David said his two favorite things were music and girls, and he thought he could find both at the clubs.

At his assessment interview, James was antsy and ready to go, right away wanting to know what he was going to get out of the program. He wanted action and events that he could influence. I was impressed with James' eagerness to get involved in challenging situations—he felt he had much more to offer than was being asked of him. He rated himself quite high on all his *strengths*, just as David did. He was interested in taking karate or Tae Kwon Do (TKD), playing tennis, and meeting girls—especially meeting girls.

As I evaluated the information from these interviews, it appeared that I was dealing with a proactive mother, a very laid-back father, and specific inherited personality traits in the boys. In the early days of working with this family, I thought I had the whole situation pretty well figured out and that I knew how to use each person's attributes to the best advantage to accomplish our goals. However, I was soon to learn that the family dynamics of this group were considerably more complicated and complex than I had originally anticipated.

A SURPRISING MEETING

My first indication that things were not as they seemed initially came about 6 weeks after our first interviews, during David's 3-year evaluation and Individualized Education Program (IEP) meeting at school. Jessica (David's teacher), the high school special education coordinator, and I met with Jackson and Margaret in a small conference room near the cafeteria. The coordinator, Ms. Martin, sat at the head of the semicircular table with the rest of us arranged around her.

Ms. Martin began the interview with David's evaluation scores on his vision and hearing tests, as well as academic on subjects. Apparently, David had scored poorly on his vision test this time, just as he had the time before. Ms. Martin asked Margaret if they had gotten David's eyes checked yet (the previous test had been three years before). Margaret said that they hadn't because David didn't want to go—but she said they would do it soon.

David scored low on all of his academic subjects—around fourth-grade level on math and reading, and even lower on spelling and vocabulary. He had tested at the 8 to 11 age level on the adaptive behavior scale, which Jessica thought was too low. She recommended testing him again with another scale to see if there might be a problem with the test itself. Jackson and Margaret nodded dutifully. Ms. Martin said there was no doubt that David should stay in the special education class at the Educable Mentally Handicapped (EMH) level.

Ms. Martin appeared to be finished with her part and started shuffling through papers to find the ones for Jackson and Margaret to sign. Margaret began to talk in a fast, high-pitched, squealing kind of tone about her feeling that neither of the boys belonged in special education. The problem was that the school wasn't providing the kind of education that suited her boys. There was nothing wrong with them—they were as smart as anybody else. The school needed to do a better job. They were bored; that was all.

Jackson chimed in. (I was surprised here because I had hardly heard him say two words during the five or six times I had met him before.) Jackson's grievance concerned mistreatment of David in the job world. David had been bagging groceries at Harris-Teeter but hadn't received his first pay check. Jackson knew they were trying to take advantage of him because he was black and young. Well, Jackson wouldn't have any of that! He made David quit, even though he had really liked the job. I mentioned that perhaps it was a misunderstanding about the typical 2-week delay on many paychecks, but Jackson seemed to be too much into the injustice of it all to look for explanations.

Both Jackson and Margaret began talking at once, interrupting each other as they got wound up about the lack of vocational opportunities that the school system provided. David was taking bricklaying, but he had to ride a bus for an hour everyday to another school for the 2-hour class. Jackson was pounding on the table with his fist to emphasize his points, while Margaret's voice was rising to an almost hysterical peak.

I was really surprised at this outburst. Jackson and Margaret weren't actually trying to carry on a discussion about David's welfare; they were ranting and raving about how victimized they felt on their son's behalf. Though Jackson and Margaret had some good points to make, they were not presenting them in a rational enough manner to produce a reasonable response. Ms. Martin appeared calm and unruffled in the midst of the onslaught. (I could tell she had been here before.) Although Jackson and Margaret were not listening, she told them that there was no way that David would be able to keep up in regular education classes, and that she thought more vocational classes were needed, too. She recommended that Jackson and Margaret make their feelings known to the school board since hearing from parents was often quite influential. However, I could tell from the unenthusiastic tone of her voice that Ms. Martin knew that they would not do it. Jessica looked nervous and seemed very glad that Ms. Martin was there to run the gauntlet with her, even taking the brunt of it.

After about 20 minutes of almost nonsensical spouting, Jackson and Margaret began to run down. Ms. Martin pushed papers at them to sign, which they obediently did. Jessica reviewed David's IEP for this year, including a leisure and recreation section that David would complete by working with me.

Because I had already discussed David's goals and objectives extensively with Jackson and Margaret during a home visit, I stressed at this point David's choice of working with one of the school's clubs. This decision should address two of David's goals, community involvement and peer interaction, while also giving him an opportunity to practice his vocational skills in a real-world setting. I thought this might help alleviate some of the concerns about the lack of vocational training. Although I was pretty excited about the potential here, I received barely a nod from David's parents.

Jackson and Margaret appeared to be spent from their tirade and they had nothing to say about the IEP itself. They signed the papers without comment, and the meeting was over. Jessica and I walked both parents to the front of the school, while Jessica apologized to them for her inexperience as a special education teacher. Margaret waved her apology aside and said that both the boys really liked her. It was as if the outburst in the conference room had never happened. Jessica thanked Jackson and Margaret for coming and said, "Lots of the parents don't even show up at IEP meetings, you know." As we walked back to the classroom, Jessica breathed a sigh of relief and said, "At least it's over."

I learned a number of things by attending the IEP meeting. My biggest surprise was how talkative Jackson turned out to be, and how forcefully he had expressed his opinions. Apparently, he wasn't as laid back as I had thought. Also, it seemed that Jackson and Margaret had an issue agenda that they felt strongly about but that they didn't actually want to discuss in a manner that might lead to change. They just seemed to want to say their piece, and that was enough. After what I had just seen in the meeting, it seemed to me that rational, reasonable communication about topics on the issue agenda was probably impossible. I was beginning to get a feeling of "lots of talk, but no action," but at this point, I did not realize just how pervasive that attitude really was for Jackson and Margaret.

I also learned a couple of things about the school's approach to meeting with parents. They were impressed that parents showed up at all and wanted to be encouraging about that. And, the most important thing was to get the papers signed, despite what was happening to or for the student. All in all, I was not impressed by the performance on either side, but I felt very hopeful about being able to make a difference for the two boys through our program, especially because of the one-on-one, focused nature of our FLLE work.

DAVID

Although I was working with the boys simultaneously, I met with them on different days and kept my work with them separate. David's major interest was "clubbing," so I checked with Margaret to see what she thought about pursuing this activity. She said she used to go to the clubs when she was David's age and that she had had a good time. It was wild, but she thought David would be able to handle it. He had already stayed out all night a couple of times and seemed to do okay. I felt a bit dubious about the atmosphere David might run into at these kinds of places—drugs and such—but it seemed as if "clubbing" was an acceptable recreational activity for a young teenager in David's world.

David made a list of the clubs he had heard about that he thought might be fun to visit. We drove around town to find them and to see what they looked like from the outside. Here's how my field notes described the first one we checked out:

> The Barbary Coast is a hole-in-the-wall in a bombed-out looking, deserted shopping center. What used to be a supermarket is abandoned with the windows boarded up. The large black-topped parking lot is all chewed up and full of huge potholes. Several groups of black men and women were standing around the street corners nearby. I had the thought that this would be a terrible place to have car trouble. I mentioned to David that the neighborhood looked pretty rough, and I thought it would be scary at night. David said he thought it looked okay. (Field notes)

The other clubs we drove by were in approximately the same kinds of areas. I didn't think this was looking so good, but David's enthusiasm was not abated. I asked David what he would think of his dad going with him the first time he went to one of the clubs, just to be on the safe side. He said no, if his dad went he wouldn't have any fun. He thought James would come with him. I still felt reluctant because the whole situation seemed potentially dangerous to me. However, I felt that I needed to accept the dominant view of David's culture, and all the black people I asked kept telling me it would be okay.

Our next move was to find out if an underage person could get into these clubs. We divided them up—David said he would call half and I called half. At the clubs near the college, underage people could get in to listen to the music, but they couldn't buy alcohol. Kids with IDs indicating they were at least 21 years old got an ink stamp on the hand—no stamp, no drinks. But the clubs that David wanted to frequent were different. Not a single one would allow underage people to get in—not even if they were accompanied by a parent or an adult. Personally, I breathed a sigh of relief because I had never felt comfortable about David investigating that kind of night-life on his own.

The next strategy David and I devised was to check for teen clubs or activities in the area. We discovered that the three largest recreation centers had teen dances once a month on different weekends. They had DJs, refreshments, and a teen committee to do the planning. David, James, and another friend went to the next one and they had a good time. They said the DJ played good music, and there were girls—not a lot of them, but some. David was very pleased and thought the teen dances would cover his desire for music and girls just fine.

After a few dances, David wanted to get more kids to attend, so he made some posters advertising the dances to put up in the halls at school. During the 7 months that I worked with David, this was the only thing I saw him do on his own initiative. He wanted to have more people at the dances, so he figured out something to try and did it all on his own. I was impressed and pleased. Unfortunately, David got in trouble for putting up the posters—there was a school policy that nothing could be advertised at the school that wasn't sponsored by the school itself. I was able to smooth things out with the office, but David's plan was thwarted.

Then David started missing the dances. I asked him why he didn't go, and he said, "Oh, I just didn't feel like it." Since I knew how much he enjoyed going, I was surprised by his response. It was James who filled in the missing information. Apparently, Jackson had decided that David couldn't use the car on weekends anymore. I asked James why he thought that was happening, and he replied, "Oh, he [Jackson] just gets that way sometimes." When I asked David about it, he hung his head, looked at the floor, and said, "Naw-w-w, I just don't want to go."

While David and I were setting things up for the teen dances, we were also getting lined up for David to go to the Habitat for Humanity building sessions on Saturdays through David's school club. Habitat was restoring and building new homes in a battered, rundown neighborhood that the city had decided to reclaim from the drug dealers. A number of high school students from David's school participated—including a few girls. David was excited about the prospect.

Jackson had said that David could take the car to the Habitat site, or Jackson would drive him. Every Monday I checked with David to see how his Saturday at Habitat had been, but he never went. I visited Jackson, who assured me that he would see that David got a ride, but every week it was the same. Again, it was James who supplied the missing information. Apparently, when Saturday came around, Jackson always had a long list of things for the boys to do and could not let David use the car or give him a ride. The only explanation James had was, "Dad just gets like that." The problem with "lots of talk, but no action" that I had already observed in Jackson was seriously hampering my ability to work with his sons.

I had another chat with Jackson to try to get to the bottom of the situation. We discussed how helpful Habitat could be for David and what a good place the teen dances were for him to meet his peers. Jackson agreed that it was all very positive and that he would see to it that David got to go, but there was still no change. David wasn't making it to the dances or Habitat. Something strange was going on.

JAMES

All the time this was happening with David, I was also working with James. James' original request was to take Tae Kwon Do lessons, and I knew just the place. At the recreation center, a young black man named Abdul taught a beginners' class at 4:30 p.m. 2 days a week. I had met with Abdul before and had found him to be kind, understanding, strict, and extremely talented at TKD. James and I went to observe a class. Here's how my field notes tell the story:

> Just before time for class, James and I walked down to the TKD room. It is a large room with one whole wall of mirrors and a plastic tile floor. A few little kids came in dressed in white TKD outfits with blue belts. They began stretching, jumping around, and doing moves. James asked one of them to show him how they used the sticks that were standing in a corner. One kid, about 10 years old, did a routine with the stick that looked quite impressive.
>
> Then, Abdul came in. He saw us and recognized me right away. I introduced James and told Abdul I had a candidate for him and that we would like to watch for a while today. Abdul said "fine."
>
> James and I sat opposite the mirrors and watched as the class gathered and began warm-ups led by one of the kids. There were about 15 kids and one adult man in the class, with a full range of abilities. Abdul did his own warm-up in the back of the class. Abdul is beauty in motion—a beautiful sight to see with his balance and grace—it reminded me of ballet. James and I exchanged impressed glances as we watched the class progress.

Since I had told Margaret that we would be home by 5 p.m., James and I left after about 20 minutes of the class. On the way walking out to the car, I asked James what he thought, and he said, "I like it a lot!" I asked him if he would like to take those classes, and he said he definitely would. I told him that it appeared that the class was on-going, and I would check to see when he could join. He said he hoped it would be right away. I said I would check to see if he could start next week, and he looked very pleased. When we got to his house, James looked me in the eye and said, "Hey, Mary, thanks a lot." He bounced out of the car and bounded across the yard, waving good-bye. (Field notes)

James took to TKD immediately. I began working on getting the school to let James take a different bus on his TKD days so he could get off right in front of the recreation center. Margaret said she thought David or Jackson could pick him up after the class. Here are my notes from the first class:

When we got to the recreation center, James went to the bathroom to change into the clothes he had brought for TKD class. In a few minutes, he returned dressed in a long, heavy cotton T-shirt and baggy black pants. He asked me if I thought he was dressed okay for TKD. I said I thought he looked great. He smiled, looking very pleased about beginning classes.

As the other students began to gather, James and I went into the classroom. Abdul came in, and I told him that James had decided to join the class. He said "fine." As the students were stretching out and warming up, Abdul told me that he wasn't feeling well, so he wouldn't be dressing out today. Mr. Simon, the other adult in the class, often did a lot of teaching for the students who were not so advanced. The more advanced students could go through their routines by themselves.

James joined in with the students working with Mr. Simon. James was the largest child—two of the kids were 5 or 6 years old, the rest 8 to 10. James appeared to be at ease and picked up on the forms pretty well. I thought he looked as if he were enjoying himself. About halfway through the class, a father of one of the students showed up. He began helping with the class, too. Abdul said that he was in the adult class that meets on Fridays. Some of the folks in that class sometimes work out with the younger class to get in more practice, like Mr. Simon and this guy.

At one point, Abdul gave James some individual attention, showing him the moves for the first routine so he could practice at home. Toward the end of the class, Abdul handed out new colors of belts for some of the students and praised them highly for the good job they had done at a TKD tournament over the weekend. Abdul also had some TKD outfits for some of the students, and James asked if he could get one. Abdul said they would fix him up. James appeared quite pleased.

At the end of the class, the father of one of the other students came over to James and said he thought James was doing a good job with his first class. The father looked at me and said, "This guy is going to be really good." James heard him say that and beamed.

As we walked out to the car, James had quite a spring in his step, and he was smiling broadly. He said he really liked the class and that he thought he did well. I praised him, too—we were both feeling very good about the experience.

On the drive home, we went over the plans for the next 2 weeks again. I went in to the home to get Margaret to sign the bus permission slip for James to ride a different bus on his class days. James was all excited and demonstrated the first set of moves for his parents. Margaret was very pleased with how happy James felt and thanked me very warmly for helping all this happen. Jackson was smiling and nodding, too. I left feeling very good—somehow it felt like a great victory for us all.

[James' first lesson wasn't such a big deal really on the outside, but we were all feeling exceptionally pleased and good about it. I think that was mostly due to how good James was feeling—we were all "catching" it from him. Margaret appeared genuinely pleased and grateful to me for helping this happen for James. Her eyes sparkled, and she appeared to have a deepened sense of belief in what I would be able to do for her boys—as if she hadn't really understood what I was up to before and now she knew. A sweet moment!!] (Field notes)

James continued with TKD classes for 2 months. He caught the bus from school and David or Jackson picked him up after class. According to Abdul, James was making good progress and would probably be ready for tournaments in the spring. Then Jackson quit picking him up after class and he refused to let David do it. James asked for a ride home from other students a couple of times, but he didn't want to keep doing that. When I talked to Jackson, he said he would pick James up, no problem. But then it didn't happen. I was completely amazed that a father would so pointedly sabotage his son's desires, especially when it seemed to be so beneficial for James to participate. I tried to enlist the help of Margaret, but she said she was working when all of this happened, so she could not do anything about it.

James was pretty upset and angry with his father. After missing several classes, James said he would just walk home from class—it was only a few miles, and the weather was warm by then. So that's what he did. I still didn't know why Jackson was making choices that created such limitations for his sons.

Another goal for James centered on doing more things with typical peers. We checked into all the clubs that were available at school, and James chose the Fellowship of Christian Athletes (FCA) club. The group met on Thursday nights at the school for an hour. They had speakers, played games, read the Bible, planned events, and talked about Christian ideals in the area of sports. I told James that I would provide a ride to the meetings for three times to see if he wanted to continue. Then perhaps Jackson or David could give him rides after that. (Margaret worked the second shift, so she was working in the evenings.) James was doubtful, but I talked to Jackson and received assurances that James could get a ride.

I gave James a ride to his first FCA meeting. I stayed in the car until he walked into the school, and then I waited in the teachers' lounge. After the hour was over, I walked back toward the meeting room and saw James walking out with three girls. They were all chatting and laughing. James waved good-bye to them and said he would see them next week. When we met at the car, James said that was a *great* club—he really had a good time.

After I had taken James to the FCA meetings three times, it was the family's turn to take over, as we had agreed. However, when I checked with James after the meetings, he had not been able to go—no ride. Yet another "all talk, no action" situation. This time, I didn't even check with Jackson about what the problem could be. Instead, I went to the club sponsor to ask if any of the students in the club could pick James up. While I was telling the sponsor what we needed, one of the FCA members overheard the request and said he could pick James up every week. And, for every meeting until the end of school, James had a ride. Hooray!

PROBLEMS WITH FAMILY DYNAMICS

Working with David and James' family proved to be an interesting, but very frustrating, experience. We had opened some doors to potentially expanding the boys' experience in some very positive ways, only to be sabotaged by Jackson and abandoned by Margaret. David appeared to just let it all slide by, but James was resentful and angry. The more we tried to do, the more aware James became of how unsupportive his family really was. Jackson and Margaret always talked a good line about how much they wanted and would do for their boys, but when it came down to the action required, the story changed completely.

The only motivation that I could ever figure out for Jackson's behavior had to do with control over the boys. Perhaps he felt that the circumstances of his life gave him little control over his own situation, but that he could exert control when it came to the activities of his sons. Margaret expressed opinions and had high expectations for her sons' potential and achievements, but when it came time for the action that would allow them to proceed, she became power-less. She worked and brought home the money, but the running of the family fell to Jackson. I am only guessing at the motivations and personal circum-stances that caused the erratic, disabling behavior in this family, but they cer-tainly turned out to be quite different people than I had originally thought.

I did a follow-up interview with David and James a year later to see how things were going in their lives. David was in his last year of high school. Jackson had gotten him a job unloading trucks for Canada Dry, and he said he liked it okay. When I asked about his plans, he said he figured he'd just keep unloading trucks. Someday, he wanted to have his own car.

James was much more unhappy with his situation because he wanted so much more for himself. He had kept on with TKD throughout the summer and the following fall, taking the initiative to walk home after the classes him-self. He had even gone to a couple of tournaments and done well. When it got cold and he couldn't walk home anymore, he had to quit. He said he planned to start up again soon, though—as soon as it warmed up. He was almost ready for his yellow belt.

James said he hadn't been able to get involved in any clubs or other school activities that year because of the lack of transportation. He had gone out for the wrestling team in the fall, but he had to quit because Jackson had too many chores for him to do and wouldn't let him stay after school. James said he was very unhappy at home because of the way his dad treated him, and he asked me if I thought there was any way he could get his own apartment. He said that maybe a couple of his friends could go in with him. I had to tell him that I did not know of any way that could happen without his parents' permission and assistance. I told him I thought his best bet was to acquire skills so he could make his own living as soon as he was old enough. James looked down at his feet and said he couldn't wait that long.

SUMMARY

The major lessons for me in dealing with James and David's family had to do with the limitations in actually knowing a family and the limitations of being able to help a family. In the beginning, Jessica had assured me that David and James' parents were very involved and helpful with their boys. Over the course of working with this family, I learned that the school had developed this attitude only because the parents showed up for meetings, not because they actually did anything to help. Schools have to deal with parents who never show up for meetings and won't even return phone calls; so, when parents arrive for IEP meetings, they think it's a big deal.

I started out with the idea that Jackson and Margaret were going to be very cooperative with our endeavors, and it took me a while to realize that some direct sabotage was going on. Actually, as it turned out, we were dealing with a very uncooperative family. The reactions to this situation were manifest quite differently in the boys. David just gave up, took what he could get, and let the rest go. James, on the other hand, continued to grow more resentful and rebel-lious. In my follow-up meeting with both of the boys, I was distressed to see the extent of James' frustration and resentment. I was fearful of him doing some-thing drastic that might not be in his best interest. Things had turned out so dif-ferently with this family than I had first thought. It was a good lesson in "what you see may not be what you get."

The second limitation that I had to face involved the fact that I really was not able to be of that much help to this family due to the significant effect that the lack of parental cooperation, assistance, and support had on the progress we were able to make. For some students, the family dynamics can be so disabling that the therapeutic intervention may need to focus primarily on independence issues—how students can get on with their lives despite their families. With this family, an important piece of the puzzle to understand was that they were likely to say one thing, but behave in an entirely different manner. As a therapist, I learned that I could not take the family any further than its members were willing to go.

As is often the case with dysfunctional families, the ones who suffer the most are the children. I knew that David and James had great potential, and James even knew that for himself. Yet, without the cooperation of the family, there really wasn't much that we could do. In retrospect, I think that it might have been in everyone's best interest to end the intervention as soon as I was sure that the family wasn't going to be supportive. That way, expectations and hopes might not have been raised to an unrealistically high level.

7

Can't Anyone See?: When Caretakers Are Also Blind

Kathy Fletcher
Danny E. Johnson[*]

INTRODUCTION

How would you feel if you lived in a world of darkness where every step you took was dependent on the directions of another person? How would it be to live in a world where you felt you had no control? What would you do if you did not have a voice to advocate for yourself and to tell others who you are or how you felt? Although these questions may be interesting to contemplate, for people like Sara, such questions could dominate her life. This story is about Sara, a young woman who is blind and profoundly mentally retarded, who deals with these questions daily, but who has no way to reveal her answers.

The story of Sara is laced with the frustration, anger, and sadness that I experienced as I worked with her. These feelings were not directed at Sara, but at the systems that had swallowed her up. Sara had, unfortunately, been underserved for years by service providers and had been allowed to lie dormant in her home and school environments. Sara's story would not be complete without including the emotions that colored so much a part of the time that I spent

---

[*]Both authors worked extensively on this case. The first author provided the intervention and the chapter is written in the first person based on her experiences.

involved in Sara's life. Sara had been put into situation after situation where she did not get the services she needed and deserved; she was trapped in a world that caused her mother to once state, "It is just beyond me. Sara has no rights! I mean, that's [mobility training] part of her learning, you know. Sara should be getting that." Sara had regularly slipped through the cracks of system after system, with no voice to advocate for her to obtain the services that would unlock her potential.

Sara's story begins with an introduction to Sara and her school environment. Following the detailed description, the intervention planning process is described with an emphasis on the assessment procedure and results. The third section includes an in-depth discussion of the themes that emerged throughout the data collection process. The data were compiled from in-depth interviews with school and group home care providers and Sara's mother, as well as from detailed field notes gathered at each session. The remainder of the chapter includes implications for human service workers, which are developed in the form of mathematical equations.

DESCRIPTION OF SARA AND HER SCHOOL ENVIRONMENT

I was able to spend considerable time with Sara and her service providers in their natural environments. I was able to interview her mother, her teachers, and her group home workers in depth, as well as to observe Sara extensively in school, at the group home, and in the community. This allowed me to see Sara from a variety of perspectives and to begin to understand her current situation and how she had arrived there.

Sara's History

Sara was born blind and mentally retarded to a 16-year-old mother. Her mother described the beginning of Sara's life as a constant battle:

> I fought tooth and nail when she was a baby. I've fought everybody, in-laws, family, you name it, since I had that little girl. She was my little girl. I was going to make the decisions. I was not going to put her in an institution; I was not going to put her in the state institution. You know, I had all these people who were eager to give me advice, what I should do. This is my life and my child. To me, Sara's got as much right as this one [her small son], and my other son on this earth. Little things that are normal, a home . . . I had to really fight for that because I was young . . . I had social workers coming all the time, like I wasn't capable of taking care of this little blind baby. I showed them. I showed them all, and I was determined to give her a home. (Field notes)

So Sara stayed at home with her mother and received services through a specialized school for children with disabilities. She attended that school until she was 6, when she enrolled in a state residential school for persons with visual impairments. At age 14, Sara moved back home with her mother, but continued to attend the state school during the day.

At age 18, Sara's behavior at home became rebellious and too difficult for her mother to handle. At the time, Sara's mother was also rearing Sara's brothers, who were 16 and 1. Sara's mother began looking for an alternative place for Sara to live, refusing to consider institutionalization. She was told that "all the group homes out there are unavailable with long waiting lists." However, within 3 weeks, a group home manager called and Sara moved into the group home.

The transition was apparently difficult for Sara. She had behavior problems, which her mother felt constituted Sara's way of trying to get kicked out of the group home, on order that she could move back home. Sara's mother said, "So she went there, and she thought, if I do that over here and make a mess, mommy's going to come and get me and take me back home." However, the group home waited out the behavior problems, and, at the time of my intervention, Sara had lived there for 2 years.

Sara's transition from the school for persons with visual impairments to the public school and her move to the group home seemed to cause her to regress. Sara's mother, her job skills teacher, and her classroom teachers all reported that Sara had regressed from her previous level of performance since the time of her transition. Her mother stated, "To me, I saw her going backwards in that classroom." Sara's teacher commented that "Even last year, supposedly, there was a kid in the classroom she would hold conversations with. She doesn't come anywhere near that this year." Specifically, her mother recognized that Sara's communication skills had regressed, stating:

> She always, I always, communicated real well. I always understood pretty much everything she said. She just got to the point where, more or less, I was always asking her all the time, instead of her saying what she wanted. She just got to the point where she clammed up, got quiet. (Field notes)

Sara's mother also noted that Sara had previously initiated daily living skills and activities on her own, but she had regressed in her independence and now relied on others:

> You know, when she got ready to take a bath, she would go take her bath. I didn't have to say, "Sara, it's time to take a bath." It's just something she knew. She was ready to do it, and she did it. That's what she was doing, and no questions were asked. She doesn't do that anymore. (Field notes)

Based on her mother's descriptions and the teacher's knowledge of Sara, I felt that Sara might have appeared to be a very different person a few years ago. Her mother painted a picture of a person who was self-determining and independent in some areas of her life. Sara had apparently been able to communicate more effectively and have more meaningful interactions. Now, she was more dependent on her mother to give her directions, and she lacked initiative. Even Sara's teachers had information that led them to believe that Sara could hold conversations. They did not see that ability anymore.

Description of Sara

Sara was a 20-year-old, plainly dressed woman about 5 feet tall and weighing about 125 pounds when we first met. She was very quiet and did not draw attention to herself by making noises or having outbursts, as did many of the other students in the room. She did not immediately appear to me to be visually impaired, but after watching her for several minutes, she displayed the typical characteristics of a person with a visual impairment, such as self-stimulation by rocking back and forth, gazing at the floor, holding her chin against her chest, and not meeting people's eyes when they spoke to her. She also reached out her hand to identify objects and people; a couple of times she even leaned over to smell things for identification.

> Sara did not use a cane to assist in mobility [she had never been trained], so she was dependent upon other people to give her assistance or directions in moving from one place to another. She walked with a slight limp due to one leg being slightly shorter than the other. (Field notes)

Those who worked with Sara seemed unsure of her cognitive abilities. Sara's school speech pathologist told me that Sara's records showed an IQ of below 30 on the Perkins-Binet. Later, an expert in the field of visual impairment informed me that the Perkins-Binet is no longer considered an accurate test of IQ for people who are blind. The expert questioned the test scores because, she said, the Perkins-Binet had not been widely used in the last decade. I was further confused when Sara's teacher reported to me after the Individualized Education Plan (IEP) meeting that he had found a report in her records stating that Sara was actually qualified for the trainable mentally handicapped (TMH) class.

According to Sara's school records, Sara had autism, and her language skills tested at the 4 1/2-year-old level. Sara's autistic characteristics were most prevalent socially; she rarely interacted with others. She appeared content just to be alone, and she did not seek attention from others. However, as I got to know Sara, I wondered if her lack of social interaction could be the result of being in nonstimulating environments.

Sara exhibited some unusual behaviors at times. She often rocked back and forth in her chair while listening to music, although not necessarily to the beat of the music. When she was nervous or excited, she bit her hand, leaving a red callous on top of her thumb. Occasionally, Sara sat alone with a stuffed caterpillar toy, hitting it against her face and laughing.

It was often difficult to get Sara to respond to questions. Communication with Sara was sometimes further compromised when she would not answer even yes/no questions. This clearly inhibited her ability to have meaningful interactions or conversations.

> Sara's interactions were typically limited to two- to five-word phrases; she rarely formed a complete sentence. Often, she did not answer questions or [she] gave incorrect responses to questions asked. Even when she did make complete sentences or requests, other people often had difficulty understanding her. (Field notes)

On the positive side, Sara sometimes displayed a keen awareness of time and her surroundings. For example, her sense of time was exhibited in a quotation from my field notes. When I told her I would not see her the following week or the week after that, but I would see her after Christmas (in about 3 weeks), she responded, "Okay, see you in a couple of weeks."

A demonstration of Sara's awareness of her environment, even when she did not appear to be affected by the activities going on around her, is shown in this example from school:

> I asked [Sara], "Who is on your other side?" She leaned over, and I saw her nostrils flare as she smelled Mo [another student]. As she leaned back toward me, she said, "Mo." I asked her who was sitting on the sofa and, without hesitation, she said, "Wendall." I then heard Stephanie making noises in the bathroom. To find out if she could identify someone by a particular noise, I asked her who that was in the bathroom. I did not expect a response, but she immediately answered, "Stephanie." (Field notes)

Another time Sara surprised me was during her IEP meeting. She attended the meeting, but she did not appear to be aware of what was happening as she rocked back and forth in her chair. The IEP team was discussing her weight gain and the option of her bringing her own lunch. At this point, Sara nodded her head up and down. Her teacher noticed her head nodding and asked if she would like to bring her own lunch. Sara said, "Yes." I was completely shocked that this person, whom I had assumed was unable to follow our conversation, suddenly spoke up. She was able to answer the question appropriately and help us get on with the meeting.

Sara surprised me in one way or another almost every time I met with her. For example, one time when we were throwing a ball back and forth, I started to count the throws. After a few throws, she began counting every other time. I said "3," and she said "4," and so on, up to 10.

Sara's ability to learn quickly was a constant source of amazement to me. An excerpt from my field notes reads:

> I laid all the pieces (cards with differently textured materials glued to them such as sandpaper and felt) out and told Sara to start matching them. After she had matched the first pair, I took her hand and placed it to the side and told her to put the match (two cards with matching textures) to the side. She then put together another match, and I moved her hand and pieces to the side again. The next match she did not put together correctly, so I said "Are you sure they match?" Then she separated the pieces and found the correct match. After she made the match, she automatically moved the pieces to the side. Martha [a group home staff person] looked surprised, her eyes widening, as I told Sara that was good. (Field notes)

Sara also surprised me with little comments that I would not have expected her to say. For example, we were playing the game Ants in Your Pants where players flick plastic objects into a bucket on a table. She flicked an object that went in the air and landed on the floor. I did not take note of where the object landed. Out of the blue, after the object hit the floor, Sara said, "Hit floor." Obviously, she was paying close attention to where the objects were going, and she was able to identify the difference between the noise made when the object hit the floor and when it hit the table. Sara continued to surprise me as I got to know her at her school.

Sara's School Environment

When I first walked into Sara's classroom, the "severe/profound mentally handicapped" (SPMH) class at a large southeastern high school, I was immediately struck by the variety of noises that pulsated throughout the room. Several students wandered aimlessly, while others sat idly in various places around the room. As I later became aware, this was a typical afternoon for the students in this class. The eight students in the SPMH class were supervised by two teachers and two teachers' aides. A teacher's aide introduced the students to me, as we watched from the side of the room.

Hank, who was wearing a drool bib tied around his neck, was walking in circles around a large table in the middle of the room, as usual, I was told. He was nonverbal and seemingly unresponsive to others. He had big brown eyes that appeared to be completely empty.

Wendall was sitting on the sofa across the room. He was very quiet, which was unusual for him, the aide said, since he was typically walking around the room making unintelligible noises. Later, I often saw his teachers hold him down to his seat. Wendall would be told to sit, and as soon as the teacher turned his back, Wendall was up again. He, too, was nonverbal except for sounds. At one point, I heard an aide say that Wendall was "medicated," which caused him to be still and "zoned out." His eyes had a peculiar, steel-gray look, with a staring gaze.

Mo was swallowed up in a chair at the end of the table in the middle of the room. He appeared to weigh about 60 pounds. His hair was extremely thin, reminding me of children I had seen after chemotherapy. He was nonverbal except for frequent grunts and groans. Mo had a tendency to look at his hand as if it were not connected to his body. He would look at his hand, turn it in all directions, and touch his face with it, as if he had never seen that hand before.

Robert was sitting in his wheelchair next to Mo. His eyes were closed and his head was laid back to the right, off of the headrest. He was also nonverbal. The aide told me his teachers would try to stimulate him by rubbing his face with the backs of their hands. Occasionally, Robert moved his head, but mostly his eyes stayed closed, with his mouth hanging open. He appeared to be profoundly mentally handicapped.

Stephanie's yell, which sounded like a deep foghorn in the middle of the night, broke the relative quiet of the classroom. She was a heavy-set student, weighing about 180 pounds. She occasionally thrust her arm out, grabbing at anyone who was within her reach. Her cold, empty eyes were set deeply into her face and looked as if they saw nothing.

Paula was sitting in her wheelchair, making a clucking sound that could be heard only in close proximity. Paula appeared to be the only student who could sustain eye contact, although she only stared at me without responding when I said, "Hi." Later, Sara's mother said that Paula was Sara's best friend, although I never saw the two of them communicate with one another.

Trevor was sitting in his wheelchair at the table with a phone book open to the yellow pages, a common activity for him. He looked up at me and said, "Hi"; his smile brightened the room. Shortly after the beginning of my visits to the classroom, Trevor was moved into the TMH classroom across the hall, much to the chagrin of his SPMH teachers; they missed the animation and joy he brought to the room.

Billy slowly rolled his wheelchair across the room. For a moment, the teachers were not watching him, and I saw him roll up next to a grocery cart with different games and toys in it. He began pulling the toys out one at a time and throwing them onto the floor. An aide spied Billy's maneuvers and dashed over to stop him. "He's always doing that," she said. During my visits to the classroom, I never felt that I connected with Billy. Whenever our eyes would almost meet, he would look away.

Sara was sitting at a small table next to the wall, listening to the radio. She rocked back and forth in her chair, although not to the rhythm of the music. I guessed she was rocking for self-stimulation. She did not seem to be affected by any other activity in the room; even Stephanie's yell did not cause a reaction. As I looked around the classroom, I wondered with whom Sara could communicate, besides the teachers and aides.

INTERVENTION PLANNING PROCESS

A student from the SPMH class was a nontypical candidate for a leisure education intervention such as the FLLE program. After all, being able to make
choices is typically an essential part of experiencing leisure. I was afraid that I
would merely be providing a diversionary playtime for a person who might be
unable to be self-determining. These thoughts caused a personal struggle for me
as I entered into my relationship with Sara. I was initially reluctant to spend 6
months with a person who was unable to make decisions and who only required
diversionary activities.

My journey with Sara began with referrals from her job skills trainer
and her classroom teachers. The trainer and teachers were all convinced that
Sara could be doing much more than she was—that she only needed a chance to
express herself. After considerable discussion with other FLLE staff, I decided
to accept the challenge of developing and carrying out an intervention that
could tap into this unexplored ability to do more.

I began a lengthy assessment process, including formal interviews
with Sara's two teachers, her mother, and the two group home staff who had
been identified as having the longest contact with Sara; more than 50 hours of
observation; and informal interviews with Sara's job skills trainer, speech
pathologist, and habilitation coordinator at the group home. The assessment
process was lengthy and continued throughout the intervention. I was constantly
finding out new information about Sara that helped me to understand her better
and develop my intervention strategies.

I spent the first month observing Sara in her classroom, waiting for
permission from the group home director to start the formal intervention. The
group home director and the habilitation coordinator were supportive of our service, saying, "We really like to see the clients get any services they can to help
them be more independent." However, they needed written permission from
Sara's mother before I could begin working with Sara at the group home.
Unfortunately, Sara's mother was not easily accessible, and the materials had to
be reviewed first by a social worker, who was employed by the group home,
before being sent to the mother. This process took much longer than expected, so
I used this time to get to know Sara and to learn how to communicate with her.

Once I finally had everyone's permission to begin the intervention, I
started the formal assessments. Since Sara was limited in her communication
skills and incapable of responding to my assessment questionnaires, I decided
to interview the adults who were most aware of her strengths, interests, and
needs, both at school and at the group home.

Because the teachers seemed highly motivated for Sara to be
involved in this project, I decided to interview them first. Both teachers were
new to Sara's classroom and had been working with Sara for about 5 months.
Some of the information they relayed about Sara came from other sources. Both
teachers were very positive and willing to give me any information I needed. I

met with each teacher separately after school for a little over an hour. I transcribed verbatim the interviews later. Sara's teachers both talked about the inappropriateness of her placement in their classroom. Stuart stated:

> She [Sara] should be with other blind people, with people who have been trained to work with blind people. You know, it's frankly ridiculous that you have this lone blind child in the S/P [severe/profound] room with other kids, all needing one-on-one attention. I don't have the facilities; I don't have the expertise. . . . She slipped through the cracks some years ago, and it's too bad that it ever happened. (Field notes)

He identified her strengths as:

> Her ability to learn things. She can do that. Her desire to work with adults or to have a relationship with [an] adult . . . I think as she gets to know you, she'll want to do things to please you . . . that's like the foot in the door. And she is actually, you know, pleasant. She is fairly cooperative, you know. She wants to do well. (Field notes)

I also asked about Sara's needs. One of her teachers stressed that a strong need for Sara was to become involved in community activities with other blind people. Both teachers were concerned about Sara's social and communication skills. In response to a question about Sara's initiative, Stuart said:

> I think if she's able to talk and truly interact, initiative would come. I mean, right now, why have initiative? She'd get into trouble. . . . She's not in a place where initiative is going to get her anything because there's nothing to have initiative for. She listens to the radio. She could show initiative and go and sit in front of the TV. There's no reason for her to have it, at this point in time. (Field notes)

It seemed to me that he was saying that Sara would somehow be better off without being able to make her own decisions and act upon them. If she developed initiative, she would require more assistance and supervision, which in turn would mean more work for her care providers. In her present state, she was very easy to care for because her care providers could sit her in a chair where she would listen to music for hours without disturbing anyone or requiring attention.

Both teachers were concerned about Sara dealing with emotions appropriately. They felt that she had a full range of emotions but that she did not always respond appropriately. One teacher stated:

> [Sara] has anxiety, she has likes and dislikes, and she has sadness. She has fear, and she has those, but there's absolutely no depth. . . . If it's talking about her mom, her affect is the same as if we're talking about her favorite radio station. (Field notes)

From her classroom teachers' perspectives, the most important areas to address included social and communication skills and integrating Sara into more activities for persons with visual impairments. These interviews gave me considerable information on Sara's deficits, and they brought into focus the reality of how challenging it would be to work with her. I also came to understand some of her complexities involved with a person being in environments that inhibited her growth and development. The combination of Sara's quiet demeanor and the staff's inexperience in dealing with someone in her circumstances had left her in limbo.

It took me about a month to arrange the interviews with the group home staff. The first staff person whom the habilitation coordinator recommended that I interview did not show up for our meeting, so it was rescheduled for the following week. Later that week, the staff person was fired. The habilitation coordinator then identified two other women who had worked with Sara for almost a year, and whom she felt would know Sara better than other staff. I met with them twice for about an hour each time.

Sara's group home staff members, Martha and Felicia, were able to identify Sara's strengths more readily than her teachers had been, and they seemed more optimistic about Sara's situation. They identified three specific areas in which Sara was in need of improvement:

1. Sara needed to learn to take more initiative: "to get more into it, instead of just sitting. Taking some initiative, to get up to do stuff, without having to be told,"
2. Sara needed to learn to expand the types of social interactions she experienced:
    > Felicia: "She's probably always going to have to have somebody with her at all times, so she always will have companionship, but building friends, knowing the difference in friendship."
    > Martha: "I think it would bring her out. If she had a friend, some body like a companion." (Field notes)
3. Sara needed to develop a better understanding of the opportunities available to her:
    > Felicia: She doesn't really take advantage of her opportunities. She could do a lot, but she doesn't really ask for stuff, like to go places, like Russell. (Field notes)

Martha and Felicia stressed during the interview that Sara was heavily influenced by routine, consistent with her diagnosis of autism. Felicia pointed out that Sara was sometimes apprehensive about going on outings because she was asked to break her routine. She talked about the routine at the group home and how that differed from a regular home:

... not to mention, she's gotten so used to the same routine that often after dinner, she just wants to get ready to take her bath and go to bed. That's why sometimes I get upset when I have to do the same thing over and over. Sometimes I need change. 'Cause at home, you don't do the same thing over and over and eat dinner at the same time. Sometimes you might not feel like eating dinner at this time. So, when everybody else is eating, you're doing something else. You might have somewhere to go. But around here, they do the same thing, at the same time, day after day. (Field notes)

Martha and Felicia were describing a world that was artificial. Sara's life was dictated by a well-meaning schedule that squelched self-determination. The group home schedule was missing the natural flow of life that changes plans based on one's feelings, such as eating when one's stomach growls or going to bed when one's eyelids lie heavy over one's eyes. Instead, what was a well-meaning schedule was the enemy of a person who fights against a natural tendency to be rigid. Sara was dependent on that schedule, and when it was changed she became confused and communicated in any way that she could, such as by biting her hand.

Following the interview with the group home staff members, I had a more tangible idea of the types of interventions that I felt would be helpful for Sara. My initial strategies included:

1. developing activities that she could do that would get her out of her room and become more active,
2. improving language skills necessary to make requests for the games she could play,
3. helping her learn various activities where she could interact with her peers and improve communication skills.

I worked with Sara at school and at her group home for the next 4 months, once or twice a week. Through the assessment process and work on these intervention strategies, the themes discussed in the following section emerged.

THEMES

Throughout data collection and analysis, Sara's story revealed major themes that centered on her potential. Three aspects of potential for Sara were:

1. perceived potential—the capabilities that people in Sara's life saw in her, as well as, the barriers to her reaching her potential;
2. manifest potential—the blossoming of Sara's untapped possibilities that occurred during the FLLE intervention; and
3. lost potential—the lack of involvement and follow-through with Sara's progress, both during and following the intervention.

Perceived Potential

Sara's perceived potential emerged during the assessment process, informal interviews, and conversations with Sara's teachers, job skills trainer, speech pathologist, and mother. I soon learned that they perceived Sara as having more potential than she was currently expressing.

The overwhelming opinion was that Sara had the potential to learn more activities and to be more active. The job skills trainer described Sara as "a lot smarter than where she is at now." She saw that Sara could be doing a lot more and wanted her to have the chance to do that. The school's speech pathologist described Sara's potential in terms of her ability to follow directions, remember people, and understand more vocabularies than tests had indicated. Both classroom teachers agreed that Sara had the potential to go to the TMH classroom and participate in activities with her peers. Sara's mother also felt that Sara had a great deal of potential to grow, saying:

> I know this little girl by the inside out, and anything that Sara can do does not surprise me, because I believe she lives in a whole little world of her own. She has a whole life that she hasn't brought out. (Field notes)

Along with the potential that various people perceived in Sara, they also told me about a number of reasons why Sara was not fulfilling her potential. The barriers that blocked Sara from reaching her potential were:

1. Classmates and housemates who were typically lower functioning than she,
2. Her apparent isolation, and
3. Her experienced lack of choices and opportunities.

The next sections examine more closely why these three barriers were identified by Sara's service providers.

Lower Functioning Classmates and Housemates.   During interviews, teachers and related service personnel revealed that Sara's class placement was perceived as inappropriate. The speech pathologist began the interview by saying, "Sara's placement is not correct. She is much higher [functioning] than all the other kids [in the class]." One of Sara's teachers also mentioned her inappropriate placement:

> The job skills trainer here talked to the person at the residential school [which Sara attended for 12 years], and he was very surprised to find out she was in a severe/profound classroom. He really thought she would be in the TMH class. (Field notes)

The other students were not a resource for Sara to practice her social, motor, mental, and communication skills. This severely limited her ability to reach her full potential. Her teacher noted that "There is no one for her to talk to except for the adults."

I wondered how a student could be placed in a classroom that was not the most appropriate place for her to learn. Why were so many people saying that Sara should be in another classroom but not doing anything about it?

During the interviews, I heard several versions of possible reasons for Sara's original placement in the SPMH class. Lori, one of Sara's teachers, stated that she thought Sara's placement was due to her multiple disabilities. Jackie, the job skill trainer, agreed with Lori, stating that the SPMH classroom was the closest to "multiple handicapped" in this school. Cheryl, the teacher's aide who had been in the classroom before Stuart or Lori arrived, mentioned that Sara's mother had placed her in the classroom because Sara was good friends with Paula.

Sara's placement in the SPMH class seemed incorrect and was not helpful to Sara. The reasoning behind the placement seemed vague. It appeared that Sara was in a classroom that was inappropriate and her mother seemed convinced that it was the best that could be done.

Stuart's comment that it was "comfortable" for the school system to leave Sara in this classroom was distressing to me. Did this school system really keep a student in what appeared to be a restrictive environment because moving her would cause more work for the staff? Wasn't there a place for a student who did not fall neatly into the classroom categories established by the school system?

As I probed, I discovered the reason that seemed to be everybody's justification for Sara being in the SPMH environment. The last point Stuart made in the formal interview on the subject concerned Sara's vocational training:

> She's not appropriate [in this class]. Actually, I thought about it [putting her in the TMH class], but then, Jackie, who works with her on job skills, wouldn't be able to work with her anymore, getting her a job, and right now she's almost 21. She might end up in that classroom for a year, but then have no vocational placement. So, I felt that having the possibility of vocational placement would be better. (Field notes)

The situation seemed unjust to me. The system appeared to not meet her needs, and the people around her had to be satisfied with, "She needs to stay in this classroom so she can get job skills training." Though job skills training is extremely important, it seemed that Sara should have been able get the same quality of training in a more appropriate educational environment.

In addition to being surrounded by peers who were lower functioning in the classroom, Sara's peers in the group home were also lower functioning. The group home director stated during the IEP meeting that "There is no one for Sara to talk to as a peer." The habilitation coordinator for the group home described Sara as "the highest functioning person here." A group home staff member described the other clients as being inactive and lacking the skills to socially interact.

Sara's group home was quiet the first time I visited. As I walked in, I noticed that the home looked and felt sterile, not really decorated like a person's home. The walls didn't have many pictures, and the furniture looked as if it belonged in a college dormitory. I walked into a big room with a television that, I learned later, was on all the time. Paula was sitting about 5 feet from a large table, which appeared to be the dining room table. Next to Paula was Tracy, sitting in a high-backed wheelchair. She was strapped into the wheelchair, and her body appeared to be very rigid. I suspected that she was nonverbal since she did not acknowledge my greeting. Tracy's eyes were very small, and drool was dripping from the side of her mouth.

I went with Sara back to her room. The room was about 10- by 12-feet long with a dresser on one wall and Sara's bed pushed close to the far wall and underneath the window. The first thing I noticed was that the room was very empty. I expected to see stuffed animals or other tactile objects that she could hold and feel, but there were no toys and the top of her dresser was clear. Sara's bed was neatly made with one pillow on it. Against the wall, at the foot of the bed, was a stereo system in a wooden stand that looked indestructible. A wooden chair with a padded seat and a few scattered pictures on the wall completed the decor in Sara's room.

Sara and I went back into the living room and sat on one of the sofas. Lillie, another housemate, was sitting on the sofa perpendicular to us. Lillie said, "Hi." She was ambulatory and appeared to have limited language skills. One time, Lillie came up to me and said, "Ba, ba, ba, ba," while grabbing her pants and pointing at mine. I never did figure out what she meant by this gesture, but she always had a warm way about her. Sara, however, did not seem to be particularly interested in Lillie.

Gina, another housemate, was a very small woman, about 4 feet tall, weighing 100 pounds. Gina's head was very small compared to her body, and her face was always expressionless. She walked with someone holding her hand and appeared to be very distant. She never made eye contact with me or said a word while I was at the group home, preferring to rock silently in the rocking chair in the living room.

Sandy, the final housemate, was also ambulatory, using a large walker. I heard Sandy coming down the hall, dragging her feet loudly behind her aluminum walker. She passed by me, waved, said "Hi," and then blew me kisses. She looked mischievous, mumbling unintelligible words in an annoying nasal voice. Martha told me once that Sara did not get along with Sandy because Sandy was so loud and had a tendency to jabber.

In the group home, Sara's peers appeared to be more aware of their environment than the students in Sara's class at school. However, in most situations in Sara's life, she lived in a world where her peers made noises and roamed aimlessly around rooms. Her closest friend, according to her mother and group home staff, was a young woman who ground her teeth constantly, had limited communication skills, limited wheelchair mobility, and whom I never observed interacting with Sara. I wondered if Sara had given up the hope of interacting with her peers and had retreated into herself as a refuge. Stuart described her possible predicament this way:

> Maybe she was a different kid back then [when she was at the school for people with visual impairments], and she, you know, went out and felt good. Then, all of a sudden, there's this black hole she was dropped into. And she may just be reflecting that. (Field notes)

Sara was in environments that did not seem conducive to her reaching her full potential. Stuart, speaking about Sara's opportunities to have relationships, said, "No, no. I don't think she does, and I think she did at one point. From what I've heard, she did have some, but I can only base it on what I've seen." Sara had had limited exposure to people who were higher functioning than she was, other than service providers

Isolation.   Another barrier preventing Sara from reaching her potential was that she spent large blocks of time alone. Typically, when I arrived at the group home, Sara was in her room with the door closed and the lights off, the radio playing. Sara was also isolated at school, typically sitting at the side of the room, alone, listening to the radio. Sometimes she participated in her classroom in "morning group," which lasted about half an hour. She then went to "vocational skills," where she sat at a table alone, folding pieces of scrap paper and stuffing them into envelopes as practice for her job skills training.

Sara's isolation was mentioned in the interviews and confirmed as I observed her during the interventions. Sara's mother noted her concern about Sara spending so much time alone when she said, "She was, like, left to herself. Like I said, she started going in a different direction." The group home staff commented, when asked what Sara did for leisure, that she usually stayed in her room and listened to music. Martha said, "She really doesn't do much. Sometimes she will come out with the other clients, but she just sits." Again, she was alone or not interacting with peers. I wondered if her lack of interactions and being alone was connected to the "black hole" that Stuart had mentioned. Unless she was prompted to interact, Sara would sit alone in her room and listen to music, or she would sit alone at a table in her classroom.

Lack of Choices and Opportunities.   As I got to know Sara in her environments, I began to see that, in addition to being isolated, she had very few choices or options in her daily routine. Her teachers, the group home staff, speech pathologist, job skills trainer, and mother all expressed concern over Sara's lack of choices; this was one of the reasons they had asked for my intervention. Sara's lack of choices was made painfully obvious during our interviews. Out of all the above professionals who worked with Sara, the entire group could only identify music and puzzles as interests.

Sara's classroom provided almost no leisure options. When her teacher was asked what type of activities Sara could do for leisure, he drew a blank and could not come up with any activities for her to do, except for sitting and listening to the radio. Her other teacher noted that "We have only found two other games that our other kids can play, and that's not much of a choice for her" and "Games in the classroom just are not appropriate for her." The teachers pointed out that for them to have games in the classroom, they had to be appropriate for at least two students. Again, the differences in Sara's ability level and that of the other students had become a barrier in Sara's potential to play, grow, and interact.

Sara's leisure choices in her group home were also limited. The group home staff expressed that Sara had interests in music and puzzles. However, they pointed out that she was bored with the puzzles and had memorized how to put them together. When the staff was asked if she could play any other games, they stated, "No." Although Sara's habilitation plan included developing leisure activities and choices, it appeared that the staff members were not actively working on creating options for Sara.

It was no wonder to me that Sara was always sitting by the radio. It appeared that her best, and maybe only, option was music. Her mother expressed concern over her daughter's lack of options:

> Being in her room doesn't bother me near as much as sitting around that house [group home] with nothing to do. Just waiting for the next bath or whatever. They have a whole lot of time just waiting, bored. (Field notes)

Her mother felt that Sara was not being given options to demonstrate that she could make choices:

> But if you, like gave her a choice, "Sara, what do you want to do, this is your time." Given the choice, she may do something all together different. She's never really had a choice. And then, if she did choose music, fine . . . but see, she's never had choices. It's always been music. (Field notes)

Stuart, her teacher, had similar feelings regarding her current options at the group home. While he was describing the group home's approach to dealing with Sara's leisure, I could not help but think he could also have been describing his own classroom:

> I think at the group home, "Listen to music, Sara; you're out of the way and I'll deal with the other residents." So her only choice has always been music, you know, because she wasn't aware of the other ones. And so I think she just needs to be able to find more things to do, you know. (Field notes)

What would happen if Sara were "to find more things to do?" Would she choose those activities over the radio? The next section will explore what occurred when Sara was taught new leisure skills and was encouraged to be more self-determining.

Manifest Potential

As I began the intervention, I began to see Sara's potential that had been described to me during the assessment process. At first, progress was slow; communication was difficult and Sara's leisure options were limited. A few months after my original introduction to Sara, I had completed the formal assessments with her teachers and group home staff. Based on the information they supplied, my own observations of Sara, and the information from the informal interviews, I decided to focus on the following goals for Sara:

1. Participate in one community activity involving peers who are higher functioning;
2. Increase her game skills and repertoire of games;
3. Verbalize the games she has learned when asked, and choose and play the game; and
4. Use social game verbalizations, such as, "Will you play with me?" and "I am finished."

I began checking on activities for persons with developmental disabilities. Since the only activity Sara seemingly enjoyed was listening to music, I looked for an activity that focused around music. I learned of the Satisfied Singers, a local choral group for persons with developmental disabilities. The group was composed of adults with various levels of mental handicaps and met at a local arts center.

Sara's reactions to participating in the Satisfied Singers varied. Sometimes she did not appear to interact with anyone or even participate in the group, but at other times, she appeared to enjoy going to the group and participating. For example, on our first visit to the Satisfied Singers, Sara jumped right in to join the practice. My field notes from that day stated:

> Judy [the Satisfied Singers director] welcomed Sara to the group and told her that they like to warm up before they start to sing. She told the group to make a noise like when you see fire works. Sara joined in as they all went, "O-o-o-oh." Each time they finished saying "O-o-o-oh," Sara said, "Bang" out loud. (Field notes)

However, after this first time, Sara typically did not participate very much in the singing. The following was a typical experience for her at Satisfied Singers:

The next song was "Lean on Me." Sara smiled when she heard the song begin and mouthed a few words on her own. Throughout the song, I told her to sing out loud, and she would for a few words. Then she would be quiet again. The rest of the practice was similar. Sara would only sing when told to, and she would not carry the song on farther than three or four words. (Field notes)

Sara attended Satisfied Singers, but she was not fully engaged in the activity. I wasn't sure if that meant that she didn't like the activity, that she didn't know the songs, that she was shy, or that she didn't have the cognitive abilities to become involved. Because the main focus was to find something that she wanted to do, not something that I wanted her to do, the problem was figuring out how to tell whether she liked the Satisfied Singers. In the beginning, Sara was not able to tell me herself what she liked and disliked.

Since Sara did not express her delight verbally, I began to search for nonverbal cues to reveal how she was feeling. She had shown a pattern of giggling and smiling when she liked to do an activity. She had also shown me that if she did not want to do something, she would refuse to do it, or she would insist on receiving step-by-step instructions, even though she knew how to carry out the activity. I felt confident that Sara wanted to go to the Satisfied Singers when I arrived at her group home to find her feeling sick, but ready to go. My field notes stated:

Sharon let me into the back door of the group home. She said that Sara was "really excited to go to the Satisfied Singers." She said that she had talked to Sara about feeling bad, but Sara insisted on going. I went back to Sara's room. I knocked on the door and said "Hello." Sara said, "Hi" and giggled. I opened the door up and asked her what she was doing. She said, "Satisfied Singers." (Field notes)

I was surprised at Sara's immediate response to my question. For the first time, she verbalized both awareness and excitement about an upcoming event. This represented a dramatic change from having to give her step-by-step directions for each action we were about to take and to remind her about what we were doing at the time.

As soon as I was confident that Sara enjoyed the Satisfied Singers, I decided to turn the activity over to the group home staff and Judy, the Satisfied Singers' director. I discussed with the staff who would accompany Sara and strategies to help her feel included in the group. A couple of weeks before our intervention was complete, I placed a follow-up call to Judy. She reported that Sara was doing well and that she had participated in a performance with the Satisfied Singers during the previous week.

Another goal stated that Sara would verbalize games she had learned when asked, choose a game, and play the game. Based on the assessments, I was aware of Sara's limited options for engaging in activities. It was apparent to me that in order to get Sara out of her room to do anything besides listen to music, I needed to teach her the names of new games and how to play them. Stuart told me that I "could probably teach her most anything." He also observed that although Sara did not have a full awareness of her options, when her options were pointed out, she could make decisions.

It seemed to me that what Sara really needed were options, a "bigger bag of choices." Because there were few games in the classroom, I brought in some that previously had been purchased by FLLE in order to determine which ones were most suitable and interesting for Sara.

The first two games I introduced were Perfection and Connect Four. Connect Four is a three-dimensional checkers game, while Perfection is a tactile, three-dimensional puzzle. Sara appeared to be familiar with Connect Four because she put the frame together and systematically put the checkers into the frame without coaching. While she knew how to put the checkers in the frame, I did not notice her smiling or laughing at any time during the game. Sara's reaction to Perfection was different. For example, a few times after she had placed the shapes into the correct places, she praised herself by saying, "Good girl, Sara Duncan."

I continued to introduce new games to Sara throughout the intervention. I introduced one new game every week, always giving Sara enough time to learn the previous game. As Stuart had suggested, she learned games very quickly; only two games that I tried were unsuccessful.

The way in which Sara made choices changed drastically throughout the intervention. According to my field notes, she made choices in the following manner in the beginning:

> I explained to Sara, "I have three games for you to choose from. I have Simon (at that time, Stephanie had the Simon game; she had come out of the bathroom, taken the game from my bag, and was looking at the outside of the box), Perfection, and Kerplunk." I placed all the games in their boxes in front of Sara. She started to feel the boxes. As she touched each box, I told her the name of the game. I asked her to say the names of the games after me. She repeated the names after me, "Er-ection, Er-unk, and Simon." I explained to her that I wanted her to make a choice among these three games. She felt them some more, pulled Kerplunk closer to her, and started to try to open it. I asked her if that was the one she wanted to play, and she said, "Yes-s-s." (Field notes)

By the end of the intervention, Sara had ten games she knew how to play. While we were playing games, Sara was able to direct the order of games being played by requesting the game that she wanted to play next. She no longer needed to be given options; instead, she became self-determining as she asked for the next game to play. She was empowered to make her own choices by knowing the names of the games and by having more activity options. She controlled her options by having knowledge of her options and and by the improved verbal skills to identify what she wanted to do.

The following excerpt from my field notes reveals the vast improvement Sara had made during the intervention. This complete example is from one of our last sessions in the classroom:

I went back in and told Sara that we would stay in her classroom and play over by the snack table. She said, "OK." I cannot remember if I initiated it or if she did, but somehow, Trevor's name came up, and she wanted to play with him. I told her she would have to ask him to play.

I told Sara to ask Trevor to play with her. Sara said, "Trevor come play Kerplunk." Trevor nodded his head and said something I could not understand. I asked him if he wanted to play, and he nodded his head to say, "Yes."

I went over to the table in the snack area. I asked Sara to tell Trevor all the games she can play. She said each game in her typical fashion. Her typical fashion was being prompted by my asking, "Sara, what do you know how to play?" Then she would say one game at a time. I asked her what she wanted to play and she said Kerplunk.

Trevor went first and had difficulty grasping a stick to pull out. However, he eventually got it. Then I told him to tell Sara it was her turn, and he said, "Sara, your turn." He had difficulty enunciating this. Sara smiled and took her turn. I prompted her to tell Trevor it was his turn.

Jamie came over, and I asked her if she wanted to play. She said, "Yes," so I asked Sara if that was okay, and she said, "Yes." I told Sara that Jamie's turn was after hers. Sara appeared to be happy throughout the game. She smiled and laughed and would say, "Yeah" every once in a while when the marbles fell. She did require prompting for each time she said, "Your turn, Jamie." [I thought she had this down, but I guess not.]

After all the marbles fell, I asked Sara what she says. She said, "All finished." Before I could ask if she wanted to play again, she said, "Play Ants." I told her to ask Jamie and Trevor if they wanted to play, and they both agreed.

Sara appeared to enjoy the game. She smiled throughout and rocked in her seat. She needed prompting to tell Trevor it was his turn throughout the game. Trevor got a kick out of the game because Sara kept hitting Jamie with the ants. Jamie was positioned diagonally to Sara. Sara picked up on Trevor's laughter and would also laugh.

They flicked ants until Sara said, "Play Memory." [Go, Sara! She was self-initiating in changing the games.] Trevor had placed his hat on the table, so I used it to collect the ants. I gave the hat to Sara, and she took the ants out, placing them in the bucket. Then she put the hat on her head.

Steve came over and asked if he could play. He took Jamie's seat. I laid all the cards to Memory out on the table and explained the game to

Trevor. Sara took her turn and quickly matched a pair. I took her hand and guided it to place the match to the side.

Trevor took his turn and picked the plastic weave cards. As he was pulling them close to him, one of them came apart. I went to the back to glue the card back together and instructed them to keep playing. [I did not really expect them to keep playing. Trevor can barely tell Sara to take her turn, and I suspected that Sara would just sit there.]

When I came back, there was only one pair left. They had taken at least two turns each. Sara had mismatched a pair, but that didn't matter. Evidently, they had communicated somehow and kept playing. I told Sara the game was finished, and she said, "All finished." I asked her if she wanted to play Memory again or a different game. She said, "A different game."

I asked them if they wanted to learn a new game, and Trevor smiled and nodded, "Yes." Sara also said "Yes." I brought out the Donut Disaster game. I explained the game to them, and they played one game.

I told Sara the game was finished, and she said, "Play again." I separated the donuts, and they played again. Sara appeared to like the game more this time. She smiled and laughed a little. After the game was over, Sara said, "Play again."

Steve and Sara then played the game. Sara required prompting to say, "Your turn" throughout the entire game. They played twice, and then it was time for them to get ready for the bus. Sara said, "Ms. B.'s class, please." I asked her if she wanted to take the hat back to Trevor, and she said "Yes." (Field notes)

Not only was Sara self-initiating games that she wanted to play, but she was also interacting appropriately with her peers. She still was not consistent with using social game verbalizations, which was her third goal, but for the first time, she was able to continue playing a game with a peer without assistance. I observed that Sara had developed her potential to learn games and interact in a meaningful way with her peers.

Now that she had more options, Sara began to choose the activities she had learned, instead of listening to music all the time. For example, during one session at the group home, Sara had been playing games for about an hour. Toward the end of the session, I gave her the choice of listening to music in her room or continuing to play a game with one of her housemates. Without hesitation, she said, "Play again." I was surprised and pleased—feeling that Sara had expanded her possibilities and had expressed her desires.

Sara also began to self-initiate social contact with her peers. Throughout most of the intervention, I had not observed Sara initiating any type of interaction with another peer. Then, 3 weeks before our intervention concluded, Sara asked a peer to join her in an activity for the first time without prompting. My field note for that day read:

> We [Sara and I] started throwing the Koosh around. Lillie came in and sat on the sofa next to the end table. Sara was about 5 feet away from her on the other end of a sofa. Sara threw the Koosh over to Lillie and said, "Lillie, Koosh." (I was really surprised that Sara just suddenly decided to include Lillie in our little throwing game). Lillie giggled, and Sara said something like, "Catch the ball, Lillie. Good girl." The three of us threw the Koosh together for about fifteen minutes. (Field notes)

Sara had definitely blossomed during our 6 months of interventions and had shown indications of higher cognitive functioning than her label of SPMH would have indicated. She was participating in a community activity with peers who were higher functioning than she, she was verbalizing the games she knew how to play and was playing them, she was more socially engaged with her peers, and she had increased her repertoire of games. She was becoming more self-determining, as well as less isolated and alone. She had learned some skills that made it possible and interesting for her to come out of her room, stop listening to music, and be active with other people. Sara's potential was clear.

Potential Lost

After perceived potential and manifest potential, the third aspect of the theme of potential emerged as potential lost. The people who had the ability to continue tapping into her potential and helping her grow, teachers and group home staff, were showing signs of not following through on what had been accomplished.

An approach to continue exploring Sara's potential was to train her teachers and group home staff to continue the simple strategies that had proved successful. My approach during the discharge training sessions was to collaborate with the teachers and group home staff, asking how they saw the interventions fitting into their daily activities. I began meeting with Stuart and Lori, Sara's teachers, 2 months prior to the end of the intervention. To increase Sara's social interactions with higher-functioning peers, I had taken Sara into the TMH classroom to play games and socially interact with the other students. Each time I came to Sara's SPMH class, she asked me to take her to Ms. B.'s classroom, the TMH class. As she said, "Ms. B.'s room, please," she smiled, giggled, and scrunched her face in excitement. Sara's excitement about going to Ms. B.'s classroom revealed to me that this activity had some strong meaning for her. As there seemed to be so few activities in which Sara could express such enjoyment, I felt that even if she just sat in the TMH classroom, it would be good for her. Optimally, if she were given assistance, she could continue to play the games she had learned and interact with her peers.

Sara's teachers would have to provide Sara with the opportunity to continue going into the TMH classroom. I met with her teachers to discuss how to go about carrying out this goal. Stuart was not receptive to this idea and listed the many barriers he perceived regarding Sara moving to the TMH class. He pointed out that he really didn't know what Sara did when she was in the TMH classroom. He also didn't feel that the TMH teacher would be able to work with Sara in the class due to the large number of students.

Lori's reaction was slightly different from that of Stuart. When the suggestion of training someone to assist Sara in the TMH classroom was made, Lori commented, "If I could get one of those regular students back in here to work with her, that would be really good." We finally settled on a compromise. Lori and Stuart decided that they would bring peers from the TMH class into their classroom a few times a week, so they could observe students interacting with Sara.

The next step was for Stuart to observe how I had worked with Sara. One afternoon, he accompanied Sara and me to the TMH classroom and watched the intervention. He claimed that the intervention was meaningful and that he could easily continue it. He saw that my goals with Sara fit well with his goals: "Very on-line with what I encounter and what I try to do . . . getting her to respond whether its games or anything. Once I get her to respond in any area, I imagine she will generalize." I was pleased that he was able to see how Sara's accomplishments in the recreation therapy intervention enhanced her educational goals.

However, during subsequent sessions, Sara's teachers appeared to be distracted from working with her. They repeatedly said that the day was too busy to give Sara an opportunity to practice her leisure skills and decision-making. Lori commented that they "hadn't gotten around to it." Sara's teachers appeared to have scheduling conflicts with the weekly intervention, stating that they had decided to work with her only on Tuesdays and Thursdays, and since I came on those days, they just "hadn't done much" with beginning to work with Sara. "I haven't had time to play games with Sara" was a common refrain I heard when I visited Sara's classroom.

At the completion of the intervention, I recommended to Sara's teachers that they continue to help Sara integrate into the TMH class. During a follow-up phone call, two weeks after completion, the teachers were asked if they were continuing this intervention, and they commented, "After we found out that she was just going over there and sitting, we figured she could do that here. So she hasn't been going over there anymore." The teachers appeared to miss the point that Sara needed assistance when she went to the TMH class, or she would just sit and not interact. They also missed the point that going to that class meant something to Sara. Once again, Sara's needs and desires appeared to be ignored for the convenience of her service providers.

Preparing for the completion of the intervention with the group home staff was equally challenging. Six weeks prior to the end of the intervention, I met with the six group home staff members who interacted the most with Sara. At that meeting, I proposed a specific plan on how to get Sara out of her room and participating in activities. The staff did not seem very responsive, and I felt uncomfortable talking to them because they appeared to be so uninterested. However, when I found out that only two of the staff members worked during

Sara's leisure time, I concentrated my training with them, but unfortunately, Felicia was transferred to another group home. I was very disappointed because Felicia appeared to be the most interested in continuing with Sara's progress. I had to admit to myself that the group home staff was unlikely to continue helping Sara realize her potential. Like Sara's teachers, they, too, came up with excuses about why they could not continue working with Sara. The same people who originally asked me to work with Sara were now the ones coming up with excuses about why they could not give her the opportunity to practice the skills she had learned. As I said good-bye to Sara, I feared that she would once again regress.

IMPLICATIONS

The implications of Sara's story are extremely significant for people with disabilities and for those who work with them. Caution must be taken in generalizing implications since Sara was just one case, but, at the same time, I am aware that Sara is not an isolated case. Many other people with severe disabilities also fall into a plight similar to Sara's. They have considerable unexplored potential that requires one-on-one interventions to access.

As you think back over what you know about Sara, consider these implications for service providers and policymakers as provided in the form of mathematical equations.

1. Compliance ≠ Satisfaction

Sara gave the impression that she was doing fine because she did not present a behavioral problem. I never heard her complain about spending all of her time listening to the radio. She may be no different than others without options in life who become spectators. As the old adage goes, "The squeaky wheel gets the grease." Sara's silence and compliance were also the sound of a life in limbo. It should never be interpreted as satisfaction with her life.

2. Potential - Lack of Action = Lost Potential, or Said > Done

Sara was not unlike other persons with disabilities who have potential that is rarely tapped. And like others, she needed significant help in achieving that potential. It was of little value to her that people thought she had potential and then did not make sure that she had a chance to reach it. Lack of action was Sara's most significant handicap. When all was said and done, more was said than done.

3. Labeling = Limits ≠ Potential

One of the few benefits of being labeled in our society is that one is often eligible for services. In Sara's case, her label of "severe/profound mentally handicapped" only served to put her in inappropriate environments where she competed for attention with students who had more obvious needs. Little was expected of students in those environments. Day to day, minute to minute needs took precedence while Sara listened to the radio. She was in environments that not only did not support her potential, but may have reduced that potential. She was in environments of persons with less obvious potential; rooms filled with limitations. I am reminded that when I get better at something, it is because I am around others who do that something better than I do; they model, inspire, and provide me with opportunities to practice skills and grow.

4. ↓ Incidence + ↓ Services + ↓ Functioning Environment + ↓ Outcome = ↑ $

Sara had a disability that was of low incidence. She was able to receive few services directly related to her disability. She ended up in environments with persons of lower abilities, and hence she had no peers. Sara achieved little in school or at the group home. In fact, by others' reports, she was regressing. At age 20, when she could have been quite independent, she was making little progress. The result of these circumstances was that she was continuing to need more restrictive environments. Sara's prognosis was more, rather than fewer services.

5. Simple Intervention + Time = Manifested Potential

The key to Sara showing her potential was a fairly simple intervention consisting of exploring possibilities and gauging her reactions to them. Sara exhibited preferences for specific activities and differing reactions to different activities. She also chose preferred activities over listening to the radio—an indication that listening to the radio was a way of coping with her lack of choices. Time was required to learn her communication styles and to allow for exploration. The time required, although ranging over a period of 8 months, was still only a few hours per week.

6. Time ≥ Expertise

No one associated with the FLLE project had significant experience with children with visual impairments or with severe/profound mental retardation, especially in regards to leisure education programs. Although this required that we spend extra time learning about Sara and her capabilities, it also allowed us to begin with few preconceptions about what she might be able to accomplish. By seeing what she could do, rather than looking at what she should not be able to do, we were able to see a capable young woman. I doubt if that would have occurred without the commitment of time.

7. Self-Determination + Interaction = Giggling

When Sara was given opportunities to make choices, she demonstrated that she was capable of being self-determining. Sara could move out of her ruts and expand her limits. Sara also appeared to choose activities that would allow her to interact with others—in stark contrast to listening to the radio. She was capable of inviting others to participate and sustain interaction—when there was a vehicle for her to do so. The result of self-determined choice and interaction for Sara was a demonstration of the joy she could express: giggling at the opportunity to participate and interact.

8. ↓ Choices + ↓ Skills = Isolation

For people like Sara, isolation results from not having a repertoire of activities from which to chose. To invite someone to play, one must have something to play and a way of playing. When choices do not exist, one has to take what one can get—in Sara's case, the radio. No one's life should come down to that kind of option. Sara was capable of so much more.

9. Families Systems = ↓ Assertiveness

Sara's mother, like many parents of children with disabilities, was doing the best she could. She constantly ran into roadblocks from the systems set up to help Sara. State services never taught Sara mobility skills; group homes had a revolving door for staff, and schools provided minimal assistance. In the end, a parent takes what she can get and hopes that it will help. Sara's mother had run out of energy after 20 years and she had to settle for whatever was there.

10. House ≠ Home

Although the group home arrangement kept Sara out of an institution, it did not provide her with a home environment. Schedules and routines took precedence over self-determination and growth. She had a room in the house, another place to listen to the radio, but she was only renting space. What she needed was committed, consistent support for her development—the kind found in a home.

These considerations apply to many of the students with whom we have worked. It is somehow difficult for systems to take into account the individuality of each person. It is difficult to offer choices, to let them be themselves. Yet we found that when potential and options were explored, even on a limited basis, students were able to express their uniqueness. Educators and practitioners must continue to explore the reasons that this is not commonplace.

Section IV

Tell Us How We Can Do It

Chapter 8
When Enough is Not Enough
Mary Agnes Shelton
Charles C. Bullock

Chapter 9
Teetering on the Brink of Success
Mary Agnes Shelton

Chapter 10
From Drugs to Thugs to Playing
Mary Agnes Shelton

Mom and I have used this to make three plans since you were here. We went to the movies, to the library, and to my cousin's house. Is that okay that we used it without you?

—Keisha (chapter 9)

.

8

When Enough Is Not Enough

Mary Agnes Shelton
Charles C. Bullock*

Sometimes you just want to keep your head buried in the sand; it hurts too much to know the truth.
— Diane, Marilyn's mother, about school inclusion

THE FAMILY

Michael and Diane were the parents of a 10-year-old girl, Marilyn, who was born with brain defects resulting from problems with the fluid in the cranial area. Marilyn's first few weeks of life were spent in a neonatal intensive care unit, and it was touch and go if she would survive. Ten years later, Marilyn was healthy and strong but she had limited cognitive abilities and a tottering gait. Diane said she felt that Marilyn was approximately at the cognitive level of a 2 year-old. Marilyn could talk, learn words and letters, and even write her name, but she couldn't carry on a conversation or follow progressions of thought. She liked people and she enjoyed activities, but she wanted to do whatever she

---

*Both authors worked extensively on this case. The first author provided the intervention and the chapter is written in the first person based on her experiences.

wanted to without restriction, even walking into the street with no sense of danger. Marilyn would be cooperative about half of the time; the other half, one would have to "deal" with her behaviors. Marilyn still wore diapers. She had to be watched all of the time unless she was in an enclosed space which was free of harmful objects.

Michael and Diane were an upper class couple in their mid-40s who lived in an up-scale middle-class neighborhood. They had another daughter who was a bright, talented, typical adolescent named Leslie. Michael was an active professional who traveled extensively. Because of this, most of the day-to-day child rearing was left to Diane.

I received a referral to work with Marilyn from her special education teacher, Jean, because she felt that Marilyn's parents wanted more for their daughter than they were getting through the school. Jean felt that there would be no problem with parental involvement since Michael and Diane were active members in a volunteer organization for people with disabilities.

My colleague, Dan, and I met with Michael and Diane over lunch at a gourmet restaurant in a nearby town to discuss the possibilities of Family Link in Leisure Education (FLLE) working with Marilyn. Dan and I reviewed with Michael and Diane some of our current FLLE cases and the kinds of things we worked on with other students. Diane and Michael were interested in inclusion for their daughter since the school she attended, Hillcrest, was reported to be one of the leaders in inclusion of elementary students with disabilities into regular classrooms. Diane expressed having doubts about how the inclusion was actually working, however, since her visit to the school at Thanksgiving. Diane had expected to see a model of inclusion, with her daughter actively engaged in the "goings on" of the class. She had expected to see involvement at some level with Marilyn's nondisabled peers. What she saw, however, was all of the students in the classroom participating in the preparation of a large Thanksgiving lunch—all, that is, except for the two students with disabilities and the teacher's aide, who always accompanied them. They were sitting in a corner at a table watching the action, but not being involved. When Diane questioned the regular classroom teacher about this, the response was, "Oh, we just have so much going on today, and the special kids require so much attention." Though Diane was sensitive to the amount of attention her daughter required, the situation seemed anything but "inclusive" to her. She wondered how often "inclusion" meant allowing Marilyn to sit and watch the typical children have a good time. She was demoralized. Diane and Michael hoped that FLLE would be able to help them address this issue within the school and in the community.

ASSESSMENTS

As with all of our students, we began working with Marilyn by conducting our separate assessments with the parents, the teachers, and the student herself. As revealed in the parent assessment, Marilyn's *strengths* centered on her willingness to interact with people and her friendly disposition. The areas of need on which Marilyn's mother focused were:

1. Finding things to do,
2. Having more people with whom to do things, and
3. Being included at school.

The special education teacher's assessment added "Learning appropriate activity skills" and "Improving social skills" to the needs list. Interestingly, Marilyn's regular education teacher's assessment provided little useful diagnostic or prescriptive data. Clearly, the regular education teacher—the teacher in Marilyn's inclusion classroom—had little information about Marilyn at all.

The assessment with Marilyn was different than any other assessment that I conducted during the FLLE program. Marilyn was not able to respond to any of the usual assessment questions in a verbal way, or even to understand any questions about herself that were directed to her. I decided to try to get a general picture of Marilyn and her interactions by observation. With the intention of exploring the inclusion situation while I observed for the assessment, I visited her classes at school often.

Following the completion of all of the assessment data, the parents, Marilyn's special education teacher, and her regular classroom teacher agreed on these goals:

1. To increase inclusive experiences for Marilyn at school,
2. To create access to a computer for Marilyn at home, and
3. To develop a community Circle of Support for Marilyn.

Michael and Diane were delighted with the goals, but the regular classroom teacher had some reservations. She felt fine about the computer and "circle of support" goals, but she thought that everything that could be done with inclusion at school was already being addressed. Nonetheless, all those involved agreed on the goals so that Marilyn could become more engaged in her life.

MARILYN'S STORY

I worked with Marilyn and her family for about 8 months. During that time, most of the energy of the project was directed toward inclusion issues, specifically, the lack of genuine inclusion at the school and the potential for genuine inclusion in the community. These two topics comprised the major themes of Marilyn's story.

The Illusion of Inclusion at School

As soon as I started visiting Marilyn's classes, the problems with what the school was calling "inclusion" became immediately apparent. Students from the special education class were sent out into the regular school in pairs, accompanied by a teacher's aide. Regular teachers volunteered to have the "special" students in their classes for 2 hours per day, but preparing or adapting lessons for them was not part of the bargain. My field notes tell how one of the classes looked to me:

> I walked into the inclusion classroom where Marilyn spends 2 hours of every day. I stood in a corner trying to look inconspicuous, as Ms. Hughes, the regular teacher, and I had agreed. John, the other special education student, looked at me and waved. Hillary, the inclusion aide, said something to him and he looked away. Marilyn apparently didn't notice, or didn't recognize me.
>
> Marilyn was sitting in the far corner of the room with Hillary and John at a table all by themselves. There were some books on the table and some writing paper and markers. All of the other typical students were divided into groups of six at other tables on the other side of the room. The closest typical student was at least 10 feet away from Marilyn.
>
> The regular class was working on spelling words that start with "d-is." Ms. Hughes would say a word, and a student would spell it. Since all of the words started with "d-i-s," each student was spelling "d-i-s," followed by some more letters. Marilyn was watching the regular students across the room and as the students spelled out "d-i-s," Marilyn would repeat each letter after them. Everyone was ignoring her—it was as if she weren't there. Even though Marilyn was attempting to participate and join in with the activity of the class, no one even acknowledged her presence, much less encouraged her.
>
> After about 10 minutes of this, Hillary, Marilyn's inclusion aide, took Marilyn's hand and shook it to get her attention. Hillary shoved a book in front of Marilyn and forced her to look at it. Marilyn looked at the book for a few minutes and then went back to looking at the other kids. This time, Marilyn didn't talk though, she just looked. (Field notes)

During the whole time that I was in the classroom that day, and indeed on most other days, I never saw any typical student interact with any of the three people from special education. Even Ms. Hughes completely ignored them. There was absolutely nothing "inclusive" going on. The students from special education just sat in the room for 2 hours, but it was as if they were invisible or, perhaps, pieces of furniture.

This kind of scene turned out to be quite usual for Marilyn and her special education comrades. I visited many times, and it was always the same. Even in art, dance, and gym, the special education kids were separate, over in a corner with their adult aide trying to keep them quiet and making sure they didn't disturb the other students. I never saw any activity specifically adapted so that Marilyn or John could enjoy it, too.

Michael, Diane, and I had quite a different idea from that of the teachers in regard to what inclusion means and what the potential is for inclusion in the school. We expected involvement at some level in the regular education process, interaction with typical peers, and an adapted curriculum that would include the special education students. We agreed that it might require extra time and an investment of energy from the teachers, but we felt it would be worth it for Marilyn, for the other special education students, and even for the typical students as well.

Marilyn's IEP. About the same time we were developing our plans, Marilyn's annual Individualized Education Plan (IEP) came due. Diane and Michael agreed to try to use that meeting to address some of our inclusion concerns. For that meeting, I arrived at the special education classroom for the IEP meeting at 10 a.m. Several other people filed in and sat down at a short round table in children's chairs. The people present were Jean, the special education teacher; Brennen, the physical therapist; Leon, the speech therapist; Hillary, the teacher's aide; Billy, the special education teacher; Michael and Diane; Wanda, the music therapist; Kristi, the occupational therapist; and I.

Jean began the meeting by reviewing the goals from the previous year's IEP. These goals included such things as being able to state age and birthday, count objects past two, name body parts consistently, sort objects, identify letters, and say when she had to "go to the potty." Long discussions ensued about Marilyn's progress and what the new goals for the coming year should be. During these discussions, it was agreed that Marilyn did better at tasks when other kids were around. It was agreed that when other kids were around, it kept Marilyn's attention better. That brought up the topic of Marilyn's Circle of Friends at Hillcrest.

Marilyn had had a Circle of Friends at school for 2 years. It was made up of eight typical students who volunteered to meet with Marilyn and play with her once a week for half an hour. They got out of their other classes to be with Marilyn. Jean was in charge of this project. The Circle of Friends at school had actually met with Marilyn only a few times during the previous year and not once during the current year, even though it was then January. Diane, who had high hopes for the Circle of Friends in the beginning,. was quite disappointed with how it had actually worked out.

Diane attempted to express her feelings of disappointment without being accusatory toward Jean. It was a rather tense moment. Jean said the Circle of Friends had been very slow at getting started that year. The children were set up, but time and space had been the problem. Jean said they were going to get on it since the holidays had passed.

Diane asked about Marilyn being so separate from the other kids in her inclusive class. She talked about her being seated over to the side all of the time and not really being included in the action. Even at Thanksgiving, Marilyn was seated off to the side at a separate table, while all of the other kids were together and participating. Jean said it had to do with not having enough desks in the classroom and that was the only space for Marilyn. She said they would look into it and see if they could transfer another desk from another classroom. Diane tilted her head sideways, as if she weren't quite buying this explanation. I didn't buy it either.

During the IEP meeting, I sensed strong resistance from Jean to delve into the inclusion issue, just as Diane had mentioned might happen. It also seemed pertinent to me that Ms. Hughes, the regular teacher from Marilyn's inclusion classroom, didn't even attend the meeting. Jean was pleasant enough to talk to, but when the status quo was challenged, she seemed to tighten right up. I sensed that she felt she had more than enough to accomplish, and she did not want to have to do anything more.

The Plan for Inclusion at School.   In collaboration with my colleague, Dan, some strategies were developed for trying to address the inclusion-at-school issue. We planned to suggest adapting three activities per week in the regular classroom to include Marilyn and John. I would handle the adaptation process. Dan and I also intended to try to get a member of Marilyn's "Circle of Friends" to accompany her to gym, art, and music once a week, so that Marilyn could hang out with the typical kids during these classes. We hoped that a member of Marilyn's regular classroom would volunteer to eat lunch with her at least once a week. We felt that, perhaps, the teachers would be more receptive to inclusion if I handled most of the additional work.

First, Dan and I discussed with Michael and Diane the goal "of being included more at school." Again, Michael and Diane both revealed their frustration with trying to get inclusive situations happening for Marilyn at school. They knew she sat to the side with Hillary and John and was rarely involved with the typical students. I explained the plan that Dan and I had devised to try to get Marilyn included in three activities per week in the regular classroom. I would work with Ms. Hughes to figure out which activities could be adapted to include Marilyn and John, and then I would facilitate that. Also, I planned to arrange for Marilyn to be accompanied at lunch and in art, gym, and music by kids from her Circle of Friends, or even by other students in the class.

Michael and Diane really liked this approach. They thought that, with such direct intervention and personal attention to the situation from me, perhaps we could actually be successful. We all talked about our observations that the school seemed to agree to come up with the very least rather than the most they could do for the special education students. We knew it was hard, but that didn't seem to be much of an excuse. Dan and I talked about the reluctance we had experienced at Hillcrest, mostly from Jean, and we explained that we wanted to proceed slowly so that we wouldn't alienate anyone.

Diane said that getting anything to happen at school was such a battle for her. Sometimes she felt that she would have preferred not to know what was going on rather than have to feel that it was so inadequate. She said, "Sometimes you just want to keep your head buried in the sand; it hurts too much to know the truth."

Dan told Michael and Diane that we would be telling the school staff that we were responding to parental wishes; inclusion was what the parents wanted us to work on. Since we were allowed into the school through the agreement of the principal and teachers, we were not in a very solid position to be rocking the boat too much. Michael and Diane wholeheartedly agreed.

The next week, I approached Jean, Billy—the second special education teacher, and Hillary, the inclusion aide, at Hillcrest. I went over the strategies such as classroom adaptations and typical student accompaniment and interaction that Dan and I had come up with to try to get more inclusion happening with Marilyn in the school. Jean said that they were already doing all they could to help Marilyn be included with typical students and that she felt their program was entirely adequate. "These kids have disabilities, you know," Jean said. Hillary said, "I go to art and gym and lunch with Marilyn, and we always sit with the other kids. It seems to me that should be enough." I asked if it would be okay for me to go ahead to see what I could do, and Jean and Hillary reluctantly agreed. Billy was quiet during the whole discussion.

Later, Billy stopped me in the hall when we were alone. He said he knew what I was talking about and that he felt Hillcrest's inclusion was "pretty much of a joke." However, he said he didn't think there was much I could do about it because the commitment to make inclusion really happen just wasn't there. He thought I would be better off to focus my attention on working things out for Marilyn in the community. I told him I appreciated the advice.

A couple of days later, I approached Ms. Hughes, the regular classroom teacher where Marilyn spent her inclusion time, to discuss the inclusion goal. Ms. Hughes was not pleased with this goal either. She said she didn't think that there were any activities in her class in which Marilyn and John could participate. She said,

> I don't mind them sitting in my class, but I don't have any extra time. I have too much to handle already. Twenty-eight 9- and 10-year-olds every day keep me plenty busy. (Field notes)

Since I felt completely blocked in my attempts to improve Marilyn's inclusion experience at Hillcrest, Michael, Diane, and I decided to begin concentrating most of our attention on community goals at this point. We were all disappointed with the school and their inclusionary practices. And this was supposed to be an exemplary program? It all seemed to be a lot of talk and pretense. Without the support and encouragement of the teachers and administrators of the school, we did not feel that inclusion at school was even an option.

Michael and Diane felt that they had pushed all they could. Enough for the school staff was just not enough for Marilyn!

Potential for Inclusion in the Community

The second major theme of Marilyn's story resulted in the development of a "Circle of Support" in the community. The following is a description of a "Circle of Support" from TBI Project STAR, Circle Manual (1996):

Circle of Support

A Circle of Support is a group of people who meet regularly to help a person with a disability and her family realize their dreams and reach life goals. The Circle does not replace service providers, but its support can reduce an individual's dependence on the service system.

Philosophy

- People with disabilities belong in the community, engaged as active members.
- Relationships are what make a community
- people can receive the support they need without having to rely entirely on the traditional service system.
- "Systems don't solve problems—people solve problems."

WHO Are the Members of a Circle?

- Family, friends, co-workers, neighbors, fellow church and club members, and service providers are Circle members.
- The only qualification for members is that they care about the focus person.

=   ### WHAT Does a Circle do?

- It creates a vision of the future with the focus person and her family.
- It helps identify fears and "nightmares" and plans to prevent those from happening.
- It identifies problems, and works together to solve them.
- It brings their community connections to the Circle.
- It celebrates accomplishments, holidays, and special events.
- It organizes the resources of the community to support the focus person and her family.

Marilyn's Circle. Diane and I began discussing the tasks involved in developing a Circle of Support. We reviewed material from the TBI Project

STAR that was running a number of successful Circles (Cooper, 1996). The information included suggestions about inviting and gathering Circle members, writing invitations and newsletters, developing protocol for meetings, and developing a system for arriving at a plan of action.

The system suggested for use by the members of a Circle of Support was designed to help the members become acquainted with the family and the focus person's needs through a process called the McGill Action Planning System (MAPS). This process required several sessions to complete, and it provided an in-depth look at the family's situation, which led to planning and action. Here is an overview of Marilyn's MAPS process:

MCGILL ACTION PLANNING SYSTEM

History

The family, Michael, Diane, and Leslie, told the story of Marilyn's birth and all the difficulties that they had experienced during that time. They showed pictures of Marilyn in the hospital ICU and described a couple of her near-death experiences. Then, people in the group described their past relationships with Marilyn, when and how each person had met her.

Who is Marilyn?   During this MAPS step, Circle members wrote three adjectives that they thought best described Marilyn. As we went around the Circle and read our lists, we compiled a master list of words that we all felt said the most about Marilyn. "Happy, friendly, energetic, and determined" were the words repeated most often to describe Marilyn.

Dreams.   In the Dreams step, Circle members declared what they would most like to see happen for Marilyn in the present and then in the future at 5- and 10-year intervals. Members were directed to release limitations and to come up with their very best wishes.

Nightmares.   Although not particularly pleasant to discuss, the MAPS system also recommends discussing Nightmares, so that fears, hesitations, and frustrations are brought out in the open and thus cannot direct choices and actions through the members' lack of awareness. Circle members are encouraged to be fearless with this step because just speaking a fear can greatly lessen its power..

Gifts.   During this step, Circle members were asked to list and share the talents, unique qualities, and special offerings that Marilyn displayed in her life and how that impacted the lives of the Circle members.

Needs. Here Circle members made a list of the three most important needs that they perceived for Marilyn in the present and in the future. Then the lists were compiled, and the most frequently mentioned needs were listed.

Action Plan. Using all that the Circle members had shared and learned about Marilyn and her family from all of the previous steps, the Circle of Support formed a plan of action. At least three immediate action steps were proposed by the Circle to facilitate accomplishing the needs, hopes, and dreams of Marilyn and her family. Members of the Circle decided by whom, how, and when the action steps would be implemented. As the Circle of Support continued over time, new steps in the action plan were developed, implemented, and accomplished.

Rather than discussing the entire Circle process for Marilyn in detail, I discuss the themes that emerged during the process.

Themes in the Circle of Support

Two major themes emerged from the data concerning Marilyn's Circle of Support. The first theme involved Diane's reluctance to believe that it could actually work and that people would want to be that generous with her family. The second theme concerned the enthusiastic response of friends and the effect of this on the family.

Diane's Reluctance to Believe

As we discussed the plans for the Circle of Support, I noticed Diane's reluctance to believe that people would really want to put out that much effort for her family without any kind of compensation. She often asked me if I thought that people would really want to be in the Circle. She was fearful of imposing on people and having them agree to participate because they thought they "should" rather than because they wanted to.

Over and over again we talked about the Circle of Support. Diane kept coming back to the church as the basis for their family's community network. She did not think there was anyone in the neighborhood who would be interested. We discussed talking with Wanda, the music teacher whom Diane had hired to work with Marilyn, and Diane thought that was a good idea. I said I would visit their church with them the following week to meet the people. Diane was pleased with that idea, too.

I noticed that after one of our discussions about Circle members, Diane looked flushed and radiant with excitement. She seemed fearful to hope that we could really get all of this to work, but she wanted to believe it could happen. I told her I thought we could get people to act on the recent interest in "community" that we all keep hearing about. Diane said she hoped so. She seemed pleased with the possibilities, but I could still sense her reluctance to believe it could really happen. She did not want to be disappointed.

With Diane's guidance, we agreed to meet those people at Michael and Diane's church who would be most willing to participate in the Circle of Support. I attended church with them one Sunday and met a number of the teachers and students in the children's Sunday School class. The church members appeared to be very tolerant of Marilyn's unpredictable behavior, and the other children treated her more as a peer. The following is an excerpt from the field notes about the church experience:

> Marilyn messed up her tights, and Joan, a teacher in the children's class, had to take them off in the bathroom. This upset Marilyn quite a bit because she didn't want to put her shoes back on without socks. When Diane came back after services, I helped her carry her things and Marilyn's clothes out to the car. Diane carried Marilyn, who was distraught and whining loudly. Diane had to carry her wailing 10-year-old child right through the middle of the socializing crowd after church. I checked people's faces and apparent attitudes as we went by. People that we passed on the way out were all fine with the slight disturbance. They appeared to be used to her. Diane loaded Marilyn and the stuff in the van, and I waved good-bye as they drove off. (Field notes)

I thought it was quite helpful to meet the people at church. The real test will be if they want to actually help out with their time and attention.

Diane and I spent the next couple of sessions developing our list of people to invite to join Marilyn's Circle of Support. We selected a date for the first meeting and invited people from the church, the disability organization, and teachers and aides from Marilyn's school. We also invited Wanda, the music teacher, and a couple of neighborhood people that Diane thought might want to come. Diane said she wanted to call all the mothers of other kids with disabilities to let them know that she would understand if they felt they didn't have enough time to participate in Marilyn's Circle, and she wouldn't feel hurt. Diane was nervous about sending out the invitations; I think she felt that folks might feel imposed upon. In fact, Diane was hedging her bets. Since she was reluctant to believe that others would be so generous to her family, she invited like-minded people. She invited mothers of other kids with disabilities. By hedging her bets, she was less likely to be disappointed.

A week after the invitations went out, I called all of the people who had received them. I asked if they had questions about what a Circle of Support would entail or how it worked, and if they would be able to participate. I was delighted by the responses! Almost everyone we invited was very pleased to become involved and thought it was a great idea. People from the disability organization and from the church were very supportive. One man declined the invitation because his wife was having health problems and he felt he couldn't spare the time. Another fellow from the church was in graduate school and regretfully declined. All of the other people we invited were happy to accept. Diane was quite moved by the widespread, positive response. Sure enough, her community had responded resoundingly. In spite of her reluctance, there were people who wanted to be part of Marilyn's life—part of her natural supports.

The Enthusiastic Response of Friends

Diane and I were both a bit nervous as we prepared for the first meeting of Marilyn's Circle of Support. Diane had made some lovely desserts to serve after the first meeting, and I set up the flip chart to use in illustrating the topics brought up by the participants. When all of the new Circle members had arrived, we had 18 people sitting in a circle in Diane's den. Diane's face was glowing as she seated the last guest. She was so pleased to have all these people gathered to focus on Marilyn with herself and her family.

A large portion of that first meeting was spent on getting to know one another—our work, our families, and how we knew Marilyn. A number of the stories about people's involvement with Marilyn were quite moving. One of the Sunday School teachers told how inspiring it was to see the typical children in the class assist Marilyn and look after her. A mother of another child with a disability described her feelings of tenderness when Marilyn and her child related to each other. The accounts continued for quite some time. They were interesting and informative. It was important for all Circle members to hear all of the relationships and the connections and interconnections. After the meeting, everyone lingered over the refreshments and had a chance to get acquainted and chat. Diane and I felt that the first meeting had been very successful.

The highlight of the second Circle was during the *History* section. Michael and Diane told the story of Marilyn's birth. They had pictures of Marilyn in the hospital and revealed how traumatic the whole situation had been for them. Leslie told her story, too—how it had all felt to a 6-year-old. She described the fear that she felt when an air ambulance had to pick Marilyn up one time when her shunt failed. There had been several near-death experiences in Marilyn's short life, and the family shared how terrifying those times had been. Many of the Circle members had not heard those stories before, or had even known the basis of Marilyn's disability. It was a moving and compassionate time for us all, and we felt a bonding happen as we shared these intimate moments.

All of the Circle members shared their personal histories with Marilyn. There were lots of touching stories about Marilyn and the impact she had had on various people. One mother told about Marilyn coming up to her to see her new baby. The mother had felt hesitant because she wasn't sure that Marilyn would know how to handle an infant. Marilyn surprised her by touching the baby very delicately on the cheek and making little cooing noises. A Sunday School teacher told how Marilyn stood close by a new student in the class who was nervous and shy all during the session. Marilyn didn't say anything to the new girl, but the teacher could see the student relax as Marilyn befriended her.

Our next MAPS step was called *Who Is Marilyn?* It involved every-one in the Circle offering adjectives, which described Marilyn. The four words repeated most often were *happy, friendly, energetic,* and *determined.* Other words mentioned more than once were *engaging, independent, curious, loving,* and *vibrant.* This was a very uplifting part of the meeting, too. Toward the end of that meeting, Marilyn, who had been outside with the respite care provider hired to take care of Marilyn during the meeting, began knocking on the patio door. The respite care provider stuck her head in and said, "I'm sorry, but Marilyn just really wants to come in." Diane said, "That's okay. We are almost finished, and after all, the Circle is for Marilyn." My field notes tell about this part:

> Marilyn came in and sat on the floor in the middle of the circle. Then she went over and sat with Diane for a bit. Next, she sat by Leslie; then she just kind of moved around among the Circle members. It was very cool that we were talking about her, this was her Circle, and she was participating and involved with the people. At one point, Marilyn started going around the Circle patting people on the head and saying, "Duck, duck, duck." She was playing "Duck, duck, goose." We figured that was because everyone was sitting in a circle. It was really delightful!

When Diane and I discussed the meeting later, Diane said,

> I really felt great about it. I almost wish we could end with this one—every-one had such a neat story to tell about Marilyn. As a parent of a child with a disability, you just don't know what people's initial reactions are toward your child. "Keep your child under control," or whatever. But, you know, it was so interesting that everyone had such a positive perspective on her. I really felt good about that. (Field notes)

Since summer scheduling was difficult for nearly all of the Circle members, we decided to have a picnic potluck at the park for our summer meet-ing. As it turned out, we had a great day, with more than 30 adults and children attending—the Circle members, their spouses, and all their children. The food was delicious! People gathered in small groups and chatted. The typical chil-dren and the older ones looked after the toddlers as well as the children with disabilities on the playground, giving the parents time to relax and to talk to each other. We all agreed that we couldn't have had a better July picnic. As Diane was leaving, she mentioned how deeply supported she felt by the out-pouring of love and caring that she and her family were receiving from these wonderful friends. Diane's eyes glistened as she turned to me and said,

I've never felt so supported with Marilyn. I always felt I had to do it all myself. You know, these people really want to help. I feel truly blessed! (Field notes)

The enthusiastic response from Diane and Michael's friends was a deeply moving experience for them, especially for Diane who was primarily responsible for Marilyn's care. For the first time in her 10 years with Marilyn, Diane felt her burden being shared and lifted. Diane was well on her way to becoming a believer. There was indeed an enthusiastic response from the people who had become members of Marilyn's Circle.

CHANGES

During the summer, some changes occurred with my work situation. As it turned out, I was going to move across the state in the Fall, and I would not be able to continue facilitating Marilyn's Circle anymore. The original plan was that I would facilitate it for at least a year. Diane was very disappointed. I felt badly that I was not able to continue with my commitment, but I felt hopeful that we could find another facilitator to continue the Circle.

After my move, I stayed in touch with Diane and learned that she had not been able to find anyone else with whom she felt comfortable. They had tried a paid facilitator, but she charged too much for them to continue with it. And they couldn't find anyone to do it as a volunteer, or even for a reasonable cost. There was some funding for Circles through the disability organization to which Michael and Diane belonged, but Michael felt it would not be acceptable for him to use it for his child since they were involved in the leadership of the organization. Diane felt very badly about having to let her Circle go. The last I heard nearly a year later, Michael and Diane had not been able to reconstruct Marilyn's Circle of Support. A really good start had been made, but no one was available to continue. Once again, all that was available was just not enough.

SUMMARY

The two major themes of Marilyn's story included the illusion of inclusion in school and the potential for inclusion in the community. Inclusion in the school that Marilyn attended was virtually nonexistent. Allowing special education students to sit in a typical classroom separately from the other kids for 2 hours per day seemed to be quite the opposite of inclusion. We felt frustrated and blocked when we tried to improve the situation. We learned that the commitment for genuine inclusion must come from the school administration and the faculty, with the cooperation and prodding of parents if it is really going to happen.

The Circle of Support in the community got off to a great start. We were all very pleased and enthusiastic about making it happen. Diane was deeply moved by the outpouring of kindness and the attention that people wanted to bestow on her family. With my paying job being to facilitate the Circle, all was well, and I devoted many hours a month to helping the Circle happen. When I left, the energy to keep it all going just wasn't there. Diane might have tried to take it over, but then it would just be more of what she already knew all about—parents begging to have people pay attention to their child with a disability. The real learning from the Circle for Diane had always been that she had supports, even natural supports, not that she was doing it all herself. None of the members of the Circle felt that they had time to take over the facilitation and thus the continuation of the Circle. I think we all felt that it was a very positive experience, but Circles almost always need a paid facilitator from somewhere to make them happen.

In retrospective discussions about the Circle of Support situation, we felt that before a Circle is started the paid facilitator position needs to be solidified. To get things started and then have them fall apart is very hard on all of the people involved. Perhaps a community of people with disabilities who want to see Circles happen can fund some facilitator positions that they could keep filled. One facilitator could run a number of Circles for different people quite effectively. From our experience, we came to feel that Circles of Support are a valuable, important resource and very much worth the effort. However, the facilitator is the key to making it all happen; so that is where it has to start.

9

Teetering on the Brink of Success

Mary Agnes Shelton

INTRODUCTION

Keisha bounced into the living room where her mother, Sharon, and I sat. "Come in the kitchen and see how they turned out," Keisha begged, pulling on her mother's arm. We could hear two of Keisha's friends from her class at school; they were giggling in the kitchen. Sharon and I accompanied Keisha into the kitchen, commenting on the delicious smells coming from there. Keisha and her friends had just taken the pizzas they had baked out of the oven, and they were waiting for them to cool. "These pizzas look real good," Sharon said, smiling at the girls and hugging Keisha's shoulders.

When we were back in the living room, Sharon smiled at me and said, "This is just what I was hopin' for, Keisha in there doin' things with her friends. I think she's beginning to feel lots better about herself."

The pizza party was one outcome of working with Keisha and her mother, Sharon, for about four months through the Family Link in Leisure Education (FLLE) program. This Saturday afternoon represented the culmination of months of encouragement and preparation for the expansion of Keisha's social network. Keisha had made a plan, invited her friends, planned the cooking activity, shopped for ingredients, and arranged transportation for her friends all on her own, with minimal prompting. Sharon said she was very proud of Keisha's progress, and so was I.

Keisha was a 14-year-old African-American student who was enrolled in a special education class in middle school. She was an attractive, petite girl with shoulder-length, slightly straightened hair and a big smile, which she displayed only occasionally. I had received a referral for Keisha because her teacher, Mr. Wilson, felt that she held back in making friends and interacting with other students in the class. He said that he felt she was capable of much more and that her reluctance stemmed mainly from lack of self-confidence. Mr. Wilson saw her as a student who just needed a little help to get over the hump. She was different from other students whom he had referred; they were on the edge of trouble—Keisha was on the edge of success.

Mr. Wilson knew Keisha's mother, Sharon, and he thought she would be a very cooperative parent with whom to work. Sharon was a hard-working, single mother who was always interested and involved in Keisha's progress at school. Mr. Wilson saw Keisha's mother as a parent who would relish the structure of the FLLE program and who would follow through. She was motivated and ready for action. What she apparently needed was help in getting past the general ideas that she had about Keisha's future and in finding ways to get started with specific activities. Mr. Wilson said he wished that all his students had parents as involved in their children's lives as Sharon was with Keisha.

KEISHA AND SHARON

Keisha lived in a duplex downtown with her mother, Sharon. The houses in the area were small, older homes—a bit run down, but tidy. The duplex where Keisha and Sharon lived had no landscaping, so it appeared rather barren, but it was sturdy and clean. On my first visit, Sharon answered the door when I knocked. She was a short, stocky woman in her late 30s to early 40s with straightened, styled hair, cut short. She was wearing white pants and a sweater. Her appearance was neat and clean.

The house was rather small and sparsely furnished with an inexpensive, overstuffed couch and chair set in the living room. A small kitchen, two bedrooms, and a bathroom completed the accommodations. Everything was tidy and clean inside, as well as outside the house. Despite the severely cold weather, the house was warm and cozy.

While talking with Sharon on my first visit, I discovered she had two older sons, 21 and 22 years old—one at a state university and another in the Marines in California. Keisha's father (and his family) lived less than 2 hours away, but he saw Keisha and her mother infrequently. Keisha's paternal grandmother was involved with the family, however, and Keisha spent quite a bit of time with her in the summer. Sharon said that the grandmother tended to baby Keisha a lot, which Sharon felt was not good for her. According to Sharon, Keisha would let herself be taken care of completely if it were provided.

Sharon said her major concerns for Keisha were independence and having friends. She was concerned about what kind of life Keisha would be able to have when she grew up, and what would happen to her if Sharon were no longer around. Sharon reported that Keisha had trouble with money—it had no meaning for her, so she couldn't make change or buy things without help. Sharon hoped Keisha could get some practical experience with money.

Sharon said she felt good about her relationship with Keisha. She wished she didn't have to work at the dry cleaners on Saturday mornings so that they could have more time together. Sharon worked Monday through Friday and half a day Saturday at her dry-cleaning job—a strenuous schedule. From our conversation, I thought that Sharon appeared to be an involved, conscientious provider. She appeared to feel good about her family's situation, which I interpreted from her upright carriage, pleasant demeanor, and upbeat mood. She was interested in the FLLE program and felt that it could be helpful for Keisha and herself. I felt encouraged about working with this family, sensing a warmth beginning to build with Sharon right from the beginning.

ASSESSMENTS

As with all our FLLE clients, I began working with Keisha and Sharon by doing assessment interviews with Keisha, Sharon, and Mr. Wilson. Keisha was quite attentive during her assessment interview. She said that her strengths were primarily her willingness to try new things and her strong family support. The needs with which she wanted help were centered on interactions with peers and on doing more things in the community.

Sharon's focus on Keisha's gaining more independence was apparent during the assessment interview. Sharon hoped Keisha could expand her leisure interests at home (beyond watching TV), learn independent planning skills, and become more involved in social situations on her own. Mr. Wilson's assessment interview for Keisha mostly centered on interacting with classmates and on learning skills to increase independence in the community. Mr. Wilson felt that individual attention for Keisha could help to bring out the potential for self-determination that he sensed was latent within her personality.

The assessments for Keisha fit together very well, with significant agreement from all parties on both strengths and needs. As with many other adolescent students whom I met through the FLLE project, Keisha was primarily interested in interacting with peers and increasing her independence. Sharon and Mr. Wilson were also interested in seeing those areas expand for Keisha. Sharon had the added wish of increasing Keisha's leisure activity selections at home. She felt that Keisha's exposure to a variety of activities had been limited due to having only one parent to come up with ideas about what to do, as well as by Sharon's heavy work schedule.

GOALS AND OBJECTIVES

When the assessments were compared and integrated, the following goals were agreed upon by all three parties:

1. To learn independent planning skills for leisure activities,
2. To increase variety and participation in leisure activities at home, and
3. To increase social interactions and social activities.

The first goal, concerning independent planning skills, focused around the Leisure Action Planning (LAP) system developed by a previous project, School Community Leisure Link, to help students begin to make their own plans by exploring what is involved in planning. Sharon, who was interested in seeing Keisha develop independence skills in any area, was mainly responsible for choosing this goal. When I showed Keisha the LAP system, she said she would like to learn to use it. We used the pictures for *Who, What, When, Where, Who With,* and *Things I Need* and the plastic-pocket card for Keisha's planned activities. I provided a magnetized plastic sleeve in which the completed card could fit, and Keisha could hang it on the refrigerator. Keisha was eager to use the system to see how it worked.

Objectives for the second goal, that regarding leisure activities at home, primarily focused on introducing Keisha to a number of new activities to see which ones she might enjoy. I presented Keisha with a number of activity choices, and she decided she would like to try making paper beads and stringing necklaces, painting by number, and cooking her favorite foods—brownies, cupcakes, and pizza. Keisha agreed to try out all of the new activities for 6 weeks before deciding which ones she would like to continue.

To address the social interactions and activities goal, Keisha wanted to focus on doing things with girls at school with whom she would like to become friends. She agreed to invite two girls, Sandy and Bonita, to come to her house or to go out in the community for three separate adventures. Contemplating accomplishing this goal was frightening for Keisha because she said she was afraid to talk to the girls. Also, she said she thought they might not want to go anywhere with her, and she was afraid of being turned down. Sharon, Keisha, and I did quite a bit of processing about Keisha's fears before she felt ready to make the calls.

THEMES OF THE KEISHA AND SHARON STORY

During the months that I worked with Keisha and Sharon, I felt that three major themes emerged from the data. The first theme involved Sharon as a motivated mother who was willing and determined to take the initiative to help improve her daughter's situation. Keisha's lack of self-confidence with her peers was the second theme. The third theme involved Keisha's successes and her development of self-esteem and independence.

Motivation and Initiative

Since all of the goals and objectives complemented each other, Keisha and I began working on all of the goals simultaneously. I introduced the LAP system right away so that we could use the process as we made our plans for all of the activities we had in mind. After agreeing on the goals and objectives, the very next session with Keisha and her mother was selected as the beginning of using the LAP. My field notes describe the session that led to Sharon's remarkable demonstration of the extent of her motivation and initiative:

> Sharon answered the door and called Keisha from the TV room. I told them we would need to spread out some for what we were going to do, so Sharon suggested the kitchen. She went into the kitchen first to straighten up. Keisha sat at the table between Sharon and me. I explained about planning and said we would be using these cards and pictures to help Keisha make plans for our various projects. I got out the LAP card and pictures, explaining to Keisha how it works. We took out all the What cards and looked through them. I said that maybe to practice using the LAP system, we could plan a time for Keisha and Sharon to work on the painting-by-number project I had for them. Keisha agreed. Keisha selected the painting picture and put it in the slot.
>
> We went through all the pictures in each category. For the Who With pocket, Keisha selected a picture representing her mother and the "ME" picture for herself. She put the picture of her mother on top and started to put them in the slot. Then she took them back out, put the "ME" on top, and put them both back in the slot. She selected a picture of a house to represent "at home" in the Where slot and a picture of paints and brushes for Things I Need. We all discussed the When and decided on 4 p.m. Sunday, after Sharon and Keisha return from visiting Grandmother. Keisha wrote her own name and the date on which the plan was to occur (3/6) on a blank picture and put that on the LAP card. I gave Keisha the plastic sleeve, and she put the completed LAP in it. Keisha put the plan on the refrigerator. We were all pleased with the results. Sharon said she thought that was a very good idea. I told Keisha that we would plan our cooking adventure next week. Sharon suggested a particular drawer in the kitchen for keeping the LAP materials, and Keisha agreed. As I was leaving, Sharon said again what a good idea she thought the LAP was. (Field notes)

The next week, when I returned, Keisha proudly brought the completed LAP card to me from its place on the refrigerator. It contained a whole new plan, not the one we had put in about working on the paint-by-number picture. Keisha said, "Mom and I have used this to make three plans since you were here. We went to the movies, to the library, and to my cousin's house. Is that okay that we used it without you?"

I looked at Sharon, surprised and impressed. "You did all that using the LAP card?" I asked incredulously. "Well, it was such a good idea I thought we would just get on with it," Sharon said, smiling.

I was delighted! Among all of the parents and students with whom I had worked, this was the first, and only, time that someone picked up an idea and began using it immediately after its introduction. Most families had required constant follow-up for the LAP to become effective. They regularly forgot to incorporate LAP into their daily planning, with the result that it sometimes became a chore rather than a tool.

Sharon and Keisha continued to do all their planning using the LAP system for the next 4 months that we worked together. Sharon said that using LAP really helped Keisha learn what was involved in going on outings and in being prepared for all kinds of activities. She also thought they participated in a wider variety of things, as well as more interesting events, because they were focused on making plans. At the follow-up interview a year later, Sharon said she and Keisha had stopped using the LAP system after about 6 months. Keisha had learned what she needed from LAP, and she could now utilize the steps of the planning process as it naturally occurred.

Another example of Sharon's motivation and initiative in picking up ideas and making them her own was revealed during our session with paint-by-numbers. Since our goal involved finding interesting new activities to do at home, I brought over several projects for Keisha to try out—one was a paint-by-number picture of a teddy bear sitting in a field of flowers. Keisha and Sharon began working on the picture while I was there and agreed to continue painting on it during the week. When I arrived the next week, the picture was finished. Keisha was very proud of the picture and wanted to frame it for her room. Sharon thought it was pretty messy because they had painted outside of the lines so much. She wanted to do another one and try to do a better job.

I talked to Sharon briefly about allowing the picture to be just whatever it was rather than having a self-imposed standard that might lead to feelings of inadequacy. Sharon was responsive to the idea, and Keisha thought that sounded great. So, we set the picture up on the back of the couch and looked at it as an impressionistic idea of a teddy bear in a field of flowers rather than a realistic expression of one. We all enjoyed the picture more with just this little shift of our mind-set. Sharon laughed and said the picture was looking much better to her now. Keisha, of course, had been delighted with it all along. The following week, I saw the picture framed and hanging on the wall in the living room. Again, I was impressed with how easily and smoothly Sharon picked up an idea, adjusted her thinking to make the best of it, and proceeded to incorporate the new information into her life. Sharon's motivation and initiative were inspirational for me as a Recreation Therapist.

Keisha's Lack of Confidence with Peers

A second pervasive theme of Keisha's story involved her lack of self-confidence in relation to her peers, particularly with the other girls in her class at school with whom she wanted to be friends. Mr. Wilson had noticed her reluctance to reach out and make friends, and he was hoping she could make some progress toward overcoming her hesitancy.

One of the most noteworthy and poignant situations when I noticed Keisha's lack of self- confidence with her peers involved another activity that I brought for Keisha and Sharon to try at home—making paper beads and stringing them with plastic ones to make necklaces. The paper beads are made by cutting long strips of colored newspaper, typically the ad sections, about an inch wide at the top and tapering to a point. A line of glue runs all the way down the strip, and then it is rolled up around a matchstick or chopstick. It makes a multi-colored, elongated bead when the glue dries. Painted with clear nail polish, the beads become hard and shiny. They are really quite attractive. A similar process is used to make a type of commercial beads.

Keisha had some trouble rolling the beads. It requires a bit of a knack to make them turn out just right, and Keisha was too impatient to learn it. She enjoyed cutting the strips, though, and Sharon made lovely beads. We painted a batch with the clear polish and lined them up to dry.

The following session turned out to include Keisha's favorite thing to do at home, stringing the necklaces. I brought a bag of multicolored plastic beads to mix in with the paper beads, and we all created necklaces. Keisha made ones for her cousins, her grandmother, and the two girls she particularly liked at school, Sandy and Bonita. Keisha was quite proud of her work and felt thrilled about the idea of giving the necklaces to the two girls. The next week, Sharon told me that Keisha had given the necklaces to the relatives, who were very pleased with the gifts. They had made a big fuss over how talented they thought Keisha was. However, Keisha hadn't given the ones she made for the girls at school—she had been afraid they wouldn't like them and might laugh at her. Sharon described how Keisha had tearfully thrown the two necklaces in the trash because she felt they were not good enough. Sharon said she had tried to talk to Keisha about giving it a try, but Keisha would hear nothing about it.

Another time that Keisha's lack of self-confidence with her peers emerged was when we were making plans to invite Keisha's chosen friends over for a cooking party. This event was working on all of Keisha's goals by involving planning, the home-based activity of cooking, and expanding social activities. It was all coming together nicely until it came time for Keisha to call the girls and invite them. Keisha became quite emotional and was terrified of rejection. Sharon and I both talked to her about her fears and tried to help her be able to take the risk. Finally, the action that caused a turning point was Sharon calling the girls' mothers first to see if they thought it would be an acceptable idea. The two mothers thought it sounded like a splendid plan, and that gave Keisha the courage to talk to Sandy and Bonita and invite them over. Fortunately, both girls were sincerely delighted to be invited and assured Keisha that they would love to come. I could see Keisha's self-confidence begin to grow with the conquering of her fear and the acceptance of her friends.

Successes Developing Self-Esteem and Independence

During the 4 months that I worked with Keisha, I clearly saw the successes that she experienced begin to increase her self-esteem and expand her inclination for independence. A profound demonstration of this tendency was shown through our "cooking favorite foods" project.

The third activity to do at home, cooking some of Keisha's favorite foods, involved a number of other steps in order to prepare. Keisha and I developed a shopping list, figured costs, made a trip to the store, purchased required items, and brought everything back to the house. With encouragement, Keisha took the lead in all of these endeavors, and I offered advice when it was needed.

During the preparation stage, I guided Keisha to focus mainly on the monetary aspects of the project—the cost of items, paying for things, and counting change. Though Keisha disliked anything she thought had to do with math, she was interested in these calculations which would enable her to proceed with her project. She needed quite a bit of help with adding sums and counting change, but she felt quite successful when we had finished. The cashier at the supermarket caught on to what we were doing and counted the change out carefully and slowly so Keisha could follow along. Keisha appeared to feel triumphant when we arrived home with the goods. This sequence also provided an excellent example of the power of contextual learning in leisure education. Keisha was able to use her motivation for a chosen activity to overcome hesitancy in dealing with her deficiencies in math.

Keisha and Sharon accomplished the actual cooking part of the activity during the week. When I arrived for our next session, Keisha presented me with a brownie that she had made. It was quite good, though gooey in the middle. Sharon said Keisha had added chocolate chips to the recipe, and that made the brownies too wet to cook thoroughly, but they were still very tasty. Keisha and Sharon were both very proud of Keisha's success with the brownie project. Keisha told her mother several times how she had counted the change and purchased the items all on her own. Keisha's eyes just sparkled with the triumph of her success.

Another major success for Keisha involved inviting the girls, Sandy and Bonita, over to her house. By the time all the plans were made, the party had turned into a sleepover on Saturday night. After all the trauma of preparing for the party was behind her, Keisha was very excited about the event when I saw her two days before the big Saturday.

At our next session, Keisha told me all about the rest of her successful party. I had visited with Sharon during the afternoon while the pizzas were made. Later, Keisha said, they had rented a movie and made popcorn. They called several boys from their class at school and stayed up until midnight. Sharon nodded in agreement that it was a great success. Keisha and Sharon were both looking forward to when they could do it again. Within a couple of weeks, one of the girls had invited Keisha out for an activity in the community. Sharon was hopeful that these interactions marked the beginning of a social life and friendships for Keisha. Keisha was finally getting to have social experiences like her same-age peers.

During the follow-up interview the next year, Sharon said that indeed the pizza party had been the beginning of Keisha developing friendships with Sandy and Bonita and going out with other friends. Keisha's self-esteem and independence from her mother had expanded greatly, and Sharon was very pleased with her progress. However, Keisha had moved on to high school during the past year, and making friends had become much more difficult. Keisha tended to be moody, emotional, and occasionally depressed, which caused problems with being close with her peers. Sharon thought Keisha was doing okay though, and thought she would get more comfortable in high school with the passage of time.

SUMMARY

One of the most remarkable things about working with Sharon and Keisha for me was their enthusiastic response to ideas. As soon as I gave Sharon a new idea, she would claim it, develop it, and try it out by the time I appeared for our next session. She continually amazed me with her interest and engagement. Sharon thanked me often for the ideas that I brought her, but she was completely willing to do the work with Keisha herself.

Keisha was energetic and interested. She liked trying new things and could select which ones she enjoyed the most. She had a good relationship with her mother and liked working with her on the various projects that she decided to pursue. Though she was hesitant and fearful at first in dealing with relationships, she persevered, experienced success, and noticeably grew in self-confidence and self-esteem because of her experiences.

This family epitomized the section concerning "tell us how to do it." They were both willing and able to comprehend an idea and its benefits and proceed to act on it, expanding and embellishing on it to suit their needs. In the follow-up interview, Sharon selected individual attention and creative approaches as the two most important aspects of the FLLE program for herself and her daughter.

Families like Sharon and Keisha lead to cost effective services because they require less intensive, time-consuming intervention. They can be recognized by their motivation, their immediate follow-through on tasks, and their recognition of the value of services for their child. They are looking for services for their family, not just for their child.

Future FLLE-type programs can look for families who are motivated, on the edge of success, and who only need a slate of new ideas to get started quickly. These families may need a different flow of services spread out over a longer period of time. Teachers may be asked to refer families like Keisha's who are not desperate for services but who can benefit from an intervention that just gets them going. It is important to remember to serve families whose needs may not be on the verge of crisis, but for whom life-changing interventions can still make all the difference in the quality of the family's life.

10

From Drugs and Thugs to Playing

Mary Agnes Shelton

INTRODUCTION

Mr. Wilson, the middle school teacher for a special education class of students in the "mild" range, and I sat on the bleachers at the edge of the athletic field, watching his class of 18 African-American students play dodge ball. It was a crisp, fall day, and brightly colored leaves drifted down over us from a nearby elm as we discussed one of the students, Stephan. Mr. Wilson had referred Stephan to our Family Link in Leisure Education (FLLE) program because he was concerned about the direction in which Stephan was heading. Stephan, his single mother, and his older sister had moved to the area following a serious family upheaval. One of Stephan's uncles had been killed and another one arrested after a drug-related incident. Not knowing the full extent of family involvement, Carol, Stephan's mother, had left her large network of relatives and her ancestral home, at least until things cooled down. Mr. Wilson's fear was that Stephan saw the drug culture—and the rich, swaggering lifestyle it generated—as "cool" and worthy of emulation. Stephan also displayed a combative, explosive temper, which frequently got him into trouble.

I visually searched the scrambling, squealing group of young teens in front of us for the youth Mr. Wilson was describing. He was a slim, dark-skinned, sinewy young man with long limbs, close-cropped hair, and a wide, engaging smile. Skillfully athletic and coordinated, Stephan was about 5' 6" tall and attractive in a youthful, vigorous way. Mr. Wilson said he was a bit of a "ladies' man," with a number of girls his age displaying overt interest in him.

Mr. Wilson called the class in from the playing field. As I walked with Mr. Wilson and his class back toward the school, he introduced me to Stephan and told him that I was a Recreation Therapist who would be working with his mother and him at home. Stephan gave me a warm smile, held out his hand for a "give me five," and darted off in a "testosterone race" for the school door. Mr. Wilson shook his head and said, "I hope you can help him. He's a good kid, but a wild one."

Mr. Wilson, called "Coach" by the students because he was the track and field and basketball coach for the middle school, was a light-skinned African-American of impressive stature and kindly nature—a big, warm, huggy-bear kind of guy. His interest in and affection for his students were obvious and sincere. So many of them came from such difficult situations—Mr. Wilson shook his head sadly as he recounted some of the home lives that these young folks experienced every day. He was in favor of any kind of program that might be available to help out, especially in the community and on the home front. "If any real difference is to happen for these kids, it will have to start at home," Mr. Wilson said.

I was delighted to have such an important and influential ally as Mr. Wilson on my team. It was obvious how much all the students, and especially Stephan, respected, admired, and loved their "Coach." Mr. Wilson's strict, but compassionate and humorous way made his students respond by trying to do their best for him. Mr. Wilson's perceptive advice and realistic insights were invaluable to me while I worked with Stephan.

STEPHAN

My first visit to Stephan's house revealed much about his situation. An excerpt from my field notes described the neighborhood:

I found Stephan's street easily enough and turned down it. After one block, there was a "No Outlet" sign, and about every other house was deserted, with fluttering "condemned" notices tacked to the crumbling doors or porch railings. Windows stared vacantly, and tall grass filled unkempt yards. A number of wrecked and dismantled cars lined the street, giving the whole area a sort of otherworldly, desolate feeling. A group of four or five black men huddled around a car with the hood up—their eyes followed me as I drove slowly by, looking for house numbers. I parked under a bright street-light and silently prayed that my car would still be in one piece when I returned. (Field notes)

Despite the condition of the neighborhood, Stephan's house appeared to be sturdy enough, though the steps to the front porch were a bit wobbly and the screen door hung at a rakish angle. I knocked on the door and heard a voice call from within, "Who is it?" After I offered a fairly long description of who I was and why I was there, the door opened a crack and Stephan's dark eyes peeked out. Seeing it was truly me, he opened the door widely and called into the back of the house, "Mom, she's here!"

The living room was furnished with a massive set of overstuffed furniture—a large couch and two big armchairs—upholstered in prickly, navy blue fuzz. A large-screen TV sat opposite them with *Indiana Jones and the Temple of Doom* playing at high volume. A coffee table in front of the couch held an ice bucket and a number of brightly colored plastic glasses wrapped in cellophane and turned upside down. Clothes, blankets, and pillows were strewn around the room in a random manner. The adjoining bedroom was in complete disarray, with sheets hanging off the bed and clothes lying all over the floor.

In a moment, Carol, Stephan's mother, appeared wearing floppy slippers, knee-length shorts, and a huge, dark green T-shirt that declared "100% Black Woman." She was quite round, with a broad, dark face, a wide smile like Stephan's and big pink curlers in her hair. "You know, I totally forgot you was comin'," she said, as she kicked a stray shirt under the couch. Carol stubbed out her cigarette in the large, full ashtray on the coffee table and turned down the TV. She waved me into a chair and sank down on the couch. Stephan sat on the floor near the TV and continued to watch it.

STEPHAN'S ASSESSMENT

During the assessment interview, I learned more about Stephan's family. Jackie, Stephan's 18-year-old sister, was the only person employed in the entire extended family, including all of the relatives in their ancestral hometown on the coast. She worked part time at the dollar store in the mall and she was finishing high school at night. Carol was very proud of Jackie's accomplishments—having a job and trying to finish high school.

Carol's family was a multigeneration welfare family, having developed a whole lifestyle around the circumstances created by being on welfare. Though many of the women in this large family never married the fathers of their children (I was told that they received more welfare money as single mothers), the families lived near each other and maintained relationships as extended family members. Carol's immediate family was exceptional in that neither of the fathers of her two children had stayed around, so she had depended on brothers and uncles as the male supports for her family. When the whole drug thing exploded, Carol decided to move away from her home and her people, especially for Stephan's sake. The rest of the family gave their blessing, and now Carol and her children found themselves making a whole new life in a brand new town. Carol said she was hopeful that Jackie was going to break free of the welfare cycle, "if she just don't have no babies." I got the impression that Carol had less hope for Stephan since she looked down at him sadly and shook her head several times during this part of our conversation.

When we discussed Stephan, Carol echoed the sentiments of Mr. Wilson in being concerned about Stephan's attraction to the fast, rich lure of the drug-dealing culture and about his explosive temper. She said the neighborhood was so riddled with drugs and violence around there that she hated to let Stephan out the door, but she couldn't control him all of the time. She hoped that through working with me in our FLLE program, Stephan could find something that he liked to do that would keep him off the streets. The neighborhood recreation center that was just down the block wasn't the answer because that was where all the local drug dealers hung out and did their thing. Carol said, "We can hear them gun shots ring out from down that way all the time."

At the beginning of the current school year, Stephan's first year in the area, Mr. Wilson sent Stephan home from school on the city bus frequently because he was disrupting the entire class. Carol thought that was the wrong tactic and that Mr. Wilson should have kept Stephan at school no matter what. She said it was teaching Stephan that he would get to come home if he behaved badly. Finally, Mr. Wilson referred Stephan to the guidance clinic, where he was diagnosed ADHD and given a prescription for Ritalin. Carol said that Stephan had calmed down a lot since then, and he had not been sent home a single time after he had begun the Ritalin.

Mr. Wilson's version of this period helped explain his choices. He said that when Stephan first came into his class, he had never experienced such an unfocused, rambunctious student. It wasn't that Stephan was mean or angry, he was just unable to sit still—"this kid was bouncing off the walls." Mr. Wilson did not like the idea of sending Stephan home either, but there didn't seem to be much of a choice if class was going to happen at all. Sometimes, Stephan could be contained with one-on-one supervision at the counselor's office, but frequently, that was not possible. Mr. Wilson said he didn't like to see kids put on drugs like Ritalin, but in Stephan's case, it had literally saved the day. Although Stephan still had a hard time focusing on a particular subject matter, he was able to sit still and remain in class. Mr. Wilson had hopes for Stephan being able to develop more personal discipline through sports because he played very well and he respected the authority of the coach/athlete relationship. In fact, hoping for more sports involvement was the primary reason for Mr. Wilson's referral to the FLLE program.

As Carol and I continued our discussion of how she thought the FLLE program could be helpful for Stephan, Carol revealed another important area that she hoped Stephan and I could work on. Along with redirecting Stephan's attention away from the drug scene, she was also interested in Stephan's developing independence skills, such as cooking, handling money, and taking care of clothes. Carol said, "I ain't always gonna be around, you know. He better learn somma that stuff for hmself."

Carol said there was no need to work on independent transportation skills because Stephan already knew how to get around town riding the city bus. In fact, I was to learn later—when Stephan and I were driving around in my car—just how good he was at getting around town. After having lived in the area for only a few months, Stephan knew many shortcuts and back roads to places, and he had a clear picture of the layout of the whole city. I was quite impressed with his sense of direction and place and his memory for details. With much more time logged driving around town, I was much less efficient at getting across town than Stephan. It appeared that when Stephan was focused and interested, his cognitive limitations disappeared, and his street savvy revealed a sharp, quick mind.

As we were nearing the end of the assessment interview, Carol squirmed in her seat and yawned. She shook her head and said, "I don't know why I'd be sleepy—I slept all day." I took this as my cue to wrap it up. When I walked back out into the night, I saw my car sitting there under the streetlight, just fine.

I completed thorough and comprehensive assessments with Carol, Mr. Wilson, and Stephan. I was impressed with how open and revealing Carol had been about her difficult and chaotic life—telling intimate, personal details about herself and her relatives without apparent shame or embarrassment. Mr. Wilson filled in my picture of Stephan with academic and athletic information, adding some strong suggestions about positive directions in which he thought Stephan and I could head. Stephan was less revealing about a "big picture" focus for himself, but he was definite about playing lots of basketball and taking Tae Kwon Do (TKD) lessons. He also thought his mother's idea about learning to cook was a great one—he wanted to make lasagna just like his mother. "My momma makes the best lasagna there ever was," Stephan said proudly.

THE INDIVIDUALIZED LEISURE EDUCATION PLAN

After comparing and compiling the assessment interviews, I developed an Individualized Leisure Education Plan (ILEP), which was agreed upon by Carol, Mr. Wilson, and Stephan. The Plan focused around three main goals:

1. Improving personal planning to include time for selected leisure pursuits,
2. Increasing community involvement through athletic activities, and
3. Improving independent living skills in the home setting.

During the next few weeks, I assisted Stephan in developing objectives for his goals and making plans about how to implement them. For the first goal, which concerned planning his time to include selected leisure activities, I introduced Stephan to the Leisure Action Plan (LAP) system that I often used with FLLE clients who had difficulty planning and following through on activities. Since Stephan could write and spell fairly well, he used the written form to plan his activities and to schedule his time weekly after school. Stephan did quite well with this planning process, and he proudly showed Carol what he had written out. Although she was encouraging about Stephan's work and praised his writing skills, Carol was not particularly impressed with the need for scheduling and planning. She said that she didn't do any of that in her life and couldn't see why Stephan would want to. I explained that I felt it would be helpful to do some planning and scheduling to help Stephan focus on specific activities which would be more in his best interest than whatever he thought up just in the moment. Carol said, "Well, maybe," but I could tell she didn't buy it. Stephan wrote out plans and schedules whenever I asked him, but he never did it on his own. Even though I requested it, Carol never appeared to have helped or to have encouraged him to do it either.

The second goal, increasing community involvement through athletic activities, was Stephan's favorite, and he knew just what he wanted to do— TKD lessons. He had taken TKD lessons with his uncle once before and had really liked it—he felt he was quite good. He still had the uniform he had used and was quite excited when we found an after-school class at the local Parks and Recreation Center.

I took Stephan to meet the TKD teacher, Abdul Raman, before class to ask if we could sit in and observe. Abdul was a very "cool," 19-year-old African-American with deep brown, twinkling eyes, a warm, friendly smile, and a "with it" way of talking to Stephan. He was just as confident and at ease talking to me, too. He said he'd be pleased for us to watch his beginners' class.

The class was composed of about 15 students, mostly boys, with ages ranging from 6 to 16. About one-fourth of the class was African-American, one-fourth Asian, and the rest Caucasian. The classroom, with polished hardwood floors, had windows all down one side with the opposite wall completely covered in mirrors. The students began their warm-up routines, facing the mirrors, before Abdul entered. I was impressed with the agility and balance of some of these tiny little kids.

Then, Abdul came into the classroom and began his warm-ups. What a show! He was graceful, balanced, and as light as a feather. He did a number of moves that appeared to defy the possibilities of human bodily movement, as well as gravity itself. Abdul's performance was breath-taking! I looked at Stephan—his face wore an expression of awe, complete with round eyes and gaping mouth. I was sure mine did, too. Abdul glided over to us with a big smile. He could easily see how impressed we were. "Just a little preview," he said, winking at Stephan. Later, I heard from the lady in the office that Abdul was training for the Olympics in a few years and had won many national awards and honors. She said they were very proud to have him as an instructor.

Stephan loved the TKD class and Abdul. When he spoke his new instructor's name, it was with reverence and respect. He said he would like to be a TKD instructor someday, just like Abdul. Fortunately, since the recreation center was within walking distance of Stephan's school, we worked it out so Stephan could walk to class once a week and then ride the city bus home afterward.

Stephan was excited, and it was all looking great. He attended one class successfully; then, realities created by Stephan's personal programming and lifestyle set in. He just couldn't put it all together to get to class. I began to see how the lack of structure and scheduling affected the broader aspects of Stephan's life. Stephan did not seem to have a "big picture" of his life that he could fit pieces into. He had dreams—like being a TKD instructor, but he didn't really believe them, nor did he have any idea about how to make them happen—through perseverance and hard work.

Stephan's third goal, improving independent living skills in the home setting, was somewhat more successful—mostly because Carol was directly invested in it. Stephan planned menus, followed recipes, went shopping, and prepared a couple of dishes. Carol supervised the food preparation since Stephan wanted to learn to cook like his mother.

Stephan worked on money-handling by figuring out how much certain recipes would cost, paying and getting change when we went out to eat, and paying for food items in the grocery store. He knew all the coins and values, and although he remained a bit slow at counting change, he improved quite a bit in his ease with using money.

Since Carol wanted Stephan to take better care of his own clothes, Stephan agreed to add that as an objective to his goal of improving independent living skills. He wasn't actually very interested in doing it himself, but he did like pleasing his mother. With my assistance, Stephan and Carol made a list of things he needed to do to take care of his clothes—the primary task being to hang them up rather than to throw them on the floor. Carol also taught him to do laundry at the laundromat.

Although Stephan's ILEP goals and objectives were fairly routine, the experiences we had and our level of accomplishment were very uniquely related to Stephan, who he was, and the patterns in his life that influenced his choices and behavior.

INFLUENCING FACTORS

During the 7 months that Stephan and I worked on his ILEP goals, I became more and more aware of how various factors in Stephan's life influenced his behavior, his options, and his potential. The three factors that appeared to have the most far-reaching affects were Stephan's inconsistent, unstable relationship with his mother and family; attitudes that Stephan had learned due to his family's social and financial situation, a "get what you can when you can" kind of mentality; and learned helplessness. In looking back over my experiences with Stephan and his family, I felt that I learned how important the awareness of cultural/familial influences were in understanding and assisting Stephan in ways that would actually work for him.

Family Relationships

During my weekly meetings with Stephan and Carol to plan our strategies, I observed a complicated, variable relationship between them. On the one hand, they appeared to be close and affectionate with each other. Carol said that both Stephan and Jackie thought of her as more of a sister than a mother. According to Carol, they all hung around together as pals and enjoyed each other's company.

Carol and Stephan showed an affectionate ease with touch that seemed unusual to me for a teenage son and mother. An early excerpt from my field notes reveals this story:

> As I was going over the list of activities with Stephan, he began getting a bit bored or restless. Carol said, "He's getting tired." After a few minutes, Stephan lay down on the couch with his head in his mother's lap. She put her hand over his shoulder, and Stephan took her hand in his. Stephan continued answering questions while he moved his mother's hand over his face and held it next to his cheek. (Field notes)

I was surprised by this affectionate, physical display by a 14-year-old boy toward his mother, especially in front of someone else. It seemed a bit babyish, yet it was also natural and warm.

A week after observing this affectionate episode, I was to learn about the flip side of the coin. I arrived for an appointment to discuss strategies and found that Stephan wasn't home. I proceeded to talk over some plans with Carol. After we had finished with my agenda, Carol wanted to talk about how things were going between Stephan and her. Here's how my field notes recount this scene, including the personal comments at the end which I made at the time:

> Carol began with the story of how she had beaten Stephan with a broom handle for not coming home right after school. Several times last week he

had come home after 8 p.m. without checking in after school. Carol said she couldn't beat him with a belt anymore because he was too tough. Now she was using a broom handle. But she wouldn't beat him with" a rubber hose like her mother used to beat her—that was too much. Carol said some white woman one time had tried to tell her not to beat her children, that she would call the law on her. Carol told that woman she didn't know what she was talking about—you had to beat your children. The Bible told you to— "Spare the rod and spoil the child." Carol said, "I'm not gonna spoil no child of mine."

[Carol seemed to have no sense of brutality or abuse in this situation— no sense that violence begets violence, that abuse creates an abuser. She spoke as if this were the way everyone behaves.] (Field notes)

Then, describing the addition of psychological violence to physical violence, Carol had more to say. During that same conversation, Carol said she was planning to let Stephan have a puppy from a litter down the street. The field notes tell the story like this:

Carol thought getting a dog would help teach Stephan responsibility. He used to have a dog, but it growled at everyone. It growled at Carol, too. She told Stephan if that dog growled at her one more time, she would shoot it. It did, so she got the gun, went out back, and shot it right in the mouth. She hauled it down the street, trailing blood, and buried it in a field. Stephan screamed and cried. Carol wrapped up the story by saying, "He wouldn't speak to me for a month. I reckon he hadn't forgiven me for that to this day, but I wasn't gonna have no dog that growled at me." (Field notes)

I had quite a bit of difficulty dealing with the recounting of such overt violence occurring in Stephan's home. I discussed the situation with my colleagues, who pointed out that I had not seen any direct physical harm being done to Stephan or noticed any physical damage on his body. Perhaps by continuing contact with the family, I would be able to exert some positive influence on this behavior.

When I arrived at Stephan's the next week, there was a fluffy little chow-looking puppy tied to a bush on a 6-foot rope in the front yard. He yipped and jumped up and down at the end of the rope when I walked up. I hoped for his sake that he never learned to growl.

Later, Stephan's staying out behavior escalated to days at a time. One weekend, he didn't come home from school on Friday, and Carol couldn't locate him until he returned on Sunday night. His story was that he had gone home with a guy from class whose mother said she would drive Stephan home later that evening. Since Carol's phone had been disconnected for lack of payment, he couldn't call his mother to let her know. He thought it would be okay. The friend's mother got drunk that night and couldn't drive him home. The next day she was mean and wouldn't do anything for anybody. It wasn't until Sunday evening that she agreed to drive Stephan to his street where she dropped him off. At least, Carol said, that was Stephan's story. Carol did know that boy's mother though, and she did drink. Carol punished Stephan anyway, just to be sure.

Subsequently, Stephan was missing for 2 days again, and Carol told me she had found him hanging out with some old drunken men and drug dealers in the neighborhood. Carol said, "They was treatin' him jus' like one a them. I took out my pistol and waved it at them men, and told 'em to leave my boy alone or I'd shoot 'em in the mouth jus' like I did that dog. Boy, they didn't say nothin' then." Carol said she had decided not to beat Stephan anymore because it only made him mad and it didn't change his behavior. I sensed that my concern on this topic had affected her behavior. Now she was going to keep him in the house all of the time so he couldn't run off.

I felt concerned that Stephan would respond to being kept at home all the time by taking off for good. I asked Carol if we could set up some kind of schedule for Stephan to do a few supervised activities, such as beginning track practice with Mr. Wilson at school and Tae Kwon Do lessons with Abdul. That way, Stephan would have some healthy things to do and not get too bored. Carol thought that would be okay, as long as I checked it all out. Stephan was delighted with the compromise and promised to do exactly what he was supposed to do. If he didn't have a scheduled activity, he would come right home after school. I pointed out to him several times how important it was that he stick with these rules, at least for a while.

The following Tuesday, Stephan was supposed to stay after school to begin track practice with Mr. Wilson, who was both the track coach and Stephan's teacher. Mr. Wilson had been filled in on the circumstances and had agreed to send Stephan right home after practice. When I saw Stephan at school on Wednesday, I asked him how track practice had gone, if he had gone straight home, and if Carol was feeling good about his behavior. He said everything had gone as planned, and his mother was pleased. I couldn't find Mr. Wilson that day to corroborate Stephan's version of the story.

Since Carol had no phone, it was 2 days before I caught up with her. I arrived all smiles, thinking we were right on target with our strategies. Carol had quite a different story for me. Track practice had been canceled on Tuesday, and not only had Stephan not come home that night, he hadn't reappeared until Wednesday night. Here's what my field notes said about it:

> Carol said she didn't want to call the police or the school when Stephan "goes missing" because she gets blamed for being a bad parent and for not knowing where her child is. She said now all she can do is keep Stephan home all the time, no track or Tae Kwon Do. If she had a car, she would take and pick Stephan up at school, but she doesn't. Carol said she knew beating him wouldn't work—it only made him mad and resentful. She said her relatives all tell her to beat him, but she won't. Carol said she had told Stephan that if he gets in trouble, not to call her—she has no money to help him get out of any mess he gets into.

[I was really nonplussed. Here we had made all these great plans—it appeared to be coming together for Stephan, and he had blown it the very first day! I felt sad.] (Field notes)

Since beatings, threats, and attempts to keep Stephan at home had not been successful, Carol decided to allow Stephan to experience consequences on a larger scale. If he got into trouble with the police or with some of the unsavory characters he was hanging around, he would just have to learn what his actions brought down on him. I was still hopeful of finding activities that would interest Stephan enough to keep him from getting himself into too much hot water.

Since Stephan had not been able to stick to a schedule enough to attend TKD classes with Abdul, I asked him if he would be interested in seeing what was going on at the YMCA, which was about a mile from his house. Stephan thought that was a good idea, and we agreed to see what Carol would think of letting Stephan out of the house to go to the "Y." It took some convincing, but Carol finally agreed to let Stephan and me check out the kinds of programs which were offered at the "Y" and how much it would cost to go there. We found out that, due to Stephan's low socioeconomic status, he was eligible for the fee waiver program—he could have full access to the "Y" facilities for $5 per month. I made an appointment for Stephan and me to tour the "Y" and to meet the folks who worked there. Here's how the field notes tell the story, including my personal comments made at the time:

At the "Y," we asked for Stewart at the front desk, as had been arranged. Stewart is a tall, red-haired, good-looking young man, probably in his early 20s. He is quite open, energetic, and "hip." He connected with Stephan and directed his conversation to him, introducing him to people and showing him all through the facility. I just followed along. Stewart challenged Stephan to shoot some baskets, which Stephan was excited to try.

[I was quite impressed with how tuned in Stewart was with Stephan's world—he talked the talk and walked the walk, and he wasn't even black. It didn't seem phony or pretentious either, and Stephan seemed to appreciate it.]

After a thorough tour of the "Y," Stewart talked to me about the discount that Stephan could get since his application for financial aid had been processed. For $5 per month, Stephan would have full access to the facility, including basketball courts, weight room, gym, track, swimming pool, and more.

[Sounded like a great deal to me, and Stephan appeared enthusiastic, too.]

I went in the house with Stephan, and we both told Carol and Jackie how great the "Y" was and all the opportunities it could offer Stephan. I told Carol about the $5 fee per month, and she looked dubious. However, she said she would take Stephan to the "Y" on Monday and pay the fee. She thought it would be good for him. (Field notes)

During the last few months of our work together, the "Y" worked out great for Stephan. He got his bicycle up and running and could ride to the "Y" in about 10 minutes. There was always an open gym "pick-up" basketball game going in the afternoons that he could join. He liked the weight room, too—a weight coach was available for guidance and instruction. As it turned out, when Carol backed off from trying to control his decisions and behavior, Stephan became much more cooperative. With an exciting, interesting outlet for his energies and less anger and upset at home, Stephan was much more content with his situation. Apparently, having the flexibility to go to the "Y" whenever he wanted to was a key point to Stephan's success there. Scheduling was just not part of Stephan's framework.

Mr. Wilson and I were particularly pleased with the kinds of role models and mentors with whom Stephan was associating now—ever so much better than the drunks and drug dealers. Mr. Wilson knew some of the guys who worked at the "Y," and he checked in with them now and then on Stephan's progress. The feedback he got was that Stephan was fitting in very well.

Get What You Can When You Can

Another major factor that I felt influenced Stephan's life concerned the attitudes he and his family had developed due to their social and financial situation. As I spent time with the family and began to observe their behavior patterns and belief systems, I became aware of certain behaviors that I felt had been developed to accommodate being on welfare and having to get by on whatever was available.

The "get what you can when you can" attitude was revealed most profoundly, I thought, when we were working on the goal of improving independent living skills by having Stephan learn to cook. Stephan and I planned the shopping outing, listed the ingredients of recipes, and budgeted for the costs. As we prepared, Stephan and I were getting pretty excited about our impending adventure.

The day for our shopping trip and cooking lesson arrived, and I stopped by Stephan's house to pick him up. As I drove up to the house, I noticed that Carol was standing on the porch with Stephan. When I stopped the car, Carol led Stephan down the steps and told him to get in the back seat while she climbed into the passenger seat next to me. "Stephan said he wanted me to come, too," Carol said, without looking at me. An excerpt from the field notes tells more:

> Right away, Carol began giving directions and monopolizing the conversation. Several times when I directed comments to Stephan or asked him questions, Carol answered for him. She seemed to be more into this behavior today than usual. We drove to Byrd's Supermarket, and Carol showed me two short cuts. She said she has walked it often enough to know all the

ways to get there. The store is probably at least a mile from their house, and with groceries, that could be quite a haul when you're walking. As soon as we got to the store, Carol grabbed a cart and took off down the aisles. It was obvious that Carol planned to do some shopping while she had a ride home available. Apparently, she planned to take full advantage of her opportunity. Carol knew her way around the store, and Stephan and I followed in her wake. She picked up a box of doughnuts and told Stephan that they were only for her, and he better not touch them. She picked up fruit, bread, noodles, and several other items before we shopped for the lasagna ingredients. Carol told Stephan what to get before he even had a chance to try to figure it out for himself. She completely took over our shopping trip. (Field notes)

This example of Carol taking advantage of an opportunity to fulfill her needs despite what was on the agenda for anyone else was repeated a number of times during my work with the family. Carol needed a ride to the corner for cigarettes; she needed me to pick Stephan up after school; she wanted me to give Jackie a ride to work. I tried to be accommodating because I could imagine how difficult it must be to get around town without a car. Public transportation ran infrequently with limited hours, and it was pretty expensive over time. However, the more I tried to help, the more Carol wanted from me. I got the feeling she felt she had found the "golden goose." It appeared to me that Carol's circumstances had led her to develop a habit of trying to grab the most she could from whatever resource appeared in her life.

Finally, Carol asked me to pick Stephan up after school the next day to take him to his appointment at the guidance center. I would have had to drive into town, a round trip of over 40 miles, and use half of my working day to accomplish this. I told Carol that there was no way my boss would allow me to use my time to give people rides around town. I tried to be tactful and kind, but Carol was upset. She set her jaw, refused to look at my face, and stalked into the house without saying good-bye.

For the next two appointments with Stephan, Carol wouldn't talk to me, but only grunted in my direction when I spoke to her. She had been friendly with me until then, even affectionately calling me "my white woman" to her neighbors. By our third meeting, Carol seemed to have forgiven me for not accommodating her wishes and once again became friendly.

Stephan also appeared to display the behavior of trying to get all he could from me when we were together. No matter what kind of outing we were on, he typically hinted broadly about being hungry and wanting me to buy him food. A couple of times when we went out to eat, I gave Stephan the money to pay for his food so he could practice counting money and ordering for himself. When we got back to our table, Stephan pocketed the change until I asked for it back. It was indeed a learned culture of "get what you can when you can."

Learned Helplessness

A third influencing factor that I felt Stephan had developed was learned help-lessness. Several times I saw situations where Stephan could have taken a proactive stance and greatly improved his circumstances without huge amounts of effort on his part. Repeatedly, he declined to take situations into his own hands to get what he wanted. The most dramatic occurrence revolved around Stephan getting a job.

Stephan and I talked about the possibility of his getting a job so he would have some spending money of his own. He knew of a grocery store a few blocks from his house that hired neighborhood kids to stock shelves for $5 an hour after school. One of the guys who lived near him worked there regularly and told Stephan they would hire him, too. Stephan thought that sounded like a good idea, but he never followed up on it as long as I worked with him. I even asked if he would like for me to help him check it out, but he said, "No."

A couple of weeks later Stephan's class took a field trip to the NC Zoo in Asheboro. Thinking that Stephan would be gone that day, I stopped by to see Carol. When I drove up, there was Stephan in the front yard. I asked him why he wasn't at the zoo with his class, and he said that his mother couldn't afford the $8 that each student was supposed to contribute for the trip. He looked very sad that he hadn't been able to go. Carol said, "I feels bad, but no money is no money—he might as well get that straight."

At a subsequent appointment, I talked to Stephan about how he could have made enough money for the zoo trip in just one afternoon at the grocery store. If he wanted things for himself, he was going to need to figure out how to make them happen. Stephan nodded his head, but as far as I know, he ever did anything about it. [As is often the case, the school would have provided the $8 for the trip if Stephan had asked.]

I felt that these behaviors—trying to get all he could out of me and being helpless about helping himself—were traits that Stephan had learned and developed in response to his world. He took cues from his mother, who appeared to try to squeeze all she could from opportunities that required the least from her. I was hopeful that perhaps Stephan would observe and develop some more pro-ductive, self-motivating habits from his peers and mentors at the "Y."

FOLLOW-UP

A year later, I returned to Stephan's neighborhood for a follow-up visit. I was quite surprised as I turned down Stephan's street. The trashed cars, littered streets, and condemned houses were all gone, and several new houses were under construction, part of a Habitat for Humanity Project. The whole neighbor-hood had undergone quite a face-lift and was looking ever so much better.

Stephan's house looked about the same, except that a great big, brown chow dog was tied to the bush in the front yard. He didn't get up or growl when I walked up. A wise move on his part, I reflected. I knocked on the door, but no one answered. The neighbor lady across the street walked toward me and said, "Hey, ain't you Carol's white woman from a ways back?" I said that I was. She told me that Carol had a job now, as well as a phone and a car. She gave me Carol's number.

Within a few days, I had contacted Carol and had made an appointment to see her at home. When I arrived, she was dressed up and looking quite spiffy. She greeted me warmly, saying that she was leaving for work soon, but that she had a few minutes to talk. Carol told me that she worked at a large motel as a receptionist, a job she did well and enjoyed. Jackie had graduated from high school and was taking nursing classes at the community college.

Stephan had finished middle school and would start high school in the fall. He was doing really well. He still went to the "Y" regularly and had quite a few friends from there. Carol said she thought that hooking up with the "Y" had been a turning point for Stephan. Putting his energy into sports instead of the street scene was just what he had needed. The other teenage boys that Stephan had met at the "Y" had shown him an energetic, interesting lifestyle that he could relate to and enjoy. Next year, he was planning to go out for the basketball team at his high school.

Carol said that things had improved so much for her family that they were going to stay in town and not move back to the coast near her relatives. She said the influences on Stephan's life were much better here, and she had hope for both of her children being able to create a better life for themselves than they had known so far. Carol also said that she felt really good about having a job.

I accompanied Carol to her car as she was getting ready to leave. She proudly showed me the inside of the car and pointed out important features. I commented on how improved the neighborhood looked, and Carol said they were certainly fixing it up. She was glad it was happening and felt safer now, but she also commented, "They sure better not raise my rent!"

SUMMARY

In looking back over my work with Stephan and his family, I feel that the intervention with Stephan came at a very crucial time in his life. Stephan was at a turning point of deciding which direction he was going to take—one toward education and sports or one toward dropping out and the drug scene. With some "hit and miss" tactics and natural maturing on Stephan's part, we were able to help steer Stephan toward a safer, more promising future. Hooking Stephan up with the resources that worked for him and getting him involved with positive role models seemed to be the most important accomplishments for Stephan through the FLLE program.

Even though Stephan's family offered him virtually no assistance, Stephan's story still turned out well. Since Stephan was a savvy, energetic, independent kind of guy already, just giving him a bit of a push in the right direction proved to be the help he needed. I have strong hopes for Stephan's ability to create a positive, pleasing life for himself in the future.

Section V

Implications for Working with Students

Chapter 11
Lessons From the Front: The Family Link in Leisure Education Projects

Danny E. Johnson
Charles C. Bullock

Once they were given "permission" to be self-determining and the skills they had lacked to be successful, choices became regular and meaningful. When given a voice, they roared. When given a chance to give, they responded. When given the freedom to be self-determining, they became more than they had been. It was our greatest lesson.

—Chapter 11, p. 222

11

Lessons From the Front"
The Family Link in
Leisure Education Project

Danny C. Johnson
Charles C. Bullock

INTRODUCTION

Family Link in Leisure Education (FLLE) was a 5-year research project that sought to understand the impact of including families of children with mental retardation in a leisure education process to increase the self-determination of students regarding leisure. Students and families were provided an individualized leisure education program based upon the students' needs, interests, and strengths. An assessment package was completed with the students, with their families, and with their special education teachers. Goals and objectives were developed from the assessments with input from all of the parties.

Over the course of FLLE, we learned much about the process of providing this unique service. Many of those lessons were learned through trial and error and came as a surprise to us. We learned about how inclusion operated in one system, the cultural nuances of African-American families, and the difficulties of being a special education teacher in this day and age. Anyone replicating this type of program may well benefit from our experiences.

Researchers involved in this project utilized a variety of data sources, including assessments with students, parents, and teachers; structured interviews; and extensive field notes of all sessions and contacts. Cases were discussed throughout the process on a weekly basis with the project coordinator, and also in a weekly staff meeting comprised of the entire research team. The following sections, utilizing data from all of the case studies, describe the surprising, and not so surprising, conclusions we reached:

1. About families,
2. The provision of family/home leisure education,
3. Schools and teachers,
4. About students with disabilities.

WHAT WE LEARNED ABOUT FAMILIES

Our data revealed that there were three types of families that emerged within this process and that are described here. Families were spread rather evenly among the three types. The types of families we identified can be useful to service providers making decisions about the provision and continuation of interventions. Knowing, for example, that families that were initially hesitant to be involved in the intervention also had poor outcomes may mean that those families would not be chosen. Or, families that can utilize information quickly can have shorter planned interventions.

Several aspects of our work with families were surprising to us. We found families to be reasonably unchanged by the process, in direct contrast to the significant changes in their children with whom we worked. We were also struck by the impact on parents of having to deal with their children's disabilities, as well as the impact families had on their children's successes and potentials.

The Three Types of Families

Data from the study revealed that families fell into a pattern of involvement characterized by the following categories:

"Tell Us What We Are Going To Do Together." Families in this category sought partners in improving the quality of life of their children. They invited us into their homes and lives, generously sharing their family's history.

Families in this category, while providing rich information for a research project, were very time-consuming. Planned 1-hour interviews often turned into 3-hour interviews as attempts for closure led to more stories about the child. These families were time-consuming for the therapist, as they desired considerable information and structure to get started. Over the course of the intervention, though, the time requirements were reduced as the families and their children became more independent.

Families in this category were quick starters and slow finishers, often not following through as completely as we would have expected. High motivation, we believe, lulled us into expecting more out of them. Established goals were often very complicated and required extra effort from these families.

Families in this category liked to talk about their children. They especially seemed to revel in the fact that someone else saw potential in their children; that someone saw the twinkle in their eyes and the joy they could bring to others.

Families who are highly knowledgeable about their children's disabilities seem to be more motivated, whether they are or not. Long discussions, especially about the potential of their children, led us to believe they were willing and able to do whatever it took. Their frustrations with schools and social service agencies further led us to make big plans for the intervention.

Families in this category were generally middle- to upper middle-class families with two parents and ample financial resources. They had often received high levels of services in the past. What was hard to realize at the time was that although they could talk about their children by the hour, they were still exhausted by the enormity of raising children with disabilities. When it came time for more effort, it often was not there. In Barney's case, we would have expected, after our assessment, that providing a computer communication program and a consultant in literacy and disability to a father who worked in interactive telecommunication, would have hit a bullseye. We were wrong. At this point in the father's life, it may have been too much.

"Tell Us What You Are Going To Do." Families in this category wanted services for their children, but they were not interested in being deeply involved in the process. They wanted anything that might help their children and any activity that we did with the children. But what they did not seem to want was any changes that might affect them.

Families were short-sighted (sometimes blind) in seeing the benefits of self-determination for their children. They tended to see activity and involvement as separate from the family's life. What they did was something like sending them to school—"You do whatever you do, and then send them home to us."

This lack of involvement was problematic for a variety of reasons. Families in this category did not learn how to integrate what the children had learned into the families existence. Gains made by the students were separate from home life—something done for the family, not with the family. These families also did not experience the children's gains in self-determination. They did not see their children growing and learning. Even when they saw successful self-determination, it was not significant enough for them to change.

Families in this category did not follow through on the students' gains. They did not go out of their way to see that activities and dreams continued. They did not see or want to see the children any differently, or to significantly change their behavior. There was a comfort, somehow, in the lack of potential of their children. That comfort, however, significantly handicapped these children.

For example, Eric's family did not want to change their Saturday schedule of grocery shopping. Sara's group home workers did not want to structure her time individually. Sara's teachers did not want to change their routine to see that she moved to a classroom with higher functioning students. David and James' parents would not see that they got to places that they jointly agreed would be good for them.

What surprised us was that the responses of these families did not occur early in the process. Their responses occurred, instead, in response to their children's successes. All the parents and teachers claimed the children could be doing more, but once they did more, the parents and teachers failed to do anything to keep the success going. Often this occurred despite specific training for the teachers and parents by the project staff to help the children.

Although Eric's parents were initially reluctant, we believed they would change if he were successful. Eric's efforts with Habitat for Humanity were in complete harmony with his parents' dream of him working in carpentry when he got out of school. His behavioral changes were greater than they could have imagined.

Surely, Sara's workers would respond to her new-found abilities to be self-determining. Surely, James' parents would be thrilled by his successes in Tae-Kwon-Do. Yet, in the face of these successes, it was the parents who could not change. It was not the child with mental retardation, not the child who was blind; it was the adults who could provide the support for continued success who fell apart.

Although intervention success is an obvious goal, success of a child with a disability has several difficult and not-so-obvious implications for families.

1. Success requires them to deal with different behaviors. Self-determination leads to more self-determination. Did Sara's group home workers really want her to have choices and to have to deal with her choices?

2. Success removes the excuses, such as that other people are not doing enough for their child. David and James' parents would have to deal with the successes of their sons rather than the failures of the school.

3. Success means students must be taken seriously as individuals, and planning and preparation must be for an individual, not for a group or a label. Sara's teachers could no longer leave her by the radio for hours, if they acknowledged her abilities.

4. Success may mean more independence. James' father was somehow bothered by his independence and was not supportive of David's efforts. He decreased their independence and maintained his control by refusing to let them use the car to get to activities.

5. Success means more effort toward new goals. Eric's parents would have to drive him to Habitat and interact with the supervisor. The "dream" of carpentry would be a reality—maybe too much of a reality.

6. Success means dealing with a new person—a new image. Sara could no longer be the quiet girl, content to listen to the radio; she now had preferences for both activities and activity partners.

7. Success means you can't be neutral anymore. Eric's parents could no longer wonder if he was capable of more, or think that eventually he would grow out of this. Not following through lets one go back to neutral and not deal with the realities.

8. Success may mean realizing that this could have been done much earlier in their lives. In Sara's case, she was able to make significant gains quickly. Does it make workers consider what they could have accomplished long ago?

9. Success may be realizing that the family is responsible for continued support. For students to continue to be more self-determining, the family must be supportive. Short-term efforts by human service workers lead to the need for long-term efforts for the family.

10. Success may mean a child must be taken seriously and action must be taken. Eric would have to be dealt with as a teenager, not that far removed from the workforce.

It is important to recognize the "costs" of a student's success to a family and how they may not support and may even sabotage a student's efforts to be self-determining. If success means more work and change to the family, they must become an even more significant part of the equation in this type of intervention.

"Tell Us How To Do It." Families in this category were seeking information about which directions to take with their children. They were actively involved in their children's lives and needed facilitation from an outside source to succeed—a "jump start." They were often very independent in their follow-through, requiring less intensive follow-up from us. Their high level of motivation led to success as they integrated the program into their daily lives. Keisha's story is an excellent example of the independence that a family can sometimes achieve quickly.

Some families in this category had just become "stuck" from dealing with the day-to-day hassles of raising a child with a disability. Fighting for services with systems that tried to provide minimal programs left many of them frustrated and tired. Others found that their children, although labeled "disabled," had few services readily available. Families within this category were likely to be African-American, single-parent families of children with mild disabilities. Often, they had received few human services in the past. A fresh outlook, in this case, from the recreation therapist, was all they needed to get moving again.

Several families in this category profited from resource information about programs, facilities, and financial assistance. Other families seemed to benefit from being reminded of the importance of play and interaction for their children. The questions on the assessment triggered a renewed value of play and interaction with peers. Some parents seemed to be relieved not to be talking to a professional about their child's difficulty with addition and subtraction; instead, they were talking about how their child could become part of the community through the child's interests and strengths. These families did not use technical disability language, nor did they tend to talk about their child as being disabled. They described their child by his or her qualities, not according to their labels.

Families in this category were typically warm and caring. They asked specific questions and wanted specific direction. They seemed concerned with their children's home activities and involvement with peers, especially in their neighborhood. Parents wanted to be independent and for their children to be independent in "normal activities." They wanted their children to not be behavioral problems to others. They also did not want their children to fall through the cracks—to be forgotten.

Families, like these, who are looking for direction, can be slotted for less intensive interventions. They may require a less intensive assessment process. They also seem to benefit from a jump-start and can then do well with follow-ups spread over a long period of time—more to touch base and answer questions, then to re-engage in the intervention. These families would seem to be candidates for a greater proportion of printed materials that could be utilized independently. Their desire for results and action meant the recreation therapist had to quickly proceed with a plan, striking while the iron was hot.

One explanation of why families fell into this category may have been cultural and racial differences. In each of the three cases documented in this book, the families were African-American and the therapist was a middle-aged, Caucasian female. Families who sought direction and information may have been choosing a safe mode of interaction, with less intense directing in the process from the therapist. Quick directions kept the interactions on an equal level for the families. Another explanation might be that most of the students had mild disabilities and were fairly independent, accustomed to relying on their instincts and making the best of situations. Direction from the recreation therapist made this process more efficient for them and increased the likelihood of better outcomes.

Another explanation would be that, as we talked to parents on a nontechnical level, we kept things more simple and manageable. It may have been easier to follow-through—easier to see immediate accomplishment.

Families are Stable in Their Behaviors

Our experience with the FLLE project was that families exhibited little change in their behavior over the course of the project. Those families that were motivated stayed motivated. We were merely a vehicle for their motivation. They did not change; they just were now able to do what they had wanted to do anyway.

If parents waffled at the beginning of the process, they were likely to still be waffling at the end. They continued to express interest, but they did not show the commitment necessary to be active participants. This noncommittal stance endured despite a student's obvious progress and successes, and in the case of Eric, despite his plea to them for their involvement and support.

Difficulty getting started was a harbinger for later difficulties. Missed appointments, multiple changes in appointments, lost consent forms, unreturned phone calls, all signaled problems. Only in the later stages of the project did we learn to just let families go that could not respond.

It was extremely difficult for us to deal with families' ambivalence. The "helper," with all his or her naivete, thought people would respond, rejoice, and revel in their children's efforts and successes. In retrospect, we should not have worked with Eric. It was just too hard to see the inevitability of the family's failures when we saw the potential in Eric's eyes. Our efforts were just not going to be enough; the family needed something we could not offer.

Those families that had difficulty dealing with their children's disabilities did not significantly improve their coping. Those that could not or would not see their children differently stayed that way. Those who had imposed limits to potential also remained unchanged.

This may be explained by the focus of the family involvement in the process. The goal of FLLE was to involve the family members in the program, so they might support their children's efforts, they would understand their roles in continuing the children's chosen activities, and they would experience the children's progress. The goal of FLLE was not to provide family therapy, but rather to educate and involve the family.

Families are Worn Down by Systems Designed to Help Their Children

What do you say when your child suffers rejection by his or her peers and his or her only occupational therapy goal is to make better loops in written letters? What do you say in your child's 12th IEP meeting, after they tell you, in great detail, what your kid cannot do? What do you say when your teenager with a disability gets no vocational preparation? What do you say when your child is provided with minimal services?

Often, parents are happy to get any services; they are just glad the child has *someplace* to go. Some parents assert themselves when the child is young, but they tire of the process. One parent remarked that it seemed like a full-time job to obtain appropriate services. Parents who work and single-parent families eventually just seem to give up and take what they can get.

Parents are forced to fight continually for services against school systems often ill-prepared to provide and fund those services. Parents eventually seem to tire of the battle and just sign the IEP. Programs such as FLLE can provide hope for parents who desire more for their children; who want their children to be connected to their community—who want their children to be active and have relationships. Elementary school is probably the ideal setting for programs like FLLE—working with parents before they are burned out on systems.

Families Determine Their Children's Potential

Simply put, families who wanted their children to succeed found success. Conversely, families who expected little got what they expected. These realities cannot be overstated. Sally's and Stephan's parents found success through high expectations. Sara's and Eric's families had decided their children's potential was limited and did not even see the success that occurred. Neither wanted to deal with a child with higher potential. It was too much work and too many changes in the routine.

Students with disabilities must rely on their families for support, motivation, and cheerleading. Students with disabilities are dependent on families, more so than nondisabled students, for transportation to and supervision during activities. They often do not have the support of peers for these functions, as do nondisabled students. Families, oddly, also become the "peer" support system in the absence of friends. Families can become the chief providers of self-esteem for the child with a disability. It is little wonder that parents become exhausted.

This dependence also means that students with disabilities are enormously affected by the perspectives of their families, both negatively and positively. Eric's limits were not self-imposed; his family placed those limits. Eric had dreams and expectations far greater than his family had for him, but he was dependent upon them to reach his goals. On the other hand. Sally would have probably been content to sit on the sidelines her whole life, if her mother had not been motivated for her to do more. Both Eric's and Sally's families made the difference, albeit in different directions.

Families Become Used to the Notion That
Their Children are "Special" and Need Help

A student's self-determining behavior is clearly affected by a family's perception of the student's potential or ability to be self-determining. A family can get caught in a rut of thinking of the their child as a "special person," one in need of constant assistance in both actions and decisions. Over a period of time, they come to believe many things about their child, including:

1. The child must be supervised and led.
2. The child cannot participate in activities without help.
3. If the child is with same-age peers, a peer or a group of peers must assist him or her.
4. Independence is considered a possibility.

5. Relationships with others are always of a helping nature, unequal.
6. The child will not participate in normal activities.
7. "Special" becomes synonymous with "nonself-determining."

Parents do not intend to think in these ways; it just becomes a "natural" part of the course of the disability experience: devalued persons do not make valued choices. If people only talk about their children's limitations, they think of them only in those terms. Parents experience their children's difficulty relating with others. While they see their children's special qualities, they are overwhelmed by the "specialness."

Parents need help to get beyond this—to expect more, to allow for more, to insist on more. They must be supported to see their children differently. They need support to fight systems. Sometimes they need help overcoming themselves.

Some Families May Need Relief Rather Than More Work

Families, especially those with older children, may become overburdened by programs such as FLLE that ask them to expend more energy. Programs may be advised to phase in parental effort, as the child becomes more active. Programmers and teachers must learn to quickly assess parents' willingness to take on more effort. This issue should become a topic for discussion as parents decide their willingness to become involved.

In our zest to see the potential of children, we often did not see the potential for parents to become tired of all this. Despite their belief in their child's potential, it still came down to the fact that it would be more work for them. Parents who desperately want more services for their children may have difficulty seeing the increase in effort as a barrier.

A better strategy for working with some parents may be to provide very simple ideas and plans that are not overwhelming. Other families may benefit from recreation programs for their children which do not require the family's attendance. Some families may not be able to benefit from programs like FLLE, and instead should be referred to respite programs or family therapy.

Agreement to Participate and Commitment to Change Are Two Different Things

Our protocol for participation in the program was to explain the goals of the research and to obtain the parent's consent to participate. Parents were given an overview of the process and some descriptions of what other students had done and accomplished. At this point, they were asked if they wanted to participate.

In retrospect, a better option may have been to complete the assessment and goal-setting process before asking for a commitment. The parents could then have made a commitment or not, based on the goals and objectives for their children and their roles and responsibilities in the intervention. Parents could then see specific plans and not have to rely on anecdotes of other families.

There is probably a tendency in research projects with limited samples to describe the process too simply and to accentuate other participants' outcomes, rather than to fully describe the work and the commitment necessary for these changes. Pressure to enlist families when there are few choices may lead to less than desirable situations. A family like Eric's would probably not have ended up in a program in a nonresearch situation. In ongoing programs like FLLE, parents must be fully committed, or little is accomplished in the end.

WHAT WE LEARNED ABOUT LEISURE EDUCATION

Leisure education is the process of teaching various recreation- and leisure-related skills, attitudes, and values. Individuals develop skills and knowledge for leisure participation during early years of development. They are exposed to a variety of opportunities to explore and develop new leisure skills and awareness of a variety of leisure possibilities. They often take leisure and the skills for participation for granted simply because it is a natural part of growing up. Unfortunately, children with disabilities often do not have the same opportunities to explore and learn about leisure. Through leisure education, students learn the knowledge, skills, and attitudes necessary to participate in leisure activities of their choice. Consequently, they are more able to derive the benefits of participating in satisfying, enjoyable, and developmentally appropriate leisure activities. Leisure education curricula include units on leisure awareness, leisure resources, social skills, leisure decision making and planning, and recreation activity skill instruction.

FLLE staff worked with students and their families to provide the necessary skills for satisfying and successful leisure experiences. Activities were freely chosen and supported in their natural settings, and they were orchestrated to enhance the students' educational goals. By facilitating leisure experiences that were contextual and person-centered, the goals of FLLE were to enhance and expand the students' community membership and acceptance, and their ability to follow through on personally chosen and planned leisure experiences.

The natural contexts for learning were primarily in the students' homes and in the community. Each learning plan was based on the student's interests and his or her desire to explore specific activities and interactions. Students and families were encouraged not to limit themselves to recreation programs or activities typically provided for students with disabilities, such as Special Olympics and special populations recreation programs.

We learned a variety of things about providing leisure education in the FLLE project.

Leisure Interests Need to be Explored, Not Inventoried

Students with disabilities are often at a loss to identify leisure interests. This may be caused by lack of exposure to activities, limited physical skills, difficulty in cognitively understanding an activity, and limited access to "normal" recreation programs. In most studies of the activities of persons with disabilities, watching television, listening to the radio, shopping, and eating out are most commonly identified.

Interests need to be explored with students who have limited experiences with activities. Responses to typical interest inventories tend to be that they are interested in everything or nothing, or that they are interested only in what they have done or are doing.

Our approach to identifying interests yielded surprising results, even to us. Students were encouraged to identify activities that they had seen on television or in movies that they found interesting. They were asked to identify interesting activities in which relatives and neighbors were involved. The CTRS and the student often spent considerable time examining newspapers, recreation brochures, and visiting recreation facilities. Students were encouraged to interview recreation programmers to find out if they were interested in the activity and to find out if they were comfortable with and welcomed by the instructor.

When students were able to explore interests, they chose activities similar to their same-aged peers. They chose sports, art, music, dancing, camps, and martial arts, among other activities. This approach to exploring leisure interests opened the world of possibilities for students and allowed them to dream. When they identified dreams, they identified real interests.

Come Early, Stay Late

Students and families seemed to benefit more the earlier the intervention occurred in the child's life. Factors, such as labeling, history of failures, length of time in segregated special education classrooms, and tired parents, all seemed to point to a poorer prognosis in the leisure education process. When students were in elementary settings, parents clearly had more energy and hope that their children could succeed.

We learned that the artificially set intervention time of 1 school year needed more flexibility when considering an on-going program. There was great variance in the time and attention families needed. There was also variance in the needed length of service. Families such as Barney's could have benefited from a less intense intervention, but one that was spread out over a longer period of time to provide more support. Several students, like Stephan, could have benefited from "booster shots" at a later time, to check-up, encourage, and to re-teach concepts. Some families, such as Eric's, may have benefited from several years of intervention, to see if the family could become more involved.

Contextual Learning is Effective

School may be the least effective setting for a program such as leisure education. It is in our communities and among our families, that we live and where there are opportunities to learn. We must recognize the importance of these contexts and look for ways that learning can occur and can be enhanced. Learning that occurs in the context of a person's life is more likely to be integrated into his or her life. It is easier to learn skills in the context in which the person lives than to learn them in a classroom and hope that they will be transferred. For many years, special education teachers and researchers have insisted that students with disabilities receive community-based, as well as school-based, vocational training. To learn a job by doing that job has been shown to be more effective than learning that job in a contrived classroom setting. The same is true in other areas of students' lives. One context that is often overlooked, even devalued, yet which is extremely important, is the area of play, recreation, and leisure.

Students with disabilities often do not have the opportunity to learn and practice play, recreation, and social skills. Others, because of developmental delays, require interventions to be able to develop them. Playing and participating in recreational activities, planning for those activities to occur, and making self-determined choices about one's leisure are central to one's growth and development.

Students involved in self-determined leisure activities at school, at home, and in their communities are learning in context to prioritize time, budget and use money, explore interests, develop skills, and identify and utilize transportation and community resources. For example, a student who participates in a martial arts class after school is learning how to socialize and cooperate with his or her peers and schedule time for homework, as well as to develop and practice self-discipline, respect, and gross motor skills.

Successful leisure experiences can provide opportunities for students to learn and practice skills that enhance their educational outcomes and which are already regularly included in their Individualized Education Programs (IEP). Academic and life skill goals and objectives, which can be facilitated through leisure experiences in contextual learning situations, are easily integrated into IEPs.

If leisure skills are learned in context, they will often include the family in various parts of the contextual learning process since the family, by definition, is part of the context in which that person lives. As most leisure occurs outside of school, the average student spends much of his or her leisure time at home with the family.

In inclusion school settings, we found that it was even more important to work with the student outside of school. By going into the inclusion classroom or by pulling the student out of the regular classroom, we only succeeded in once again highlighting that the student was different from his or her regular education peers. The special education students in an inclusion setting have enough problems assimilating; they do not need separation within that classroom in any shape or form.

Raise Everyone's Expectations (Even Yours)

Students were consistently more capable of learning and succeeding in their choices of activities than was reflected in their parents' and teachers' portion of the FLLE assessment. As "outsiders," it was easier for us to see student's capabilities. We saw them in a variety of situations that allowed them to behave positively and show their strengths. These positive thoughts must be passed on to others who have become complacent or overwhelmed.

Students sense clearly when limits are placed on them or when expectations are low. They also respond favorably when expectations are high and effort is rewarded. When parents and teachers are overwhelmed, it is critical that someone else be able to step in and present a different viewpoint of the child. This viewpoint maintains higher expectations, loftier goals, and an emphasis on the student's strengths. This viewpoint could often come from related services professional, such as a certified therapeutic recreation specialist.

The Community is Embracing, if Prepared

We found that, not only was the community not prejudiced against persons with disabilities in regard to participation in recreation activities, they welcomed students with open arms. The key to this success was the planning process and preparation for involvement.

Students were often highly involved in the process of seeking out resources. This allowed students to speak to recreation leaders about the activities and determine how the activity, as well as the leader's style, would fit their interests. Recreation leaders did not require intense training to work with a person with a disability. What they did require was a sense that this activity was important to this particular person.

Another key factor in the successes of community involvement was that the student chose activities. When a student was committed to pursuing an activity, it was apparent that recreation leaders could sense the commitment and thus commit themselves to welcoming and accommodating the participant. There is a marked difference between showing up for an activity and carefully exploring the activity on a personal basis. Activities were chosen because of the

TABLE 11.1
Community Leisure Learning Contexts

Habitat for Humanity	Bicycling
Swing Dance Club	Community center teen dances
Volunteering at a day care center	Community recreation and parks department
Community sports league	Scouting
Tae Kwon Do	Summer science camp
YMCA fitness	Golf lessons

meaning they had for the students. Activities were not chosen because they were the only "special" activities available. They were chosen because they were important to that individual. Table 11.1 shows activities in the community that were chosen by students.

Resources are Sometimes the Keys

Families can get stuck in helping their children find meaningful activities and companionship when they are unaware of available resources. Several parents who were highly motivated to help their children get involved simply needed information, encouragement, and plans to get going. The following categories of resources highlight the types of resources from which families benefited.

Activities. Parents did not seem to believe that their children were welcome in regular recreation programs. Parents did seem aware of the Americans with Disabilities Act (ADA) and how that related to their children. Parents generally had little awareness of the breadth of activities available in the community. They were unaware that municipalities provided activities and that there were several active community centers. They appeared aware of special recreation opportunities, such as Special Olympics and dances for persons with disabilities, but not of activities offered by city recreation departments and commercial recreation facilities. They did not seem to know specifically that the children could take lessons and learn many activities. Families seemed to think there were few options for their children to be involved in the community and to take part in programs with "normal" people. Several parents also believed that their children must attend the city's "special" camp, rather than the camps of their choice.

Transportation. Parents were often unaware that transportation services were often readily available for their children to get to activities. Community service agencies provided several transportation programs that could be utilized. These services were especially crucial to single parents and working families who were overwhelmed with time pressures.

One parent, in part being protective of her child, did not consider the city bus system to be a viable alternative. It took our teaching her child systematically to use the bus that made a difference in the student's life. Being able to use a city bus opened up a new world of possibilities for Sally.

Transportation was a crucial issue for Eric, James and David, Sally, Sara, and Stephan. When those issues were resolved, student self-determination flourished. When they were not resolved or not allowed, self-determination decreased significantly.

Fee Assistance. Families who were financially strapped did not know that there were fee waivers and scholarships available for their children to utilize. City recreation departments and the YMCA provided this valuable assistance, which made participation possible for several students. Once Stephan could go to the YMCA, he had a viable alternative to hanging out on streets frequented by drug dealers.

Simple Home Activities. Parents were typically at a loss to know what to have their children play at home. Several were upset that their children played the same activity over and over again or played games normally played by children of a much younger age. Several described the pressures of having to constantly deal with this issue at home, or the pressure on siblings to be constant playmates.

Parents needed day-to-day ideas for dealing with their children's free time. They often needed low-cost ideas. They needed strategies for involving the children in planning family activities. These simpler ideas in many cases were the most effective help we provided.

Printed Materials. While families seemed to know about weekly community newspapers, it did not seem to occur to them that their children, in exploring their leisure, could use these newspapers.

Free weekly local independent papers and entertainment magazines contained information on museums, camps, science programs, computer opportunities, exhibits, special events, activity classes, children's programs, and stores selling activity items. Families did not take advantage of being on mailing lists of community services and recreation organizations that would have brought them regular—rather than always "special" information.

School Activities. Parents had little awareness of after-school programs, extracurricular activities, school clubs, and elective leisure-related classes. IEP meetings never seemed to discuss these options. In high school, the special education teachers had to individually ask other teachers to get their students in to those classes, significantly reducing opportunities.

Sally's after-school involvement, James' Fellowship of Christian Athletes, and Stephan's involvement in track all provided the opportunity for student success and interaction with typical students.

Volunteering. Caught in the cycle of having children who always received help, these families did not consider the possibility that their children could become volunteers and help others. Volunteering provided several students with an opportunity to be a contributor to the community and to break the cycle of dependence. If given the chance, all students have the potential to help others. Reciprocity enhances self-esteem and self-worth.

Sally's volunteer service at a day care, another student's volunteer work at a nursing home, and Eric's work with Habitat for Humanity showed that students with disabilities could prosper in the role of helping others. Volunteerism is a powerful tool for changing how others view disabilities and allows students to display their unique qualities.

Use Manuals as Guides, Not Bibles

There are a variety of manuals and model programs that have been introduced over the last decade, including several from the Center from which FLLE was developed. We found that although these manuals generally supply quality ideas, they are only a starting point for ideas when one is providing an ILEP.

Each student and family required the utmost of individualization to succeed. Programs needed to take into account levels of self-determination, family support, family resources, cognitive levels, motivation, financial resources, history with activities, neighborhoods, schools, siblings, interests, physical condition, attitude towards leisure, resource knowledge, and personality.

Each student and family required a plan that took into account as many factors as possible and which was timed to fit the student's context and readiness to grow and succeed. Canned programs cannot possibly take these factors into account. Each individual program was developed in concert with the student, the family, and the teachers, and it was presented to other FLLE staff on a weekly basis for feedback, so that plans could be adapted instantly. Plans included exploring interests, trying activities on a trial and error basis, and making community visits. Each step led to more adaptation, as the student pursued interests and explored his or her potential. There are no short cuts.

Start at Home

Parents seemed to be more interested and involved when activities took place in the home. This convenience factor should be a part of future program planning, as it quickly involves the family. Some activities away from home facilitated by the recreation therapist may unintentionally disconnect the family, by taking the child away from home.

The further the activity was away from home, the more difficulty families had following through. When families could deliver their children to an activity and return later for them, they usually did well. When they had to take them there and participate with them, they often did not do well.

WHAT WE LEARNED ABOUT SCHOOLS AND TEACHERS

Inclusion Itself Does Not Lead to More Interaction or Friendships

In our experience with the FLLE project, placing a special education student in a regular education classroom and expecting that he or she will be accepted and included socially is unrealistic. Neither students nor teachers were prepared for this experience. Students from special education merely became a smaller class within the regular education classroom, often participating in different activities than the regular education students. Little interaction was observed, even in classes such as art, music, and physical education.

Special education students in inclusion classrooms interacted with adults, not other children. Teachers and teacher assistants were constantly at their sides, further reducing the chances for interaction with typical students. Special education students are often placed in the regular education classroom in the back desks, nearest the door, seated beside an adult.

Inclusion is about belonging, not about being in a room. Inclusion is about being treated as a peer with unique qualities. Inclusion is about having the chance to both succeed and to fail, just like any other kid. Yet, that is not what we observed.

Teachers Did Not Seem to be Affected By the Process of FLLE

We found teachers to be generally interested in leisure education for their students and eager to refer them for services. They seemed to understand the difficulties their student's experience in participating in activities, especially when their peers were involved.

However, we witnessed little change in teachers' behavior toward the students as a result of the process. Teachers were unwilling or unable, it seemed, to utilize the student's progress or to see the student in a different light as the student accomplished goals. Despite intense efforts with Sara's teachers and workers, we were unsuccessful. We do not know if we just did not communicate effectively with teachers, or whether, for example, school systems made teachers' situations too difficult for them to change their approach to a student.

We also found that teachers seemed to have the lowest expectations of the student's potential. They often thought only of keeping the student busy, while parents were much more concerned with the student's happiness, and while we looked at reaching goals. This was surprising to us, but it is something for teachers, parents, and researchers to consider.

Teachers, in our limited sample, routinely failed to reinforce the student's newly found skills, knowledge, and self-determination. It seemed too difficult to reframe the student and his or her potential as it developed. Student progress often meant more work and individualization for the teacher. If it meant they had to change their routines or interact more with parents or help the students be in a more inclusive setting, they balked. Some ignored the progress; some failed to follow through on intended changes. Some even seemed to set the student up for failure in their continued improvement by not being supportive and not utilizing the training provided by FLLE. Many teachers seemed to not want to change their routines or schedules so that the students could continue to be self-determining.

Teacher Referrals

Several patterns emerged concerning referrals from special education teachers to FLLE over the course of the project. Teachers appeared to want us to work with either the with students who had the most obvious potential, with students with whom their behavioral strategies had not worked, or with students whose parents were outspoken. Students who teachers felt could be more active were most often referred. Various approaches included the following.

The "They Should be Doing More" Approach. Eric, Sara, Stephan, David and James, Barney, and Luis were all the highest functioning special education students in their classes. Teachers may have recognized the difficulty of giving enough attention to high functioning students when others in the classroom needed and demanded their attention. Disappointingly, teachers were not able to follow-up on the attention we provided and to integrate the student's self-determination back into the classroom.

The "You See What You Can Do" Approach. Several other students not used as case studies in this book had exhausted the strategies of their teachers. Teachers were looking for someone who could get through to the children.

The "Throw a Dog a Bone" Approach. Several of the referred students were from families that were extremely active in local advocacy organizations or who were vocal in IEP meetings. Teachers appeared to use these referrals to soothe parental demands.

WHAT WE LEARNED ABOUT STUDENTS

Students Are More Capable Than Reported or Labeled

In each and every case, we found that once we got to know a student, his or her capabilities were greater than we expected. They were capable of much more than teachers reported and somewhat more than parents reported. They were also more capable than they had reported. There is a great difference between what a person thinks on a day-to-day basis, days filled with schedules and paperwork, and what a student is capable of on a one-to-one intense basis. If one were to read both reports, one would think we were talking about two different persons.

Labels provided absolutely no insight into the capabilities of a student. Labels only served to identify a classroom placement for a student. Labels were not a predictor of success, capabilities, or potential. It is only when labels are ignored that a person can be seen as a person, a unique person, with unique personality, interests, and strengths. Labels served as limiting factors for everyone, including the student. When individualized services are developed to increase self-determination in leisure, a student can become a person, instead of a label. We must reluctantly admit that we have traditionally taught university students labels to help them understand disability. It is through the students and families in this project that we have learned the hollowness and indifference of labels, how they limit and compromise people and those close to them.

They Wanted "Normal" Activities

No student ever asked for more Special Olympics. No student ever got excited about "special recreation." It's not that they do not enjoy some of these activities; several looked forward to the ARC dances held every month, as an example. Few resisted going to Special Olympics bowling, but no one wanted more special activities.

The activities they pursued—when given information and opportunities in the community—were activities that anyone might choose. When given the community at large as their menu, they did not choose a limited, "special" community. When they were encouraged to be self-determining, they chose not to be limited, not what was normally "given" to them.

School Was Boring to Students

Many students expressed their boredom with school through their verbalizations and their behavior. School was full of repetition, rote learning, and videos—little related to the context of their lives. After a time, students would simply act-out on a regular basis. Others would self-stimulate, repeat activities, listen to the radio, or perfect their dysfunctional behaviors. This did little to prepare them for dealing in the real world with their same-aged peers.

Friendships Were Rare

We observed that most special education students did not have friends in school, regardless of the type of placement. Students in self-contained classrooms often had little interaction with each other. Students in inclusion classes had few interactions with regular education students. We observed most interactions to be with adults.

Students in special education appeared to have little to share in terms of activities and interests with other students. We did find that the opportunities for friendship improved when students learned new activities that they could share with their peers. The following examples are problem areas we observed regarding students with disabilities having friends:

Greetings. Special education students rarely greeted other special education students when they entered an activity or a classroom. The very act of acknowledging someone's presence was not common.

Invitations. Special education students rarely invited other special education students to play with them. Most play was of a parallel nature, with little positive interaction. Special education students tended to start an activity themselves, often following an adult's direction, and continue that activity alone. It was not unusual to walk into a special education classroom and see every student doing something different.

Conversations. Students spent little time conversing with each other about their home and school activities. They would not inquire about another student's activity, nor would they offer to talk about their own activity.

Sharing. There was little sharing of either ideas or toys. Objects, once possessed, were kept as long as possible. The sharing of classroom computers typically required an adult intervention.

Interaction on Trips. When special education students were on outings, students would typically sit in their seats, looking forward or down, speaking to no one. Teachers would have to ask specific questions to get responses from students.

In contrast, a trip with inclusion classes found the special education students talking to adults on the trip, while regular education students talked incessantly about everything the bus passed, what they had done last night, and what they were going to do on the outing.

Playground Activities. Special education students struggled on school playgrounds to play with each other. These activities resulted in a constant stream of teacher threats and time-outs. Often, students were content to sit on benches and watch other children play.

When at recess with their inclusion classes, special education students tended to interact with other special education students and personnel. They were very rarely invited by their regular education classmates to play. They could also be typically found at the end of the line when coming and going from the playground.

Motivation Amends Negative Behavior

Several students with whom we worked experienced significant behavioral problems. For the most part, this included dealing appropriately with other students at school and dealing with the public in the community. Eric's story is an example of a student who had no motivation to change his behavior around others. His attention-seeking behavior was an attempt to gain acceptance. While that behavior seemed ineffective to us, on some level it worked for him. The long-term disadvantages to him were that he was not able to participate in activities, peers in school made fun of him, and his parents did not take him out very often. All these behaviors resulted in Eric not having positive contact with others and in having few chances for self-determined activities that mattered to him.

In Eric's case, Habitat for Humanity provided him the motivation to listen to Jen and to learn more effective ways of communicating. Previously, he had no reason or motivation to change; he was not headed anywhere. Once he had a meaningful goal, in this case a leisure activity, he changed quite easily. In school, there was no reason to change.

Sara's isolated behavior of listening to the radio constantly and of engaging in other self-stimulating behaviors were, at least in some part, due to her lack of options and opportunities to make decisions. This coping style provided no motivation to change, even if she thought there were more options. At the beginning of the intervention, to predict she would learn multiple activities and invite others to participate would have been far-fetched. Sara seemingly became motivated to participate, to make decisions, and to interact with others, when given the opportunity. Her behavior improved remarkably once she had a reason to do so.

Students Thrive on Self-Determination

All students are capable of making self-determined choices about their leisure, regardless of their disability. All students have preferences for activities and a preference for playmates. Often, when not encouraged to be self-determining, students would passively not make choices and would be content with whatever was going on at the time.

Once they were given "permission" to be self-determining and the skills they had lacked to be successful, choices became regular and meaningful. When given a voice, they roared. When given a chance to give, they responded. When given the freedom to be self-determining, they became more than they had been. It was our greatest lesson.

SUMMARY AND IMPLICATIONS

The Enormity of Potential

During the entire FLLE project, students with behavior problems succeeded. Students who could not speak succeeded. Students who blended into the woodwork succeeded. Students whom others had written off succeeded. Only one student did not succeed; she wanted only to deal with getting a part-time job. Every other student had some measure of success, often far beyond anyone's hopes.

By and large, if students can succeed with only an hour or two of intervention per week, then it is the systems that are failing them. If, with just a little help, they can do wonders, then they are regularly not being asked to do enough, or they are regularly not given the assistance they need to succeed. They are simply not given the chance, because, when given the chance, they do succeed.

Keep it Simple, Flexible, and Personal

Interventions were most successful when simple ideas and activities were introduced. Families seemed to desire simple solutions, rather than more work. They could respond more quickly and follow through more often.

When people know their options and have the freedom to choose leisure experiences, they thrive. It happens because it is personal. It does not happen because they are disabled or because they are labeled or because they are in a program. It happens because they own it. Ownership brings responsibility, meaning, and connections.

It is not a gift or a service like they are used to receiving because there is something wrong with them. It is something they have chosen because it is right for them. The power of self-determination is strong.

Commit After the Assessment

In a research project such as FLLE, it is often difficult to find subjects for the study. Our protocol asked for a commitment to the program after a general overview of the project. In retrospect, it may have been better to have completed all assessments and to have developed the intervention goals before asking for the commitment. Parents and teachers could have then had a chance to see specifically what they were expected to do.

Run to the Home, Find the Community, Stay Away From School

Home is where the help is. Parents regularly sought assistance for home activities where transportation was not an issue and where they struggled to keep their children active, stimulated, and in control. They seemed to see new home activities as a break for them, a respite from constant attention-giving.

The community is where students found a place to belong, to be something other than what they were in school or at Special Olympics—something other than their label. They could pursue their interests and be "normal." Students with disabilities do well in the community when they "do their homework." For students, this included pursuing activities of real interest, being part of the process of investigating activities and resources, and meeting with recreation providers.

Schools are a place of labels and low expectations. Students with disabilities are often segregated from other students. A program such as FLLE may be effective in schools where real inclusion is practiced and where contextual learning is the rule.

Find the Ignored

Students with mild disabilities and those from low-income families in our study had typically received few services in the past. Students in these categories were ripe for quick success and action by families starved for help. Interventions were both time- and cost-effective. These students had often fallen through the cracks because they were quiet and only mildly disabled; yet, they needed services to be able to make changes that had the potential to make significant long-term changes in their lives. They were able to connect with others, to find a place in their community

Give Teachers a Specific and Ongoing Role

It is too easy for teachers to see related services personnel as people who work with their students rather than in concert with the teacher. This seems especially true when services are provided in the home and in the community. Teachers in previous programs had done well when leisure education was conducted as a group activity, but when teachers must integrate the student's self-determined leisure into the classroom setting on an individual basis, they struggle to make the necessary changes.

Remind Yourself Everyday of Students' Potential

The greatest danger for students with disabilities is that people get used to them. In many cases, that also means accepting them and expecting nothing more. While persons with disabilities strive to be accepted, this type of acceptance may include forgetting about a person's potential—to only see them as one sees them everyday, to only see them in one situation, in one role, in one place.

Potential waiting to be unlocked may have to bloom somewhere else, with someone else, where they can be someone else. Only when we see that systems can improve and allow and encourage self-determination will we truly be of help.

References

America 2000: An educational strategy. (1996). Washington, DC: U.S. Government Printing Office.

Bedini, L. A., Bullock, C. C., & Driscoll, L. B. (1993). The effects of leisure education on the successful transition of students with mental retardation from school to adult life. *Therapeutic Recreation Journal, 26*(2), 70–82.

Bell, B. (1995). Self-sufficiency: Accelerating the learning curve. *Journal of Housing and Community Development, 52*(5), 44–45.

Bregha, F.J. (1985). Leisure and freedom re-examined. In T.A. Goodale & P.A. Witt (Eds.), *Recreation and leisure; Issues in an era of change* (2nd ed., pp. 35–43). State College, PA: Venture.

Bullock, C., Morris, L., Mahon, M., & Jones, B. (1994). *School community leisure link: Leisure education program curriculum guide*. Chapel Hill: Center for Recreation and Disability Studies, University of North Carolina at Chapel Hill.

Chinn, K.A., & Joswiak, K.E. (1981). Leisure education and leisure counseling. *Therapeutic Recreation Journal, 15*(4), 4–7.

Cooper, J. (1996). *TBI Project STAR Circle Manual*. Charlotte, NC: Charlotte Institute of Rehabilitation.

Cowger, C.D. (1992). Assessment of client strengths. In D. Saleebey (Ed.), *The strengths perspective in social work practice* (pp. 139–147). New York: Longman.

Cowger, C.D. (1994). Assessing client strengths: Clinical assessment for client empowerment. *Social Work, 39*, 262–268.

Curtis, E. (1998). It's my life: Reference based planning for self directed goals. In M.L. Wehmeyer & D.J. Sands (Eds.), *Making it happen: Student involvement in education planning, decision-making, and instruction* (pp. 211–240). Baltimore, MD: Paul H. Brooks.

Dattilo, J., Kleiber, D., & Williams R. (1998). Self-determination and enjoyment enhancement: A psychologically based service delivery model for therapeutic recreation. *Therapeutic Recreation Journal, 32*(4), 258–271.

Dattilo, J., & St. Peter, S. (1991). A model for including leisure education in transitions services for young adults with mental retardation. *Education and Training in Mental Retardation, 26*(4), 420–432.

Fiene, J., & Taylor, P. (1991). Serving rural families of developmentally disabled children: A case management model. *Social Work, 36*, 323–327.

Ford, A., Davern, L., Meyer, L., Schnorr, P., Black, J., & Dempsey, M. (1989). Recreation/leisure. In A. Ford et al. (Eds.), *The Syracuse community-referenced curriculum guide for students with moderate and severe disabilities* (pp. 63–92). Baltimore, MD: Paul H. Brookes.

Granger, L., & Granger, B. (1986). *The magic feather: The truth about special education.* New York: Dutton.

Iso-Ahola, S.E., & Weissinger, E. (1987). Leisure and boredom. *Journal of Social and Clinical Psychology, 5*(3), 356–364.

Johnson, D.E., Bullock, C.C., & Ashton-Shaeffer, C. (1997). Involving families of school-aged children with disabilities in contextual learning. *Teaching Exceptional Children, 30*(2), 30–34.

Lanagan, D., & Dattilo, J. (1989). The effects of a leisure education program on individuals with mental retardation. *Therapeutic Recreation Journal, 23*(4), 62–72.

Luken, K. (April, 1993). Reintegration through recreation. *Parks and Recreation, 28*(4), 54–57.

Mahon, M. (1994). The use of self-control techniques to facilitate self-determination skills during leisure in adolescents with mild and moderate mental retardation. *Therapeutic Recreation Journal, 28*(2), 58–72.

Mahon, M., & Bullock, C. (1992). Teaching adolescents with mild disabilities to make decisions in leisure through the use of self-control techniques. *Therapeutic Recreation Journal, 26*(3), 9–26.

McCallion, P., & Toseland, R. W. (1993). Empowering families of adolescents and adults with developmental disabilities. Families in Society: *The Journal of Contemporary Human Services, 74*, 579–589.

McCann, C., & Bullock, C.C. (1991). *The parent training guide to recreation.* Chapel Hill: Center for Recreation and Disability Studies, University of North Carolina at Chapel Hill.

Moon, M.S. (1994). *Making school and community recreation fun for everyone: Places and ways to integrate.* Baltimore, MD: Paul H. Brookes.

Munson, W., Baker, S., & Lundegren, H.. (1985). Strength training and leisure counseling as treatments for institutionalized juvenile delinquents. *Adapted Physical Activity Quarterly, 2*(1), 65–75.

Negley, S. (1997). *Crossing the bridge: A journey in self-esteem, relationships, and life balances*. Beachwood, OH: Wellness Reproductions & Publishing.

Parnell, D. (1996). Cerebral context. *Vocational Education Journal, 71*(3), 18–21, 50.

Peterson, C.A., & Gunn, S.L. (1984). *Therapeutic recreation program design. Principles and procedures* (2nd ed.). Englewood Cliffs, NJ: Prentice-Hall.

Poertner, J., & Ronnau, J. (1992). A strength approach to children with disabilities. In D. Saleebey (Ed.), *The strengths perspective in social work practice* (pp. 111–121). New York: Longman.

Ross, C.D. (1983). Leisure in the deinstitutionalization process: A vehicle for change. *Journal of Leisurability, 10*(1), 13–19.

Saleeby, D. (1996). The strengths perspective in social work practice: Extensions and cautions. *Social Work, 41*(3), 296–305.

Selz, L., & Bullock, C. (2000). Introduction to therapeutic recreation: An evolving profession. In C. Bullock & M. Mahon (Eds.), *Introduction to recreation services for people with disabilities: A person-centered approach* (pp. 267–302). Champaign, IL: Sagamore.

Shain, M. (1978). *When lovers are friends*. Philadelphia, PA: J.B. Lippincott.

Tinsley, H.E.A., & Tinsley, D. J. (1982). A holistic model of leisure counseling. *Journal of Leisure Research, 2*, 100–116.

Voeltz, L., Wuerch, B., & Wilcox, B. (1982). Leisure and recreation: Preparation for independence, integration and self-fulfillment. In B. Wilcox & G. Bellamy (Eds.), *Design of high school programs for severely handicapped students* (pp. 175–209). Baltimore, MD: Paul H. Brookes.

Ward, M. (1996). Coming of age in the age of self-determination: A historical and personal perspective. In D. Sands & M. Wehmeyer (Eds.), *Self-determination across the lifespan: Independence and choice for people with disabilities* (pp. 3–16). Baltimore, MD: Paul H. Brookes.

Wehmeyer, M. (1994). Perceptions of self-determination and psychological empowerment of adolescents with mental retardation. *Education and Training in Mental Retardation and Developmental Disabilities, 29*(1), 9–21.

Wehmeyer, M., Agran, M., & Hughes, C. (1998). *Teaching self-determination to students with disabilities*. Baltimore, MD: Paul H. Brookes.

Wehmeyer, M., & Schwartz, M. (1998). The relationship between self-determination and quality of life for adults with mental retardation. *Education and Training in Mental Retardation and Developmental Disabilities, 33*(1), 3–12.

Contributors

Candace Ashton, PhD, CTRS, is an associate professor in the Department of Health, Physical Education, and Recreation at the University of North Carolina, Wilmington. She is a former research associate at the Center for Recreation and Disability Studies, University of North Carolina, Chapel Hill.

Charles C. Bullock, PhD, is a professor and chair of the Department of Health Ecology at the University of Nevada, Reno. Bullock is the former director of the Center for Recreation and Disability Studies at the University of North Carolina, Chapel Hill. He is also the project director of the Family Link in Leisure Education Project.

Jacqueline Cavadi, MS, TRS/CTRS, is the project coordinator, Beach Ability, for the North Carolina Easter Seal Society, Raleigh. She also served as a therapeutic recreation graduate research assistant in the Department of Leisure Studies at the University of North Carolina, Chapel Hill.

Kathy Fletcher, MS, TRS/CTRS, is the coordinator of the Virtual Buddies Program at the Charlotte Institute of Rehabilitation. Fletcher is a former therapeutic recreation graduate research assistant in the Department of Leisure Studies at the University of North Carolina, Chapel Hill.

Danny E. Johnson, PhD, TRS/CTRS, is an assistant professor in the Department of Health, Physical Education, and Recreation at the University of North Carolina, Wilmington. Johnson is also a consultant for the New Hanover County Schools and a research coordinator of the Family Link in Leisure Education Project.

Jennifer Laughrun, MS, TRS/CTRS, is an integration specialist for employment opportunities in Raleigh, North Carolina. She is a former therapeutic recreation graduate research assistant in the Department of Leisure Studies at the University of North Carolina, Chapel Hill.

Mary Agnes Shelton, MS, TRS/CTRS, is a recreation therapist for North Carolina Independent Living in Boone, North Carolina. Shelton serves as the intervention coordinator of the Family Link in Leisure Education Project.

Author Index

229

Subject Index

Printed in the United States
24886LVS00005B/109-135

9 781572 734807